JAMAICA KINCAID

Critical Companions to Popular Contemporary Writers
Kathleen Gregory Klein, Series Editor

V. C. Andrews
  by E. D. Huntley

Maya Angelou
  by Mary Jane Lupton

Tom Clancy
  by Helen S. Garson

Mary Higgins Clark
  by Linda C. Pelzer

Arthur C. Clarke
  by Robin Anne Reid

James Clavell
  by Gina Macdonald

Pat Conroy
  by Landon C. Burns

Robin Cook
  by Lorena Laura Stookey

Michael Crichton
  by Elizabeth A. Trembley

Howard Fast
  by Andrew Macdonald

Ken Follett
  by Richard C. Turner

Ernest J. Gaines
  by Karen Carmean

John Grisham
  by Mary Beth Pringle

James Herriot
  by Michael J. Rossi

Tony Hillerman
  by John M. Reilly

John Irving
  by Josie P. Campbell

John Jakes
  by Mary Ellen Jones

Stephen King
  by Sharon A. Russell

Dean Koontz
  by Joan G. Kotker

Robert Ludlum
  by Gina Macdonald

Anne McCaffrey
  by Robin Roberts

Colleen McCullough
  by Mary Jean DeMarr

James A. Michener
  by Marilyn S. Severson

Toni Morrison
  by Missy Dehn Kubitschek

Anne Rice
  by Jennifer Smith

Tom Robbins
  *by Catherine E. Hoyser and
  Lorena Laura Stookey*

John Saul
  by Paul Bail

Erich Segal
  by Linda C. Pelzer

Amy Tan
  by E. D. Huntley

Anne Tyler
  by Paul Bail

Leon Uris
  by Kathleen Shine Cain

Gore Vidal
  by Susan Baker and Curtis S. Gibson

JAMAICA KINCAID

A Critical Companion

Lizabeth Paravisini-Gebert

CRITICAL COMPANIONS TO POPULAR CONTEMPORARY WRITERS
Kathleen Gregory Klein, Series Editor

Greenwood Press
Westport, Connecticut • London

Library of Congress Cataloging-in-Publication Data

Paravisini-Gebert, Lizabeth.
    Jamaica Kincaid : a critical companion / Lizabeth Paravisini
-Gebert.
        p.   cm.—(Critical companions to popular contemporary
writers, 1082–4979)
    Includes bibliographical references and index.
    ISBN 0–313–30295–2 (alk. paper)
    1. Kincaid, Jamaica—Criticism and interpretation.   2. Women and
literature—Antigua—History—20th century.   I. Title.   II. Series.
PR9275.A583K566   1999
813—dc21   98–55341

British Library Cataloguing in Publication Data is available.

Copyright © 1999 by Lizabeth Paravisini-Gebert

Library of Congress Catalog Card Number: 98–55341
ISBN: 0–313–30295–2
ISSN: 1082–4979

First published in 1999

Greenwood Press, 88 Post Road West, Westport, CT 06881
An imprint of Greenwood Publishing Group, Inc.
www.greenwood.com

Printed in the United States of America

The paper used in this book complies with the
Permanent Paper Standard issued by the National
Information Standards Organization (Z39.48–1984).

10 9 8 7 6 5 4 3 2 1

To my grandmother
María Luisa Santiago
on her 100th year

Contents

Series Foreword

The authors who appear in the series Critical Companions to Popular Contemporary Writers are all best-selling writers. They do not simply have one successful novel, but a string of them. Fans, critics, and specialist readers eagerly anticipate their next book. For some, high cash advances and breakthrough sales figures are automatic; movie deals often follow. Some writers become household names, recognized by almost everyone.

But, their novels are read one by one. Each reader chooses to start and, more importantly, to finish a book because of what she or he finds there. The real test of a novel is in the satisfaction its readers experience. This series acknowledges the extraordinary involvement of readers and writers in creating a best-seller.

The authors included in this series were chosen by an Advisory Board composed of high school English teachers and high school and public librarians. They ranked a list of best-selling writers according to their popularity among different groups of readers. For the first series, writers in the top-ranked group who had received no book-length, academic, literary analysis (or none in at least the past ten years) were chosen. Because of this selection method, Critical Companions to Popular Contemporary Writers meets a need that is being addressed nowhere else. The success of these volumes as reported by reviewers, librarians, and teachers led to an expansion of the series mandate to include some writers with wide critical attention—Toni Morrison, John Irving, and Maya Angelou, for example—to extend the usefulness of the series.

The volumes in the series are written by scholars with particular expertise in analyzing popular fiction. These specialists add an academic focus to the popular success that these writers already enjoy.

The series is designed to appeal to a wide range of readers. The general reading public will find explanations for the appeal of these well-known writers. Fans will find biographical and fictional questions answered. Students will find literary analysis, discussions of fictional genres, carefully organized introductions to new ways of reading the novels, and bibliographies for additional research. Whether browsing through the book for pleasure or using it for an assignment, readers will find that the most recent novels of the authors are included.

Each volume begins with a biographical chapter drawing on published information, autobiographies or memoirs, prior interviews, and, in some cases, interviews given especially for this series. A chapter on literary history and genres describes how the author's work fits into a larger literary context. The following chapters analyze the writer's most important, most popular, and most recent novels in detail. Each chapter focuses on one or more novels. This approach, suggested by the Advisory Board as the most useful to student research, allows for an in-depth analysis of the writer's fiction. Close and careful readings with numerous examples show readers exactly how the novels work. These chapters are organized around three central elements: plot development (how the story line moves forward), character development (what the reader knows of the important figures), and theme (the significant ideas of the novel). Chapters may also include sections on generic conventions (how the novel is similar to or different from others in its same category of science, fantasy, thriller, etc.), narrative point of view (who tells the story and how), symbols and literary language, and historical or social context. Each chapter ends with an "alternative reading" of the novel. The volume concludes with a primary and secondary bibliography, including reviews.

The alternative readings are a unique feature of this series. By demonstrating a particular way of reading each novel, they provide a clear example of how a specific perspective can reveal important aspects of the book. In the alternative reading sections, one contemporary literary theory—way of reading, such as feminist criticism, Marxism, new historicism, deconstruction, or Jungian psychological critique—is defined in brief, easily comprehensible language. That definition is then applied to the novel to highlight specific features that might go unnoticed or be understood differently in a more general reading. Each volume defines two or three specific theories, making them part of the reader's understanding of how diverse meanings may be constructed from a single novel.

Taken collectively, the volumes in the Critical Companions to Popular Contemporary Writers series provide a wide-ranging investigation of the complexities of current best-selling fiction. By treating these novels seriously as both literary works and publishing successes, the series demonstrates the potential of popular literature in contemporary culture.

Kathleen Gregory Klein
Southern Connecticut State University

Acknowledgments

I am most grateful to the many friends and colleagues who took time from their busy schedules to share their thoughts on Jamaica Kincaid's work with me and read parts of the manuscript for this book. From among them I must single out Kevin Meehan, Nora Gaines, Margot Mifflin, Joan Dayan, and Elaine Savory for the generosity and intelligence of their contributions to my work. My family—Gordon, Carrie, D'Arcy, and Gordon Jr.—were models of patience and understanding, for which they have my gratitude and my love.

Abbreviations

The following abbreviations have been used in text citations for works by Jamaica Kincaid. Full citation information can be found in the bibliography at the end of this volume.

ABR   *At the Bottom of the River*

CBY   *Current Biography Yearbook*

JKNY   "Jamaica Kincaid's New York"

MB   *My Brother*

PMT   "Putting Myself Together"

PP   "Plant Parenthood"

SP   *A Small Place*

1

The Life of Jamaica Kincaid

Elaine Cynthia Potter Richardson, the woman known to readers around the world as Jamaica Kincaid, was born at Holberton Hospital in St. John's, the capital of the small Caribbean island of Antigua, on May 25, 1949. Antigua, although the largest of the British Leeward Islands, is a small territory, with a land area no larger than 108 square miles. Its deeply indented coastline is cut by numerous coves and bays; its interior is characterized by gentle hills covered by dryland scrub, the result of intense plantation-era deforestation. Once an agrarian society with an economy dependent on the cultivation of sugar cane, during Kincaid's lifetime it has been dependent on the tourist industry, which accounts for more than fifty percent of all employment. Since having achieved its political independence in 1981 it has been part of the British Commonwealth, but its government, which has been controlled by the Bird family for more than thirty years, has been plagued by corruption and frequent scandals. Its population of 65,000 is chiefly of African descent.

Kincaid's childhood and adolescence were spent in St. John's. Despite Antigua's small size and relatively short distances from village to village, she did not travel beyond the capital until her return to the island for a visit after many years in the United States. The members of her family, by her own description, were "poor, ordinary people" disconnected from the mainstream of economic and political life—"banana and citrus-fruit farmers, fishermen, carpenters and obeah women" (Cudjoe, 399; JKNY,

71). Her mother, Annie Richardson Drew, a homemaker and one-time political activist (she had a brief but intense period of political activity as an opponent of the Bird regime), belonged to a family of landowning peasants from the neighboring island of Dominica. Kincaid's maternal grandparents—a Carib Indian and a part-Scot, part-African Dominican policeman—would serve as inspiration for the central characters in her third novel, *The Autobiography of My Mother*.

Kincaid did not meet her biological father, Frederick Potter—a taxi driver later employed by the exclusive and racially segregated Mill Reef Club of Antigua—until she was an adult. She has described him in interviews as a type of Antiguan man proud of fathering children for whom he will show no interest or bear any responsibility; perhaps as a result, their relationship would never move beyond that of distant acquaintances. The man she acknowledges as her father in her nonfiction (and from whom the father figures of most of her autobiographical fiction derive) was in fact the man her mother subsequently married, David Drew, the island's "second best" carpenter. Her stepfather's presence cushioned whatever minor unease Kincaid may have felt about her illegitimacy—to which she has alluded, albeit obliquely, in her writing—and they appear to have enjoyed a mutually supportive relationship until his illness during her early adolescence forced her into relinquishing her schooling and leaving Antigua for the United States to work as an au pair.

The family's circumstances were those of the tropical poor. Her stepfather was self-employed and, as long as his health allowed him to work, the family was moderately prosperous, part of the genteel lower-middle class. Their small house on Nelson Street—named "after an English maritime criminal" (SP, 24)—had no electricity, bathroom, or running water, but these conditions were the result of the slow development of the Antiguan urban infrastructure and not necessarily a reflection on the family's financial situation. Until her three brothers were born in quick succession during Kincaid's early adolescence and her father's health deteriorated, the family's circumstances were easy enough to allow for occasional private schooling, books, lessons, and new dresses. Their situation determined Kincaid's role in the household; her relatively light chores revolved around arranging for the "night-soil men" to collect and replace their outhouse tub when full, fetching buckets of fresh water in the morning and early evening, trimming, cleaning, and replacing the kerosene in the oil lamps, and later helping her mother care for her three younger brothers (Garis, 44). Her one bounty was the great natural beauty of the island—which she always felt was unappreciated by her neighbors, too accustomed to radiant days full of sunshine, proliferating hibiscus and flamboyant flowers, and too much sea.

The family was Methodist, her grandfather having been a lay minister; but they were surrounded by a community that practiced Obeah, "a system of beliefs grounded in spirituality and an acknowledgment of the supernatural and involving aspects of witchcraft, sorcery, magic, spells, and healing" (Frye, 198). Obeah touched on Kincaid's life directly because both her mother and grandmother were believers and, consequently, its beliefs and practices were an everyday part of her life. Her mother made her wear protective sachets in her underwear and she often had special baths to thwart the evil eye, prescribed by the Obeah woman her mother consulted every Friday. She remembers her family preserving a small dried piece of her youngest brother's afterbirth to pin to his clothes as protection against evil spells. The family, moreover, had long sustained the belief that the death of her mother's younger brother from a painful illness during which a parasitic worm had nested in his leg had been the result of an Obeah spell. Once, fearing that the mother of a classmate with whom Kincaid had had a confrontation would put a spell on her, her mother sent her away to her grandmother's house in Dominica, reassured that evil spirits would not follow across water and that "the obeah practiced in Dominica was far superior to the kind practiced in Antigua" (MB, 75). As a child she had believed in *jablesses* and *soucriants*, fearful creatures who could transform themselves into animals and sometimes attacked and sucked the blood of unwitting victims. During her visits to her maternal grandmother, her contemplation of the Dominican landscape at twilight was often marred by her conviction that the deep shadows moving in the distant horizon were *jablesses* roaming in search of victims. Kincaid claims to have hated "the whole thing" while expressing nostalgia for its loss: "[T]he layer of obeah life doesn't work anymore . . . that world which turns out to have been so rich is lost. So rich in your imagination and imagination led to words" (Simmons, 9).

Kincaid was a precocious child who had been taught to read by her mother before she entered the Antiguan government school system in 1952. In school her favorite topics were history and—despite the cruelty of the Englishwoman who taught the subject—botany. The two interests have informed her writing in profound ways: her fiction and nonfiction have been increasingly concerned with the question of how to write about the Caribbean's history of slavery and colonialism; botanical topics have been frequent in her writing, and since the early 1990s she has been writing about botany and gardening and their relationship with colonialism and empire. Although she gave every sign of being a gifted child, she recalls with bitterness the lack of recognition she received from her parents and teachers. Her mother encouraged her voracious reading, but failed to realize, to Kincaid's lasting frustration and disappointment, that her daughter's special gifts could be nurtured into channels more challenging or rewarding than a career as a seamstress or secretary. She witnessed with growing disillusionment her mother and stepfather's great expectations for her brothers' professional futures and what she saw as indifference to her own prospects. "No one expected anything from me at all," she would comment ruefully after her success as a writer had been assured. "Had I just sunk in the cracks it would not have been noted" (Garis, 70). Her humiliation at being apprenticed when she was twelve to Miss Doreen, a seamstress, still rankled many years later.

Her precocity, along with a boldness often bordering on impudence, did not endear her to teachers and fellow students. She was frequently punished for an impatience with the islanders' subservience to Antigua's British colonizers that was seen as rebellious behavior. Once, as a punishment, she was forced to memorize long passages from John Milton's *Paradise Lost*, echoes of which still resound in her fiction. She also failed to make long-lasting friendships with her classmates. "I was very bright; I was always made fun of for it" (Simmons, 6). She had always been tall and thin—she would grow to be almost six feet tall—and being thinner and taller than her peers, they mockingly called her "Daddy Longlegs." Too often, for reasons she never fully understood, groups of classmates would take advantage of lonely stretches of road on her way home to beat her up. Once she had to be rescued by her mother, who gave her torturers an even worse beating than the one they were inflicting on her daughter.

Around the age of thirteen, just as she was on the threshold of taking qualifying exams that could have led to a university education, she was removed from school. Her stepfather had been ill and unable to work and her mother argued that she was needed in the house to help with the small children. She reacted to these circumstances, which demanded that she relinquish her dreams of education and achievement, with profound and lasting bitterness. "I was always being asked to forego something or other that had previously occupied my leisure time, and then something or other that was essential (my schooling), to take care of these small children who were not mine," she wrote in *My Brother*. "At thirteen, at fourteen, at fifteen, I did not like this, I did not like my mother's other children, I did not even like my mother then; I liked books, I liked reading books, I did not like anything else as much as I liked reading a book, a book of any kind" (126).

Kincaid has often spoken of growing up in the shadow of a domineering mother, but her relationship with Annie Drew before the birth of her three brothers (the first when Kincaid was nine) was a happy and loving one. She has described the early years of their relationship as years of blissful oneness, a "love affair" whose end left her feeling shattered and betrayed. The nature of their intimacy may strike some who have read descriptions of her mother chewing up Kincaid's food for her when she would not eat or using her mouth to clear Kincaid's nostrils when she had a bad cold as bound to make the inevitable separation of mother and daughter more traumatic than is normally the case. The "love affair" came to an end in 1958 when her brother Joseph was born.

Kincaid has never been shy about describing the catastrophic impact Joseph's birth had on her life; she associated it with the loss of her mother's love. "I thought I was the only thing my mother truly loved in the world," she once told an interviewer, "and when it dawned on me that it wasn't so, I was devastated" (Listfield 1990, 82). She felt "cast out of paradise." The impact of this alienation from her till-then beloved mother was "a sort of nervous breakdown" (Mantle 1996). She fictionalized the episode in "The Long Rain" chapter of *Annie John*, where she uses the description of an illness she had suffered when she was seven (a serious case of whooping cough) as a metaphor for the isolation and pain she endured as an adolescent mourning her idealized relationship with her mother. Two other brothers—Dalma and Devon—had followed Joseph's birth in fairly quick succession, claiming more of her mother's time and attention. She vividly recalled her mother's unsuccessful efforts to abort her youngest brother Devon, an experience that will resonate through her fiction and nonfiction, from *At the Bottom of the River* through *My Brother*. Her parents' marriage also underwent a change around this period—perhaps as a direct result of his illness, financial problems, the burden of three young children, and the stress created by Kincaid's own adolescent rebellion—and she believed her mother and stepfather no longer liked each other.

Just entering adolescence at the time, the young woman felt the withdrawal of her mother's affection keenly. The relationship switched from one of approval and understanding to one of frequent scoldings, lies, and punishments as Kincaid struggled to assert her independence against a mother determined to make a well-behaved, soft-spoken, proper Afro-Saxon girl out of her. Propriety demanded that Kincaid not become "the kind of woman who the baker won't let near the bread," as Kincaid wrote in "Girl" (ABR, 5). Her mother's efforts were focused on instilling in her daughter the sort of "famous prudery" that characterizes many Antiguan women, leaving Kincaid "alienated from her own sexuality and . . . to this day . . . not at all comfortable with the idea of myself and sex" (MB, 69). Her mother "had to be more rough with me than with the boys," Kincaid has said, "because I was a girl" (Kaufman, 110). She repeated to her daughter, as a sort of perverse mantra, that all these efforts were aimed at making sure that she would not end up having ten children by ten different men. But her mother's penchant for control went beyond directing her daughter's sexuality, extending to almost every aspect of her life and leading Kincaid to conclude with bitterness that her mother was a "horrible person" who "inflicted 'incredible little cruelties' upon her and her three stepbrothers" (Jacobs, 57). Despite her mother's obsession with instilling in her daughter a sense of proper sexual behavior, however, Kincaid's own experiences suggested a more nuanced awareness of sexuality. In "Just Reading," one of the gardening pieces she published in the *New Yorker* before she resigned from her position as a staff writer, she narrates how a woman in whose care her mother used to leave her when she was a child would take her to visit a male friend into whose house she would disappear—"to have sex, I realize some time later"—leaving her to while away her time dancing up and down the rows of portulacas blooming outside, "pretending I was a little girl from somewhere else" (54).

As she reached adolescence Kincaid began to withdraw more and more into the world of books, reading her favorites, like Charlotte Brontë's *Jane Eyre*, over and over. Books gave her "the greatest satisfaction" she was to know during her difficult teenage years, providing a refuge into which she could escape from the family's declining fortunes and her growing alienation from her mother. As a child she had been accustomed to going to the St. John's library with her mother every Thursday evening. The library—one of several Carnegie-sponsored libraries built throughout the Caribbean (the one in Roseau had been a favorite refuge of Dominican writers Jean Rhys and Phyllis Shand Allfrey)—was an old wood building facing the sea, with a broad verandah and large open windows. (The building, damaged by the earthquake of 1974, still had not been rebuilt when Kincaid visited in the mid-1980s, prompting her to write of its state of disrepair as symbolic of the depth of corruption and mismanagement in Antigua.) The weekly visits to the library in the company of her mother had been part of the pleasant harmony that had marked Kincaid's rapport with Annie Drew before their relationship turned sour: "then she took me everywhere she went and we were such a little couple, people used to comment on it ... and I would sit there with the *London Times* and one day I could just read it" (JKNY, 71). It had been the beginning of a craving for books that later seemed to her to have "saved her life." By the age of nine she had already read all the books in the children's section and would borrow her mother's card to choose books from the adult selections.

Kincaid has repeatedly described the great lengths to which she would go to satisfy her passion for acquiring books, which included sneaking them out of the library or stealing the money with which to buy them. She stole books she had already read, mostly the nineteenth-century British novels that formed the core of her knowledge of literature, because once she had read a book she "couldn't bear to part with it" (SP, 45). She would later explain that, having read no contemporary authors, she thought that writing was something that had gone out of style and that, consequently, there were no living writers. Until well into the 1980s Kincaid seemed unaware of the vibrant tradition of West Indian writing in English. It was evidence of the disintegration of good relationships between Kincaid and her mother that the latter began to see her daughter's passion for reading as evidence of weakness of character. "I would read books then," Kincaid wrote in *My Brother*, "and reading books would drive my mother crazy, she was sure it meant I was doomed to a life of slothfulness" (43).

Her delight in English books, the revered *Jane Eyre* in particular, belied a growing rebellion against the legacy British colonialism had left on Antigua, a British territory that did not become independent until 1981. Kincaid's childhood and adolescence coincided with the most intense development of the tourist industry in Antigua, with its consequent degradation of national culture. The island's tourist industry, "largely foreign-controlled, dominated by expatriates and investors linked to organized crime," and described by the political opposition as the "modern plantation," has led to young people being "ripped from any rootedness in a folk culture" (Pattullo, 182). Kincaid, a bright, insightful child whose mother, moreover, had been passionately albeit briefly involved in opposition politics, could not have failed to notice the threat to the cultural patrimony represented by tourism and foreign development. Her political awakening and resulting rebellion coincided with the onset of adolescence and seemed aimed against both the not-so-subtle goals of colonial education and her mother's determined anglophilia. Her mother strove to give her only daughter "a middle-class English upbringing" based on notions she had culled from her readings and observations of the habits and behaviors of the island's English colonial elite (Cudjoe, 398). Of the humiliations colonial education imposed on the black colonial child Kincaid has written with passionate eloquence in *Annie John* and *The Autobiography of My Mother*. She writes with particular scorn about the rudeness and racism that characterized the behavior of that colonial elite her mother placed before her as examples of proper demeanor. In *A Small Place* she recalls with bitterness how at the age of seven she had been made to stand in the hot sun for hours so she could see a "putty-faced Princess from England" enter Government House (SP, 25). In the wake of Princess Margaret's aborted romance with Group Captain Townsend she had been sent on a tour of the West Indies to forget her heartbreak. Every building she would enter or drive by during her visit to Antigua (including the school Kincaid attended, which had been renamed in her honor) was repaired and painted for the occasion.

Kincaid's rebelliousness drew on a precocious awareness of the many ways in which British and American institutions fostered racism in Antigua. People among her acquaintance could still recite the name of the first black person to be hired by the Barclays Bank as a teller, or the name and date on which the first black person played a round of golf at the Mill Reef Club. The institutional racism was mirrored in the English and European professionals with whom Kincaid and her family had frequent contact. Her mother would take her to be treated by a Czechoslovakian doctor (trained as a dentist but practicing as a pediatrician) whose wife would inspect patients before they were brought in to see him to make sure they were clean and did not smell, so that nothing "apart from the color of our skin" would offend the doctor (SP, 28). The mistress of the girls' school she briefly attended would tell her changes "to stop behaving as if they were monkeys just out of trees" (SP, 29). It is not surprising, given Kincaid's overwhelming feelings of powerlessness as a child and a colonial, that the "overarching theme" of her fiction would be the relationship between the powerful and the powerless. As the black child of a domineering mother in a British colony, Kincaid felt "at the mercy of everybody" (Kaufman, 110). "In a society like the one I am from," she wrote in *My Brother*, "being a child is one of the definitions of vulnerability and powerlessness" (32).

Kincaid's response to the daily humiliations of colonial life was a forthrightness perilously close to rudeness itself, an unwillingness to mince words or acknowledge hierarchies designed to leave those like her— black, native, female—in a marginal space. If she had been a slave, she has said, "I would have been dead within 10 seconds" (Kaufman, 111). Given her awareness of the nuances of power in colonial Antigua, she had learned early the ways in which language could be used as a weapon to maintain the likes of her in the margins. As a result, she seems to have determined at a very early age to avoid the idiosyncrasies of Antiguan English in favor of an elegant control of middle-class Anglo-American English. Her relationship to Antiguan English, consequently, is ambivalent at best. In *My Brother* she describes how, when hearing it spoken after her return home after a twenty-year absence, she could not understand what was being said. Caribbean critics have always considered her attempts at recreating West Indian speech in her novels and nonfiction as the most problematic aspect of her writing.

Kincaid has often described her adolescent impatience with the stifling provincialism of life in Antigua and with her countrymen's obsession with "Englishness" as the one factor that reconciled her to her parents' decision to send her to the United States in 1965. They had heard of a family looking for a live-in baby-sitter and presented the idea to her as a wonderful opportunity. Kincaid's family had been struggling financially since her stepfather's illness had made it impossible for him to work; her income was expected to help them weather the crisis until he was back on his feet. So at the age of seventeen she left Antigua to work as an au pair—a "servant," in her words—for the Masons, an affluent family in Scarsdale, a wealthy suburb of New York City. Despite her employer's being "very nice and protective" and her being in America, "the place I had always wanted to be more than any other place in the world," she described herself as "depressed and hopeless" (JKNY, 71). She did not take well to the cold air, which she associated with a darkness foreign to her familiar surroundings.

She left the Mason household after just a few months for Manhattan, where in answer to an ad in the newspaper she found another au pair job, taking care of the four young daughters of *New Yorker* writer Michael Arlen and his first wife. She would remain with them for three years. After the publication of *Lucy*, her novel about the young West Indian au pair and her relationship with her employers, the parents of four young girls, Kincaid was taken to task by many friends and colleagues for what was seen as her exposing of the intimacy and privacy of that family as the marriage broke up. Kincaid's experiences as an au pair in Manhattan were punctuated by her growing fascination with New York City and her transformation from colonial provincial girl to up-to-date young black American. She remade herself in the image of the African-American girls she had seen in *Tan* magazine: "The girls in *Tan* magazine looked to me to be tough and bad and worldly, and in my mind girls like that didn't live in Chicago or Detroit or Cincinnati. Girls like that lived in New York" (JKNY, 71).

While living with the Arlens Kincaid had obtained a high school equivalency diploma and began to take courses in photography at the New School for Social Research. In 1969 she left Manhattan for Franconia College in New Hampshire, to which she had won a full scholarship to continue her photographic studies. But her attempts at obtaining a college education were, in her words, "a dismal failure." Although she was barely into her twenties, she felt, by her own admission, too old to be a student, and it was too cold—so she returned to New York City within two years without completing her degree.

During these years Kincaid had broken all contact with her mother. Annie Drew had wanted her to study nursing, a career Kincaid rejected because she hated the sight of blood and was too prone to feel the onset of every symptom described to her. She had decided instead on following the more difficult path of the artist, trying her hand first at photography, later at freelance writing. To her bitter disappointment, her mother's approval, support, and sympathy had not been forthcoming. In *My Brother* she describes writing to her mother "seeking sympathy, a word of encouragement, love" when her early efforts to become a writer had led to pennilessness, hunger, and a cold apartment, only to receive a cold rebuff as a response. "It serves you right," she recalls her mother answering, "you are always trying to do things you know you can't do" (MB, 17). While in Scarsdale she had left her mother's letters unanswered. When she moved to Manhattan to work for the Arlens she left no address, thereby cutting off all communication with her mother for two years. She would not see her again for almost twenty years.

Back in Manhattan after her aborted college career, Kincaid went through a succession of low-paying, unchallenging clerical jobs that she quit or was fired from with expected regularity. She started to write, in fact, because she "couldn't hold a job" (Kaufman, 110) and freelance writing allowed her the independence she needed from the dull routine of office work and the problems occasioned by her outspokenness and outlandish style of dress. Her appearance then was as remarkable as her attitudes were uncompromising: "I use to look like a punk before punk," she has explained. At nearly six feet tall, Kincaid could be an arresting figure without trying, but her friend George W. S. Trow, a contributor to the *New Yorker* magazine who brought her to the attention of William Shawn, its legendary editor, described Kincaid as having gone to great lengths to make herself unforgettable, dyeing her hair blond and cutting it very short, often wearing a tam-o'-shanter and "a kind of red, red lipstick, a very vibrant lipstick. It was just as extreme a statement as a person could make that this was someone who did not necessarily fit anyone's conventional idea of who she would be" (Garis, 78). Her somewhat gaudy fashion combinations included jodhpurs and motorcycle boots, plaid shorts and saddle shoes, a Mets uniform, often (for street wear) white pajamas and a Brooks Brothers blue and white cotton seersucker bathrobe. Of these early efforts at self-invention she would write in 1995 that she had embarked on "the making of a type of person that did not exist in the place where I was born" (PMT, 93).

By the early 1970s Kincaid had started to make inroads into the New York publishing milieu, beginning to establish a reputation as a freelance writer for magazines like *Ms., Ingenue*, and the *Village Voice* weekly newspaper, for which she wrote pop music criticism. Her first published piece had been an interview with feminist movement leader and *Ms.* magazine editor Gloria Steinem, part of the "When I Was Seventeen" series she developed for *Ingenue* magazine in the early 1970s. It was at this stage in her career that, finding her given name not sufficiently evocative of the West Indies, she changed it to Jamaica Kincaid. The surname was apparently inspired by a reference to a character in a George Bernard Shaw play. Of her change of name she has said that it was like assuming a disguise, "a way for me to do things without being the same person who couldn't do them—the same person who had all these weights" (Garis, 78). A pseudonym assured her a certain degree of secrecy because she did not want her parents to know she was writing: "I would have been laughed at. That would have been very wounding, unbearable" (Kaufman, 110). Her family and acquaintances in Antigua "predictably" assumed that her name change was another indication that she was "putting on airs," and did not become reconciled to what they saw as a rejection of her heritage until they came to understand fully how "the conquering world" had accepted and celebrated her as a writer.

At this critical juncture, Kincaid had met and been befriended by Trow, whose "Talk of the Town" pieces in the *New Yorker* were often based on Kincaid's commentaries on her native Antigua and her idiosyncratic reactions to New York City. Following her meeting with William

Shawn, her own short essays also began appearing in the *New Yorker*. The first of eighty-five unsigned "Talk of the Town" pieces, "West Indian Weekend," appeared in 1974. From 1976 until 1995, when she left in a highly publicized disagreement with editor Tina Brown, she worked as a staff writer for the magazine. Kincaid's connection to the *New Yorker*, a magazine revered as a bastion of literary journalism at its best, has been a significant factor in the development of her literary career, guaranteeing her visibility and a highly respected outlet for her prose. The *New Yorker* also had a significant impact on her writing; it molded her style and provided a specific audience unfamiliar with her fictional terrain, for which she would evoke the myriad nuances of her West Indian experiences.

Her early success as a magazine writer spurred Kincaid into trying her hand at fiction. She wrote her first short story, "Girl," a remarkable tale told in one two-page sentence, in 1978. It had been inspired, as Kincaid has often related, by her reading of Elizabeth Bishop's poem "In the Waiting Room"; but it attempted to recreate the cadences of a mother's (her mother's) voice as she addressed a litany of instructions to her resisting daughter. The short story appeared in the June 26, 1978, issue of the *New Yorker* and later became the opening story for Kincaid's collection *At the Bottom of the River*, published in 1983. "Girl" was quickly followed by "Antigua Crossing," published the same year in *Rolling Stone*. The publication of *At the Bottom of the River*, which incorporated the stories published by Kincaid in the *New Yorker* between 1978 and 1982, made Kincaid the toast of literary New York. She was hailed by critics as one of the most important young writers of fiction of the decade. Tulani Davis, writing in the *New York Times*, called the book "a collection of gorgeous, incantatory stories of young life in Antigua." The book won the Morton Dauwen Zabel Award of the American Academy and Institute of Arts and Letters and was nominated for the PEN/Faulkner Award.

In 1979, with her writing career well on its way, Kincaid had married classical-music composer Allen Shawn, son of *New Yorker* editor-in-chief William Shawn. She credits the domesticity of her marriage and impending birth of her first child with the more linear narrative style of her first novel, the autobiographical tale of *Annie John*, published in 1985, the same year her daughter Annie was born and the year the family moved to Vermont, where her husband had accepted a teaching position at Bennington College. The novel, whose chapters were initially published as a series of stories in the *New Yorker*, was a critical sensation and became one of three finalists for the prestigious Ritz Paris Hemingway Award.

In January 1986 Kincaid returned to Antigua for the first time since her departure for the United States twenty years earlier, a visit prompted in part by one of her many short-lived reconciliations with her mother, this one following the birth of her daughter Annie. Kincaid's ambivalence about her home island is a frequent topic in her writings and interviews. She is drawn inexorably to the island and cannot resist returning to it, yet finds the prospect of a visit profoundly disturbing. At the heart of her discomfort is the presence of her mother on the island. She claims that she would be comfortable visiting Antigua without seeing her mother, but her children are fond of their grandmother, who dotes on them, and avoidance is impossible. She has described herself as "so vulnerable" to her family's needs and influence that she has to periodically withdraw completely from them. She had also had, until her return to Antigua in 1996 to help care for her AIDS-stricken brother Devon, a persistent memory of Antiguans as people who relish being cruel to each other, as people incapable of offering sympathy and affection for one another at times of suffering or loss. She has articulated the poignancy of her situation thus: "When I am in Vermont, home is Antigua; when I am in Antigua, home is Vermont" (Mantle 1996).

For her first visit home after a twenty-year absence "she wanted to have large boxes of things to take back," like the many West Indian immigrants who return home for visits laden with the goods easily available to them in America to lavish on their poorer relatives back home (Mantle 1996). But she did not have the money to take things back, nor did she have the inclination to play the part of the rich prodigal daughter. Instead she returned to reestablish her uneasy relationship with her mother and to come to know, albeit superficially, the three brothers who had been young children when she left and whom she now met again as adults. Devon, the only one of her siblings still living at home at the time of her visit, found the tall and thin woman reappearing into his life after twenty years an oddity, and enjoyed much merriment in mocking her Anglo-American accent and inability to understand local speech and marveling at her not being fat as expected.

One result of this visit was a book of nonfiction, *A Small Place*, written with the support of a Guggenheim Fellowship Kincaid had received in 1986. The essay presented a shatteringly critical view of the corruption and mismanagement of the island's postindependence government and was considered so scurrilous by many influential Antiguans that she found herself informally banned from the island. *A Small Place* was one of the few Kincaid pieces not published by the *New Yorker*. William Shawn, her mentor and father-in-law, had liked it and bought it for the magazine, but he had been replaced as editor by Robert Gottlieb who refused to publish it, deeming it too angry. So did critics when it was published as a book by Farrar, Straus & Giroux in 1988. They found themselves divided between those who found the anger vented at the evils of government-fostered tourism and corruption in Antigua refreshing and those who were appalled and repelled by the vitriol with which Kincaid had addressed both the government of Antigua and the tourists (most of them American) who by their presence on the island colluded with the government's oppression and abuses. In *A Small Place* Kincaid voices, intentionally or not, the concerns of the Antiguan opposition, who see tourism based on foreign investment as an "elusive sort of benefit" that "reinvents the economic and social relations of slavery" (Pattullo, 201). "In Antigua," Kincaid writes in *A Small Place*, "people cannot see a relationship between their obsession with slavery and emancipation and their celebration of the Hotel Training School (graduation ceremonies are broadcast on radio and television)" (55).

A Small Place changed the public's perception of Kincaid as a writer. It was a clear departure from the "charm" of *Annie John* and the somewhat abstract lyricism of *At the Bottom of the River*. The anger that had loomed below the surface in those early books—anger about the myriad forms of powerlessness she had endured throughout her life as a colonial subject, as the child of a domineering mother, as a black woman in a racist and sexist society—now bubbled over the top, and seemed to many a welcome change. It was as if the contentment she had found in her domestic life—a loving and supportive relationship with her husband, her doting on her children Annie and Harold (born in 1988)—had allowed her to safely channel her anger into her writing. Most of her subsequent writing—the most obvious exception being some of her gardening pieces—has been characterized by the in-your-face quality of *A Small Place*, and she talks of the anger in her prose "as a badge of honor" (Perry, 497). In 1990, for example, after her first visit to England, she would write in "On Seeing England for the First Time" that she "wanted to take it into my hands and tear it into little pieces and then crumble it up as if it were clay, child's clay" (16). But she denies being overwhelmed by anger in her personal life. She does not feel "any more angry than I think most people ought to be," she has explained. "I'm not Timothy McVeigh. What have I done? I've just written a book" (Kaufman, 114).

The subject of anger is one that surfaces constantly in the many interviews Kincaid has given since she gained literary fame after the publication of *At the Bottom of the River*. She seems taken aback by people's comments about there being something "unseemly" about the anger that characterizes some of her most recent writing, with frequent observations on her lack of understanding of people's fear of anger, female anger in particular. The anger in her writing, she has noted, is therapeutic, "an extension of how she feels day in and day out." As she explained recently to an interviewer, she fails to understand why she should not go through life as an angry person "when there is so much to be angry about" (Mantle 1996). Her notion of happiness is not one that requires that she be happy all the time.

Kincaid, for all the lyricism of her prose, can be fiercely political, as her most recent work has revealed. But her politics are not the politics of feminism or race, as one would expect from a black woman writer, and she refuses to be pigeonholed by those narrow categories. "It's just too slight to cling to your skin color or your sex," she told Selwyn Cudjoe in an interview, "when you think of the great awe that you exist at all" (401). She is particularly impassioned about "black" phenomena like the O. J. Simpson trial, an example of the reduction of black people, "in all their individual complexity, to the stuff of entertainment" (Lee, C10). She insists on seeing race not as an essence in itself but as "a shorthand for something broader, an imbalance of power," and can't imagine inventing an identity based on the color of her skin.

Having grown up in Antigua, where blacks are a majority of the population, Kincaid did not learn to see race as a marker of perceived inferiority until she arrived in the United States, where she learned "to be strong in the face of being things that could make you an outcast" (Mantle 1997). Having found acceptance in American society despite her race, she has lost her fear of ever being cast out again. This is particularly true for her in Vermont, where she has lived now for over a decade, and of which she speaks as a lovely place where people leave others alone, where people are "absolutely not interested in your business"—the only place other than Antigua where she forgets that she is black (Mantle 1997). More essential than race or national origin in determining one's identity, she asserts, is the ability to forget one's outward appearance and concentrate on what one looks like inside. She left Antigua in search of a private life impossible in her home island, to learn what she was like "in the privacy of her own self," a self that cannot be reduced to racial categories that are ultimately only expressions of relations of power (Mantle 1997).

In 1990 Kincaid published her second novel, *Lucy*. As with *Annie John*, the novel had originated as a series of stories published in the *New Yorker*. Kincaid has described the work as autobiographical, and it is indeed easy to read the novel as the second installment in the "imaginatively rearranged story" of the author's life (Pinckney, 28). The novel was fairly well received, despite the controversy over whether it had borrowed too closely from the intimate details of her former employers' lives, which cost Kincaid some angry remonstrances from friends like George Trow, to whom the novel is dedicated. Some critics, expecting a narrative voice similar to that of the "lively, curious and engaged child Annie," declared themselves disappointed by the "angry but disengaged Lucy" (Davis 1990, 11); but most reviewers agreed with Jane Mendelsohn's assessment that "with its subtle evocation of shifting patterns, *Lucy* reveals more gradations in the quality of possible experience than any of Kincaid's previous books" (21).

In 1990, at around the time of the publication of *Lucy*, Kincaid suffered from "something near a nervous breakdown" following a visit from her mother to her home in Vermont. During the course of the visit they had had a violent quarrel about the pain her mother had caused her and the older woman's inability to recognize how her actions had affected her daughter when young. The quarrel and subsequent explanations reopened old wounds, reawakening memories of difficulties and cruelties Kincaid herself had forgotten. After her mother's departure Kincaid suffered episodes of anxiety that needed to be treated with psychotherapy and medications and she developed a case of chicken pox, a disease she had already had as a child.

This illness may account for the gap of three years between the publication of *Lucy* and the appearance of the first installment of her third novel, *The Autobiography of My Mother*, published in 1996 to mixed critical reviews. Three excerpts from the new novel had appeared in the *New Yorker* prior to its publication in book form. The first of these, "Song of Roland," did not appear until April 1993. Kincaid, although not entirely idle during this period, published only three essays in the intervening time: two articles relating to her travels—"On Seeing England for the First Time" and "Out of Kenya"—and the first in her ongoing series of gardening essays, "Flowers of Evil."

The Autobiography of My Mother is the first of Kincaid's work not to be based directly on her life, focusing instead on characters drawn from the lives and experiences of her Dominican grandparents, interspersed with incidents from her mother's life. It drew pointed criticism from reviewers concerned with whether the anger that had characterized Kincaid's writing since the publication of *A Small Place* had overwhelmed her, thwarting her narrative voice. Yet many, even those expressing concern about the main character's overflowing anger, praised her writing for its elegance and lyricism, and many critics consider it her best work.

Shortly before the publication of *The Autobiography of My Mother* Kincaid left the *New Yorker*. The breakup came as the result of Kincaid's openly expressed distress at editor Tina Brown's invitation to sitcom actress Roseanne Barr—"as a fascinating and original feminist voice"—to serve as guest-editor of an issue of the magazine. (The idea was subsequently abandoned, although Roseanne became one of many contributors to a special issue on women.) Kincaid had stayed at the magazine after Shawn's departure despite her feelings that its owners had treated him "very brutally," but had found continued work impossible after the Roseanne affair, charging that Brown had ruined the magazine "by making it less literary and more oriented toward celebrities" (Lee, C10). She has described the magazine since as "a version of *People* magazine" (Jacobs, 57). Of Brown herself Kincaid has repeatedly stated that she created such an environment of brutality at the magazine that she felt her writing was jeopardized.

The Tina Brown/Roseanne affair underscores how combative and sometimes confrontational Kincaid can be when she chooses. Colleagues describe her as fearless and "not one to be intimidated by what others may say" (Garis, 78). Leslie Garis, in an interview for the *New York Times Magazine* that was instrumental in establishing the Kincaid persona with the New York reading public, retells an anecdote she heard from Ian Frazier, a fellow *New Yorker* writer, about a shopping trip with Kincaid to the Chelsea Charcuterie. It was an anecdote that would sear Kincaid in the minds of her readers as the perfect counterpart to her bold, undaunted heroines, contributing much to what would shortly become the Kincaid myth of the author as outspoken, dauntless, quasi-shrew—an image that Kincaid appears to enjoy perpetuating. As Frazier tells it, a man had come in with radio blasting demanding change for a twenty-dollar bill and Kincaid confronted him, insisting that he turn the radio down. The man swore he would get his gun and return to "blow you away!," to which she replied, "Yeah-yeah-yeah." Despite Frazier's entreaties to leave the store—to which her only reply was "Yeah-yeah-yeah"—she continued to shop for forty-five minutes. The man did not return. This anecdote encapsulates the feistiness, independence, and plainspokenness readers have come to associate with Kincaid's public persona. In New York literary circles, Kincaid has drawn a measure of occasional envy and disdain, as exemplified by the following parodic portrait in Gary Indiana's book *Resentment*: "Unguentina Carribou married early into an incredibly prestigious white publishing family, securing for her slender, rage-inflected memoirs of an entirely invented Carribean girlhood a kind of inflated adulation. . . . She is a surpassingly ugly woman with lumpy features and a wardrobe of frilly faded dresses worn to evoke the gentility and dignified oppression of her island forebears" (46).

Frazier has described Kincaid as "warlike," and indeed, as some interviewers have observed, she seems to enjoy making people uncomfortable. Sally Jacobs, who interviewed her in Vermont for the *Boston Globe* shortly after the publication of *The Autobiography of My Mother* in 1996, tells of how she was received coolly, "without a flicker of welcome" (57). In response to a question about her biological father, whom Kincaid barely knew, she turned the answer into what amounted to a dismissal of her visitor: "He was as real to me as you. Yes, you'll go and I'll think, was there someone here?" (57). In *My Brother*, however, we learn that this interview was conducted on the day Kincaid learned of her brother Devon's death and that in her grief "it was easy to be without mercy and answer truthfully" (101).

In January 1996, as Kincaid was preparing for her American book tour to promote her latest novel, *The Autobiography of My Mother*, her brother Devon died of AIDS at age thirty-three. Devon, the youngest of her three brothers, an intelligent, well-read child and an accomplished athlete, had drifted into the Antiguan drug culture and a promiscuous lifestyle that had included sexual relationships with both men and women. Kincaid had left Antigua when he was only three years old and their relationship had been the distant one imposed by her not seeing him again until he was in his early twenties.

Kincaid's most vivid memories of her youngest brother dated back to the first three years of his life, when she still lived in Antigua. As an infant he had been attacked by an army of red ants, an incident she fictionalized in *Annie John*. She recalled his birth as having led to a marked change in her mother's relationship to the world, turning her into a sharp and bitter woman who quarreled with everyone all the time.

In *Annie John* she wrote of the fictional mother's efforts to abort her third child. In *My Brother*, the autobiographical narrative of her brother's struggles she published in October 1997, Kincaid describes Devon's curiosity as to the truth behind that fictionalized incident. Kincaid, out of consideration for her brother, had reassured him by claiming to have invented the incident; but she makes sure the reader understands that he should not have believed her denials.

One of the most devastating incidents described in *My Brother* stems directly from Kincaid's relationship with Devon. Once, when her mother had gone out, leaving her in charge of the children, the young Kincaid had amused herself with her reading, neglecting to change Devon's heavily soiled diaper. In her fury, her mother had gathered all the books Kincaid owned—those she had stolen from the library or bought, sometimes with stolen money—and placed them on a heap, doused them with kerosene, and set them on fire. Recollections of this episode, which Kincaid had forgotten, were among the many memories contributing to her near-breakdown following her mother's visit to Vermont in 1990.

On first hearing that Devon had contracted AIDS and was hospitalized in grave condition, Kincaid returned to Antigua, bringing with her the medication that sent him into a temporary remission. Of the development of their relationship as adults, after the news and needs of his illness brought her more frequently to Antigua than in decades before, she wrote poignantly in *My Brother*. Kincaid, who for some years now has been writing about gardening, used gardening imagery to convey the relentless destruction of his body by the virus inside him: "The plantsman in my brother will never be, and all the other things that he might have been in his life have died: but inside his body a death lives, flowering upon flowering, with a voraciousness that nothing seems able to satisfy and stop" (19).

Kincaid became involved in her brother's illness in a way that was "inexplicable" to her. As she described in an interview with Larry Mantle, she felt that his life and misfortunes offered her a glimpse of "her other life," the life she would have lived had she remained in Antigua. She was inexorably drawn to his struggles, not necessarily out of love for him (although at some level what she felt for him must have been a form of love), but out of an identification with him rooted in his representing everything she had escaped by leaving for the United States: "I perhaps cared for myself," she says of her deep involvement with her brother as he struggled against the ravages of AIDS, "and he was myself" (Mantle 1997).

The tragedy of Devon's life, as Kincaid depicts it in *My Brother*, was that his circumstances kept him from knowing himself, that the culture surrounding him made it impossible for him to admit to the world a homosexuality that would have made him a pariah in Antiguan society. He, who had been so quick to laugh at other people's frailties, would have understood better than most that such an admission would have turned him into a laughingstock, a figure of ridicule. Kincaid does not learn of her brother's homosexuality, however, until some time after his death, and the knowledge becomes the missing piece that helps her make sense out of the tragedy of his life. Once she learns that he was gay, she understands the theatricality of his courtship of women, the bravura of his representation of the West Indian Don Juan, his denial of the reality of his condition. In the end, however, AIDS turned him into the social outcast he had feared becoming, and he was subject to the "incredible prejudice and scorn" with which people with the disease are treated in Antigua. Kincaid's tribute to him is that of writing to reclaim his flawed humanity, to help people understand that he was still a human being despite his looking like "one of them . . . this thinning thing" (Mantle 1997).

The circumstances leading to Devon's death, and Kincaid's frequent visits to Antigua during his illness, brought to the fore Kincaid's inability to see herself as a writer in her home island. In several interviews after her return to Antigua following her brother's death she has returned to the topic of her incapacity to write in Antigua, a place where she "lives" and "reads," but where she can never write. She can "have an experience" there, but her Antigua is beautiful "in a crippling way," and it incapacitates her as a writer. Antigua is for many a paradise, but she has always felt that "paradise was death."

Kincaid has built a different version of paradise at her Bennington, Vermont, home—a sprawling house on a knoll surrounded by a meadow about which she wrote a *New Yorker* piece in 1991—where Kincaid indulges her passion for gardening, an occupation she often describes as "an absolute luxury." The house is full of plants, and she works indefatigably on her flower and vegetable gardens, which cover much of her three-acre property. A visitor described her garden as including eight varieties of mint and "peonies big as pumpkins" (Jacobs, 57). Gardening, Kincaid says, is "an extended form of reading, of history and philosophy" (Jacobs, 57). It has become a way of life for Kincaid and her family, an occupation tied to her pleasure in domesticity. After all, she started to plant things—she embarked on the path that led her to become a gardener—when, on her second Mother's Day, her husband had given her some packets of seeds and gardening tools on her daughter's behalf. Her garden has grown over the years, away from the house, "down the hill, toward the bog, into the bog," harboring the many undomesticated species Kincaid has fallen in love with and providing many of the vegetables and spices around which she has developed a new interest in food and cooking. Of the impact of her passionate commitment to her garden on her family, Kincaid comments ruefully that her children see the garden "as the thing that stands between them and true happiness, which is to say my absolute attention" (PP, 46).

Out of her meditations on gardening and her voracious readings on the literature of the garden, Kincaid has developed a series of articles, most of which appeared in the *New Yorker* before her resignation from the magazine. Her publisher, Farrar, Straus & Giroux, plans to publish a collection of these writings, tentatively titled *In the Garden*, in the near future. Kincaid has described gardening as "one of the original forms of conquest" (Ferguson, 167), and the series, which moves uneasily between lyrical descriptions of the beauty of roses and the angry tones of *A Small Place*, addresses the thematic connections between gardening, colonialism, and empire.

In 1993 Kincaid, who was raised a Methodist, converted to Judaism, her husband's religion. She is reticent on the subject of faith, telling interviewers that "God is a private issue" (Kaufman, 114); but her commitment to Beth El, the congregation of over one hundred members of which she is president, is passionate. She is credited by its rabbi, Howard Cohen, with winning the respect of those in a position to donate time and money to the synagogue. Cohen finds "something of the prophet" in her writings: "She writes a lot about oppression and makes people uncomfortable, which is what the prophets did" (Kaufman, 114). Her children are being brought up in the Jewish faith, and Jewish traditions are at the center of the family's celebrations. A reporter arriving for an interview in the early fall of 1996 found the remains of a wooden Succoth booth, still covered in stalks of grain and leaves, built for the Jewish festival of tabernacles.

Kincaid's position as a leading American writer has been recognized in myriad ways in recent years. In 1986 she was awarded a Guggenheim Fellowship and since then has been the recipient of several honorary degrees from institutions like Williams College and Long Island College. In 1994 she joined the faculty of the prestigious African-American Studies Department at Harvard University, where she teaches literature and creative writing one semester a year. In her courses at Harvard she pursues the topics so prominent in her fiction: the evils of colonialism, the relationship between the powerful and the powerless, the links between literature and empire. In a recent course on "literature and possession" she sought to explore, through literature, "how we claim things, how we come to possess things," echoing the themes of her most recent writings.

2

From Elaine Potter Richardson
to Jamaica Kincaid

Elaine Potter Richardson's path to international fame as one of the most celebrated American writers of the second half of the twentieth century is a remarkable one. After her arrival in New York City in the late 1960s she transformed herself, in the space of a few short years, from the desperately unhappy child of a lower-middle-class West Indian family with pretensions to genteel propriety to the toast of the most exclusive New York intellectual circles. She accomplished this transformation by turning both her past and the process of her personal reinvention into the clay from which to mold an exceptional body of literary work.

Kincaid's path to becoming a writer was not a conventional one. Antigua, like many other small West Indian islands, does not have a literary tradition of distinction or long standing, and the ambition to become a writer would not have come naturally to someone in Kincaid's circumstances. Books were not readily available, even in the capital of St. John's, which by size, population, and level of development would be considered a small and not very prosperous town by American standards. Neither had she access to a broad range of literary materials. As a British colony, Antigua's educational system was under the control of the School Certificate Examination Bureau, which made few allowances for local input into the school curriculum. (The first efforts toward establishing a West Indian-based educational philosophy did not come until 1960, when the House of Representatives of the short-lived West Indies Federation [1958–1962] vowed to replace the School Certificate Examination with a system that reflected the cultures, literatures, and circumstances of the various island nations.) As a result, very few books other than those approved in the curriculum could be obtained with any ease in the libraries and handful of bookstores of the region, which stocked the English classics that became Kincaid's favorite reading: Charlotte and Emily Brontë, Jane Austen, William Shakespeare, John Milton, and the King James version of the Bible.

In "Plant Parenthood," one of the essays from *In the Garden*, Kincaid writes of her anger at being forced to memorize William Wordsworth's poem on daffodils as emblematic of the imposition on West Indian children of literary materials foreign to their surroundings—no daffodils are found in the Caribbean. One of the central chapters in *Lucy* also revolves around Kincaid's childhood recitation of Wordswoth's poem as symbolic of cultural and literary colonization. In "The Season Past," the sixth installment of *In the Garden*, she recalls how the only magazines for girls sold in Antigua always depicted girls at birthday parties with hair and clothes the golden shade of a rare yellow-fleshed watermelon she grows in her Vermont home. Reading these magazines made her wish then to be one of those golden-haired girls—"and the despair I felt then that such a thing would never be true is replaced now with the satisfaction that such a thing would never be true" (57).

In "Alien Soil," another essay from *In the Garden*, she describes how, during a recent stay in Antigua, she visited the only bookstore she knows in St. John's just to see what texts were being used in Antiguan schools and how they compared to what was taught when she was a schoolchild. To her deep regret, botany, one of the two subjects she truly enjoyed while in school, was no longer taught, having been replaced by "Agriculture." In *A Small Place* she deplores the sad state of education in present-day Antigua, and the ignorance and lack of intellectual ambition of Antiguan youth. She had found much to criticize about the British-centered colonial educational system of her childhood, but also found much to lament in the discovery that it had been replaced by a poorer system, despite the advantages of its focus on West Indian literatures and cultures. During Kincaid's schooldays, books by Caribbean authors were rarely available in Antigua and not officially sanctioned by the educational system. Kincaid's frequent assertion that she grew up thinking that writing was something that had gone out of style with the nineteenth century meant most poignantly that she grew up without envisioning the possibility that a young West Indian girl such as she was could transform herself into someone who could write books for others to read and enjoy.

It is not surprising then—given the profound personal and intellectual transformation necessary to make a noted writer out of someone of her circumstances and background—that Kincaid's early work, that indeed most of her work, has centered on the process through which a young West Indian woman moves from what would appear to be most inauspicious beginnings to a brilliant career as a writer. Indeed her early fiction—*At the Bottom of the River, Annie John*, and *Lucy*—can be read most convincingly as a portrait of the artist as a young woman, as narratives that chronicle her discovery that, contrary to anyone's expectations, someone like her could most certainly reinvent herself through art. The autobiographical nature of her work can thus be seen to stem from very interesting narrative possibilities opened by her own personal story. Not until the publication of *The Autobiography of My Mother* in 1996 does Kincaid begin to move away from her own life as the source of material for her fiction, and even then she is but one step removed from her own story, as she finds inspiration for that book in the lives and experiences of her mother and her Dominican grandparents.

Kincaid acknowledges her dependence on her own life experiences as material for her writing. "I've never really written anything about anyone except myself and my mother," she has said, offering perhaps the truest commentary about her own work (CBY, 330). As a writer she is best known for having dissected her family and its history to produce a distinguished body of writing. She describes the process of turning autobiography into art as that of conveying truth through fiction without limiting herself to writing everything down exactly as it happened. Of *Annie John*, for example, she has said that "every feeling in it happened"—"it very much expresses the life I had"—although not everything happened in the order in which it appears in the book (Perry, 494). The autobiographical element in Kincaid's work is in itself not surprising, as writers often rely heavily on their own experiences for their early fiction; what intrigues most about her work is the close connection existing between autobiography and fiction, particularly as Kincaid often offers both fictional and nonfictional versions of the same autobiographical episodes, allowing the reader to determine the closeness of the relationship between the two. Sometimes they are identical in detail and the separation between them is only a matter of style.

KINCAID'S BODY OF WORK

Kincaid is the author of one collection of short stories, *At the Bottom of the River*; three novels, *Annie John*, *Lucy*, and *The Autobiography of My Mother*; two book-length essays, *A Small Place* and *My Brother*; a handful of uncollected short stories, chief among them "Ovando"; and a number of uncollected essays, many of which will form a book tentatively titled *In the Garden*. Her work is almost evenly divided between fiction and nonfiction, and, with the exception of "Ovando," easily traceable to autobiographical episodes.

Autobiography and Writing

Kincaid's trajectory as a writer of fiction begins with two short pieces, both published in 1978, centering on the experiences of a young girl coming to terms with growing up in a West Indian colony: "Girl" and "Antigua Crossings: A Deep and Blue Passage on the Caribbean Sea." These two pieces, published almost simultaneously, already gave evidence of the themes and tensions that would characterize Kincaid's subsequent fiction. "Girl," later included in *At the Bottom of the River* (see Chapter 3 for detailed discussion), borrows the voice of Kincaid's own mother to convey the frictions between mother and daughter in a colonial setting, where the rules of behavior and social expectations have been determined by foreign cultural elements and are not native to the landscape. "Antigua Crossings," published in *Rolling Stone* magazine, assumes the voice of a young adolescent girl in a story that touches on the central themes to which Kincaid will return over and over: the powerful figure of the mother who withdraws her affection from her daughter; the dazzling natural beauty of the West Indies, here embodied by the Caribbean Sea, as the backdrop; the figure of Christopher Columbus as emblematic of the conquest of the region; the tragic history of the Carib Indians as representative of the human cost of colonization; the legacy of Obeah as emblem of resistance and healing. In addition, the story introduces various autobiographical elements—anecdotes, characters, settings, details—to which Kincaid will return in both her fiction and nonfiction: a baby who almost dies from being eaten by ants; the mother who attempts to teach her resisting daughter how to behave properly and not be an embarrassment to the family; the schoolroom as a place where history is distorted; the narrator's deteriorating relationship with her mother as she enters puberty; the earrings and bracelet of Guianese gold worn by many of Kincaid's fictional alter egos; the walk to the jetty with her father; the nickname of "Little Miss."

The autobiographical element in Kincaid's work can be traced most clearly through the centrality of the figure of the mother in her narratives. From her very first stories, "Girl" and "Antigua Crossings," through the autobiographical narrative of her brother's death from AIDS, *My Brother*, the process of severing the ties between mother and daughter has been the central theme of her writing. Kincaid sees her mother as the "fertile soil" that roots her writing. "The way I became a writer," she once said, "was that my mother wrote my life for me and told it to me" (O'Conner, 6).

The representation of the mother in Kincaid's fiction is always ambiguous—at times nurturing, but more often than not antagonistic and disapproving. There is a clear correlation established throughout Kincaid's work between motherhood and the colonial metropolis as motherland. Moira Ferguson, in *Jamaica Kincaid: Where the Land Meets the Body*, argues convincingly that Kincaid's representation of motherhood as both biological and colonial "explains why the mother-daughter relations in her fiction often seem so harshly rendered" (1). Through the mother figure Kincaid addresses both her own personal alienation from her mother and Antigua's alienation from itself because of its dependent relationship with the colonial motherland. Through her many fictional alter egos— other selves, the many variations of her former self she develops in her stories and novels—Kincaid articulates the process of separation from the mother and the motherland as necessary in order to grow into adulthood. This process of growing apart from the figure of the mother/motherland, begun in fiction in "Girl" and "Antigua Crossings," remains the central theme of Kincaid's writing, although we can glimpse traces of a new thematic direction in the essays from *In the Garden*, where she has found new approaches to the discussion of empire and colonialism.

At the Bottom of the River

At the Bottom of the River, Kincaid's first book, gathers the stories she had published in the *New Yorker* in 1978 and 1979. The setting of most of these stories is Antigua during the years of Kincaid's childhood, although two stories, "Holidays" and "What I Have Been Doing Lately," have American settings. Through them, the writer takes the reader on a voyage across the space of memory and dream, rendering through a fusion of fantasy and reality, plays of dark and light, and profuse use of poetic imagery, the nuances of a fragmented and disjointed colonial past. The prose of *At the Bottom of the River* has puzzled many readers, who consider it Kincaid's most difficult book. There is a discontinuity in the narrative and a profuse use of symbolism in the text that mirror the various narrators' fragmented spaces. Citizens of a colonized small island—divided within themselves, loving and hating their mothers, mimicking and rejecting the colonizers they have been indoctrinated into admiring, torn between Christianity and Obeah, they must carve an identity for themselves out of many disconnected strands.

Kincaid has explained in interviews that she first became interested in writing after watching *La Jetée*, a French film composed around still photographs in black and white. She would watch the film over and over, feeling "incredibly moved" by it. Its style, dependent on successions of still photographs interspersed with infrequent moving images, offered the budding writer an example of artistic expression that was not concerned with the representation of things as they are. She also found a similar anti-realistic example in the novels of French "New-Novel" writer Alain Robbe-Grillet. These influences can be gleaned readily in the stories of *At the Bottom of the River*, where they alternate with the cadences of William Shakespeare, John Milton, and the King James version of the Bible.

The prose of *At the Bottom of the River*, although asking the reader to immerse him- or herself in a textual world of reverie and daydream, is nonetheless firmly rooted in the historical reality of Antigua. There are numerous markers in the text—autobiographical elements, historical allusions, concrete details of everyday life in Antigua, descriptions of landscape, fauna, and flora—that speak to a concrete historical space and time. In these stories, despite her experimentation with narrative discontinuity, cryptic imagery, fantasy, and surreal symbolism, Kincaid nonetheless rearticulates the themes she introduced in "Antigua Crossings," constructing through the various tales a "subtle paradigm of colonialism" (Ferguson, 7). But it is a style that insinuates rather than asserts historical truth, and Kincaid was quick to see its limitations.

Three years after the publication of *At the Bottom of the River*, Kincaid published *Annie, Gwen, Lilly, Pam and Tulip*, originally written as a section of the earlier book but not included in the final manuscript. It was published in 1986 in a limited edition with illustrations by Eric Fischl.

Stylistically and thematically, *Annie, Gwen . . .* follows very closely the model of *At the Bottom of the River*, although its alternating monologues belong to a prepubescent, edenic world that precedes the adolescent conflicts of the narrators of *At the Bottom. . . .* The five friends whose voices people this text look behind to a world of blissful unity and harmony that already contains within it the seeds of its own destruction. As their own bodies betray the innocence of childhood—growing breasts, experiencing changes that will open for them a world of post-edenic sexual activity—so is the world beyond their isolated "perfect" space no longer "free of envy, pestilence, or shattering pronouncements" (unnumbered pages). The threatening presence hovering outside their protected space suggests that they inhabit a precolonial Eden about to suffer invasion and conquest, just as the preadolescent characters feel the threat to their peace and safety in their burgeoning sexuality. Like their adolescent counterparts in *At the Bottom of the River*, however, they strive to find in the memory of their pre-puberty Arcadia the tools from which to prepare to resist and endure.

In a number of interviews given after the publication of *At the Bottom of the River*, Kincaid has repudiated the style in which that book—and by extension *Annie, Gwen, Lilly, Pam and Tulip*—is written as growing directly out of her colonized education. They represent a style of writing that she has left behind. Speaking to Donna Perry, she explained her dissatisfaction with the book as stemming from its being "a very unangry, decent, civilized book," representing the success of the English people in making "their version of a human being" out of her (698–699). Her vow "never to write like that again" is firmly kept in *Annie John*, the work she started immediately after the completion of *At the Bottom of the River*.

Annie John

Annie John is considered one of the best examples of the Caribbean *bildungsroman* or novel of development. The eight chapters or stories that compose the text follow young Annie from the age of ten till she leaves Antigua at the age of sixteen, and recount her maturation as a bittersweet process of alienation and loss. Told as a work of memory, of recollections of childhood, *Annie John* owes its success with critics and the general public to the clarity and directness of its prose, which to some came as a welcome development after the elusiveness and ambiguity of *At the*

Bottom of the River. As a memoir of childhood, *Annie John* has been celebrated for the richness of its rhythms and imagery, but above all for its
gift in conveying character and its skilled evocation of the social landscape of Antigua through the highlighting of few but salient details. The
writer of memoirs, as Paula Bonnell observed in her review of the novel,
"is deeply concerned with expression of truths not conventionally acknowledged but instantly recognizable to anyone who has honestly ex-
amined his own grief and joy" (126). When first entering the fictionalized
autobiography that is *Annie John* the reader is immediately struck by the
immediacy and "ferocious lucidity" of Annie's voice (Pinckney, 29). Although the novel has been called "charming" by many critics, the charm
of the book (if we are so to describe it) is an unsettling one. It rests on
Annie's unrepentant descriptions of how through lies and betrayals she
foiled her mother's attempts at making a proper Afro-Saxon girl out of
her. The quality through which Annie retains our interest and sympathy
despite her at times too-naked honesty is her insistence on the singularity
of her experience and her refusal to compromise.

  Annie John returns to the world and incidents familiar to readers of *At
the Bottom of the River*, with one significant difference—here characters
come alive with their own quirks and idiosyncrasies, fleshed-out, so to
speak. The richness of imagination remains, but now in the service of a
distinct plot line. The concern with the destructive power of history
guides the narrative, but here it is embodied in specific characters, historical figures, and incidents. In *Annie John* Kincaid successfully anchors
her narrative in a specific time and geography without losing her ability
to make that narrative convey meaning through metaphor and symbol.
The specificities of the relationships between the characters, particularly
that between Annie and her mother, which had been too diffuse for
empathy in *At the Bottom of the River*, here carry a wealth of symbolic
meaning, serving as a vehicle for Kincaid's exploration of the struggle
between the powerful and the oppressed.

  Kincaid has described childhood as a state of absolute powerlessness,
a condition she has used repeatedly in her fiction to explore the process
of maturation and its potential for defiance and resistance. Childhood
mirrors the colonial condition, and opens fascinating possibilities for
symbolic representation. As readers we follow Annie through her dis-
continuous coming-of-age narrative as she weaves her way through the
maze of colonial myths and family expectations, seeking to define a personal identity that, given her birth in a colonial milieu, must also by
definition be a political identity. Kincaid invites us to read in Annie's

physical maturation—her breasts develop, she begins to menstruate—and emotional growth—depicted primarily through her struggles to separate from her mother—a mirror to her island's movement from colonialism to independence. It is not a triumphant process, as much is lost and many struggles end in defeat, but it nonetheless leaves Annie—and perhaps Antigua—poised to define themselves on their own terms. *Annie John* outlines the process through which a character so closely linked to Kincaid herself develops a political consciousness, thus preparing the thematic terrain for Kincaid's nonfictional polemic against British colonialism in the West Indies, *A Small Place*.

A Small Place

Jamaica Kincaid's visit to her home island in 1987, her first since having left the island twenty years before, led to a turning point in her writing. Her reencounter with the realities of political and economic corruption in Antigua unleashed a latent anger that had been glimpsed in *At the Bottom of the River* and *Annie John* but had never before found an adequate outlet. *A Small Place* offers a scathing indictment of the mismanagement and corruption that has led the Antiguan government—headed for three decades by V. C. Bird and his sons—to notoriety throughout the region for their endorsement of personal greed and the resulting disenfranchisement of the people. In *A Small Place* Kincaid assumes a new, mature voice of denunciation, and although the text provides ample links to her previous fiction through the repetition of various anecdotes and the reappearance of familiar figures (her mother chief among them), it breaks away from those earlier books in tone and approach.

A Small Place is divided into three main sections and a short epilogue. The first section discusses tourism and its impact on the local population. It addresses the tourist directly as an accomplice in the perpetuation of poverty and oppression in Antigua. A tourist, Kincaid charges, is "an ugly human being" who turns the life of "overwhelming and crushing banality and boredom and desperation and depression" of the island native into a source of pleasure for himself (SP, 14, 18).

In the second section Kincaid returns to the Antigua she knew as a child, a place of colonial rule, racism, and limitations. This pre-independence Antigua was far from an ideal space; it was what the British had made of it, a land of orphans with "no motherland, no fatherland, no gods, no mounds of earth for holy ground, no excess of love which might lead to the things that an excess of love sometimes brings, and worst and most painful of all, no tongue" (SP, 31). The third section, the longest of the book, captures Kincaid's shock at the radical changes undergone by the island during her twenty-year absence. The question that opens the section is whether the island under self-rule is better off than when it was dominated by the "bad-minded" English. The answer is a categorical no, which she illustrates by a number of "events": the Hotel Training School that does not see the irony between the Antiguan obsession with slavery and a school to teach the lucky few how to be good servants; the car dealerships, electric, telephone, and cable television services under the control of government ministers; the Swiss banking accounts fed by aid funds and the trafficking in Antiguan passports. The symbol of the impact of corruption is the ruin of the old Carnegie-built Antigua library, damaged in the earthquake of 1974 and left in disrepair, the books getting ruined in their boxes in a second-floor makeshift library.

The epilogue celebrates the natural beauty of Antigua and, in a bittersweet acknowledgment of the fallibility of human nature, reclaims for Antiguans the right to be seen as just human beings prone to error, misjudgment, and despair. Once slaves are free, Kincaid asserts, they no longer have a claim to being "noble and exalted; they are just human beings" (81).

The principal themes of A Small Place flow directly from Kincaid's previous work, here distilled through anger and presented more forthrightly without the fictional façade as mediating space: the subordination of the colonial subject to the English masters, experienced in the most mundane details of everyday life; the devastating history of slavery and colonial oppression, and its legacy of passivity and apathy; the collusion of the elites with the continued expropriation of the Antiguan people's labor as directly stemming from slavery and empire; the natural beauty of the island as a false vision of paradise that has left it exposed to exploitation by the tourist industry; the exhortation to Antiguans to rally to remedy the nefarious effects of corruption, mismanagement, and disenfranchisement. These thematic strands make of A Small Place a very angry book, but it is a controlled anger, used to great effect, rhetorically directed at Antiguans as a rallying cry to awaken them to a recognition of the many ways in which they collude in their own degradation.

Understandably, the book was not well received in Antigua, where

Kincaid was vilified in the government-controlled press and from where she was unofficially banned for years. The unpropitious reaction should have been expected, given the widespread feeling that she had relinquished her right to such frontal condemnation by her migration to the United States some twenty years before. Kincaid acknowledges having written the book "with a kind of restlessness" (Perry, 498), aware of being (and of placing herself within the text as) simultaneously an insider (when describing the Antigua she knew) and outsider (when describing her shock at what she subsequently found). Unsure of who her readership would be in the case of *A Small Place*—she had never before in her writings addressed Antiguans as an audience—she seems to write with a dual consciousness, at once covering familiar terrain and speaking to Antiguans with intimate knowledge of the geographical and social space they once shared, and addressing an American, perhaps an international audience (harangued directly as "you tourist") who knows next to nothing about Antigua but what he or she learns from travel agency posters.

Response to the book in the United States was mixed to glowing, despite the apprehension raised by the *New Yorker's* refusal to publish the piece as "too angry." Kincaid gloried in the reviews that took the book to task for lacking the charm of *Annie John*. She had not aimed at charm but at a "prolonged visit to the bile duct," which is how she refers to one lengthy passage of diatribe in *A Small Place*. But the book was generally very well received, and many critics praised the courage of her dissection of the Antiguan government's political corruption and her lucid critique of tourism. *A Small Place* was singled out from among her works for its passion and conviction, and the critical consensus held that she wrote with "a musical sense of language, a poet's understanding of how politics and history, private and public events, overlap and blur" (CBY, 330).

Lucy

Lucy, published two years after *A Small Place*, is Kincaid's most accessible work of fiction. In the character of Lucy, a young West Indian woman freshly arrived in New York City to work as an au pair for a wealthy white family, Kincaid dramatizes the political, class, and race dynamics of which she writes with such eloquent anger in *A Small Place*. *Lucy* can be read as the third installment in Kincaid's fictional recreation of her own life, as it picks up the narrative at the point of voluntary exile, of migration, as if continuing the story from the moment at which we took our leave from Annie John.

The protagonist of *Lucy*, like the typical Kincaid heroine, is characterized by her unflinching truthfulness and refusal to yield to sentimentality. In *Annie John* these traits served to distance the reader from the protagonist, keeping the reader at arm's length. In *Lucy* the abbreviated time span (the novel covers a period of two years, as opposed to the eight years of *Annie John*) and the character's isolation from her home environment serve to confer greater immediacy and psychological richness to the story. This, coupled with the narrower social canvas—the plot focuses on Lucy's relationship with her employers and develops for the most part indoors or within the domestic space—allows Kincaid to explore Lucy's dilemma from a closer, more intimate range. Lucy, courageous, reckless, and at times brutally candid, is Kincaid's most sympathetic heroine.

The American setting of *Lucy*, which Kincaid uses here in a sustained way for the first time, allows Kincaid to explore the character's isolation and lead her to a recognition of her need for human and emotional connection. Throughout the five long episodes that constitute the text, Kincaid charts Lucy's rejection of personal intimacy as stemming from the dissolution of her difficult relationship with her mother. The novel's bittersweet revelation that Lucy's determined search for independence is leading her to an emotional void is poignantly rendered in the character's realization that her struggle to detach from her mother has left her incapable of establishing deep emotional connections with anyone. "I wish I could love someone so much that I would die from it," Lucy writes at the end of her tale, and "a great wave of shame came over me and I wept and wept" (164).

Lucy's position as a black West Indian nanny in a white upper-class Manhattan setting transcends the typical expectations of relationships between masters and servants, employers and employees, serving in turn as a metaphoric exploration of the process of decolonization. Although Lucy sleeps in the maid's room, she never assumes servility as a posture; she refuses to accept any definition of herself attached to notions of race, class, or occupation, remaining throughout singular, unfettered, true to herself. Her employers, in turn, initially secured in the cocoon of their race and class superiority, functioning according to the most traditional gender roles, unravel before the reader's eyes, illustrating the fragility of those notions of power based on the exploitation of others. In the character of Mariah, drawn sympathetically despite her blindness to the cost to others of her class and race privileges, Kincaid paints a vivid portrait of the naiveté and self-absorption that has led to the exploitation of people like herself in places like Antigua. In *Lucy*, notions of colonial oppression and cultural erasure are presented without the naked anger of *A Small Place*. As embodied in characters like the naive Mariah, the self-absorbed patriarchal Lewis, or the self-decolonized Lucy, the power structures that sustained colonialism and exploitation are seen as fractured, and Lucy can see in their errors and misjudgments the dissolution of colonial authority.

Reviews of *Lucy* were perhaps the most encouraging Kincaid had received to that date. Carol Anshaw, writing for the *Chicago Tribune*, described the novel as "a graceful, complex narrative that is at the same time about sexual awakening, the construction of identity out of the scraps at hand, the elaborate misunderstandings that can arise from different cultural assumptions and the essentially harrowing nature of love" (37). Critics particularly admired the heroine's refusal to assume an identity circumscribed by race or gender. Although Kincaid owes much of her success to the reading public's interest in feminism, multiculturalism, and race, *Lucy* made clear that she does not see herself as belonging to any school and that she avoids membership in any group or "army." "I always see myself as alone. I can't bear to be in a group of any kind, or in the school of anything," she has said (Cudjoe, 221).

The Autobiography of My Mother

The Autobiography of My Mother carries the defiance that characterized Kincaid's earlier heroines to dazzling extremes. Xuela, the protagonist of this pseudomemoir, takes Lucy's emotional isolation to improbable levels. An orphan whose father leaves her, together with his dirty shirts, to be cared for by his laundress, she is destined to remain unloved, brutality being her only inheritance. Xuela's emotional deprivation is crippling, leaving her with nothing standing between her and eternity—no friends extending a hand, no blank pages to moisten with tears, no letters from her mother to leave unanswered. *The Autobiography of My Mother*, in fact, dispenses altogether with the mother figure, idealizing her in death. Instead, the father looms over her, larger than life, blighting his daughter's existence through his incapacity for love. Xuela will win her battle for survival, but it is at the cost of remaining in an emotional void.

In interviews given after the completion of *A Small Place*, Kincaid had spoken repeatedly of having developed an interest in writing about sex and smells, in not being the decent person she had been in *At the Bottom of the River*. The "decent person" of that earlier work had been the product of a colonial education, and in *The Autobiography of My Mother* she works at rejecting niceness with a vengeance. Xuela relishes the sweat and menstrual blood produced by her body as evidence of a physical existence that cannot be denied or questioned. She seems intoxicated by her own body's smells and brandishes her sexuality like a weapon, relishing its detachment from any possibility of emotional commitment. Throughout it all she leaves behind her "a trail of icy negation" (Schine, 5).

Xuela works best as a symbol, as an abstraction of the evils wrought by colonialism and powerlessness. Kincaid is at her best in this work when building on themes already familiar to readers of her previous work: the problematic relationship with a parent (in this case, the father) developed as a metaphor for colonial relationships; the correlations between sexuality and power (here turned upside down through Xuela's enjoyment of physical pleasure while refusing to surrender her emotions); the legacy of miscegenation and racism in the Caribbean (here elaborated through Xuela's complex racial legacy—African, Carib, Scottish) and the self-loathing and degradation it brings to the colonized. Despite the brilliance of its prose, the difficulties presented by *The Autobiography of My Mother* revolve around the too-heavy burden of symbolism Xuela is expected to bear. Kincaid has stacked the deck too heavily against her, and, unlike Lucy, she rarely comes off the page as believable in her isolation and pain.

Critics were at a loss as to how to respond to *The Autobiography of My Mother*. The novel's disturbing tale was balanced by the "hypnotic rhythm" of its "almost incantatory tone" (Turbide, 72). The "luminous prose" compensated for the "unrelenting, emotionally devastating" tale (Kreilkamp, 54). Despite these critical misgivings, the novel, published after Kincaid had solidified her position as one of the United States' foremost writers, received numerous awards. It was nominated for the National Book Critics Circle award in fiction, was a finalist for the PEN/ Faulkner award, and won the Cleveland Foundation's Anisfield-Wolf Award and the *Boston Book Review*'s Fisk Fiction Award.

My Brother

My Brother, Kincaid's second book of nonfiction, is the autobiographical story of her brother Devon Drew's struggle against AIDS. The book—divided into two parts, the first written while her brother was still alive, the second about a year after he was buried—tells of how Kincaid developed a relationship with her youngest brother while he was dying from AIDS. It dwells most poignantly on the waste of a bright young life to the lack of educational and employment opportunities in post-independence Antigua (a theme she had already explored in *A Small Place*) and unveils the prejudice and scorn with which AIDS sufferers are treated in the island.

In an interview with Larry Mantle, Kincaid described the process of writing *My Brother* as different from anything she had experienced. Accustomed to manipulating her autobiographical material into fictional shape, she found this book emerging with inexplicable ease because it only required complete accuracy and emotional truth. Her priority when writing the book was clarity of expression, since, given the subject matter, "clarity equaled truth." *My Brother* is in many ways as much about Kincaid herself as it is about her brother Devon. The writing of an avowedly autobiographical essay allows Kincaid to revisit material she had previously fictionalized in her earlier novels. It enables the reader to measure the fictionalized versions of autobiographical events against the real life, thus gaining insight into the "manipulation" (to use Kincaid's word) to which she submits autobiographical material in order to transform it into "fiction."

Part One of *My Brother* opens and closes with the image of Devon Drew lying in a bed in the Holberton Hospital in St. John's. These two images frame a text that interweaves two thematic strands: Kincaid's mother and her relationship with her children, and the social and political conditions that have made of Antigua a place where contracting AIDS is a sentence of quick death. The figure of Kincaid's mother and her too intense involvement in the lives of her children looms large over the first half of *My Brother*, illuminated as usual by Kincaid's abiding resentment. The episodes evoked to illustrate her mother's perfidy are those we have come to know only too well. This first part is fresher and more eloquent when bringing to life for the reader the social and economic conditions that have led to the rapid spread of AIDS in the small island. Dr. Prince Harold Ramsey, who has led the struggle against the disease, emerges in the book, in his selflessness and compassion, as the counterpart to the mother's self-centered parody of motherly martyrdom.

The second part opens with the stark statement of her brother's death: "My brother died" (87). It closes with a eulogy to former *New Yorker* editor, William Shawn, Kincaid's late father-in-law, whom she calls "the perfect reader." His death—given the fact that she knew Shawn more intimately and more significantly than she knew the brother who had been only three years old when she left Antigua—seems a greater loss to her. This section chronicles Kincaid's process of mourning for her brother and her examination of her feelings for him—not necessarily of her love, as she honestly speaks of not really loving him, but of her grief at the loss of the promise and potential he represented. She identifies with him as having lived the life that would have been hers had she remained in Antigua.

If in *The Autobiography of My Mother* Kincaid explores what would have been her mother's life had she remained in Dominica and refused to have children—borrowing from her mother's life to build a narrative of emotional vacuity—here she builds a portrait of her brother as a parallel self, one who is depicted as living the life from which she has escaped by going to the United States. Hence the themes around which the picture of her brother is woven: the lively intellect, awake to new ideas and bursting with a creativity for which there is no outlet; the promiscuity, empty of commitment, that would have been her fate if she had stayed to have the ten children by ten different men her mother had augured for her; the despair that would have been her lot if she had continued to live in a society where she felt there was little compassion for the sufferings of others. Her brother's life is played against her own, and the poignancy of his life and death emerges with stark clarity against the life she has made for herself. Her brother, this "thinning thing" we see emaciated on his deathbed, is a figure of tragedy when viewed against Kincaid, lying asleep, snuggled against her children, minutes before her husband awakens her with great tenderness, to tell her that Devon is dead.

In the Garden

Kincaid's most recent work is a series of essays on gardening published in the *New Yorker* under the general heading of *In the Garden*, material that she is currently revising for publication in book form. The first of these essays, "Flowers of Evil," appeared in the *New Yorker* in October 1992. Eight installments altogether were published in the *New Yorker*. The last one, "Plant Parenthood," appeared in June 1995, shortly before Kincaid severed her relationship with the magazine following the Roseanne Barr affair. Three additional essays have been published since then: "Flowers of Empire" in *Harper's Magazine* in 1996; "In History" in *Callaloo* in 1997; and the most recent one, "Jamaica Kincaid on Seed Catalogues," in *Architectural Digest* in 1998.

In the Garden marks a departure in Kincaid's writing. Although still heavily autobiographical, these essays on gardening are not rooted on her West Indian experiences, as most of her fiction has been, but follow her apprenticeship as a gardener in her Vermont home. Two thematic strands run through the eight essays: the evils of colonialism, a theme familiar to readers of her previous work, and the long established tradition of garden-writing. From its opening lines, "Flower of Evil," the first of these essays, addresses Kincaid's awareness of her own paradoxical relationship to a writing tradition that has more than a tangential relationship to the culture of empire. The materials she quotes—from Henry James's *Portrait of a Lady* and Tsitsi Dangarembga's *Nervous Condition*—exemplify the intricate correlations between gardening and conquest. Of the James passage she comments that it "could have been written only by a person who comes from a place where the wealth of the world is like a skin, a natural part of the body, a right, assumed, like having two hands and on them five fingers each" (154).

In the Garden addresses the long-standing tradition of English and American garden-writing, which features numerous classic guides to planting and tending gardens, essays about the joys of gardening, plant catalogues, and discussions of the principles of botany. The essays that form the basis of this new book display Kincaid's extensive readings in the field; she writes of the classics in garden-writing as if they were old friends whose charms and foibles she knows only too well. As noted before, a number of these essays explore the connection between gardening and empire, but most of them delve into her delight in being able to grow things just for the pleasure they bring, for the beauty, texture, and color of flowers, or the taste of a particularly rare watermelon or green bean. Garden-writing as a tradition has always been close to autobiographical writing, and Kincaid's essays offer numerous glimpses into her life, creativity, and sense of beauty.

Kincaid's interest in botany goes back to her schooling in Antigua, when history and botany were her favorite subjects. The botany she had studied had been a catalog of the plants of the British Empire, from which she had learned that the plants she and other Antiguans had assumed to be native to their landscape—the mango breadfruit, among them—had been brought to the island by empire-bound botanists. In "Alien Soil," she deplores the fact that botany is no longer a subject taught in Antiguan schools, having been replaced by agriculture. "Perhaps that is more realistic," she writes, "since the awe and poetry of botany cannot be eaten, and the mystery and pleasure in the knowledge of botany cannot be taken to market and sold" (50).

In the Garden reads like a natural progression of the portrait of the artist that Kincaid has been creating in her fiction and nonfiction since "Antigua Crossings." She sees gardening as intimately connected to her creativity: when she's gardening she is also writing, "so by the time I actually write, I've written what I'm putting down on paper many times in my head" (Kreilkamp, 55). In "This Other Eden" she speaks of the garden as "the most useless of creations, the most slippery of creations," since it will not accrue value with time as other forms of art will; but a glimpse at the view of woodland and beds of flowers outside her window still has "the texture of sensuality and passion and generosity" (71, 72).

These pieces, as we will see, give voice to Kincaid's most recent thoughts on history. A number of them, however, particularly those on the subject of seed catalogues and the differences between the services provided by the different nurseries, seem self-indulgently tedious. "Just Reading" opens with a recounting of how Kincaid spent a cold winter's afternoon sitting in a bathtub of hot water and reading "this little treasure," the Ronniger's Seed Potatoes Catalogue. "Earthly Delights" contains a rather pedantic list of what peonies, rhododendrons, azaleas, and roses gardeners who are at her "lowly stage of development" should wish for in their gardens. There is evidence in the essays of a struggle between those themes close to Kincaid's heart—genocide, colonialism, cultural erasure, history—and a garden-writing tradition that is in many ways a closed, almost self-absorbed world. These pieces are at their best when she analyzes issues she gleans from her rather vast knowledge of gardening literature. The discussion of Carolus Linnaeus's career she offers in "In History" is a case in point. His chapter in the history of botany, which she rewrites with huge dollops of irony, serves as a springboard for a meditation on the power of naming and the imposition of "objective standards" that turn into instruments of power.

MAJOR THEMES

The question of how to narrate and interpret West Indian history after the demise of colonialism has been an increasingly important theme in Kincaid's fiction since "Antigua Crossings." This preoccupation with the need to rewrite the history of the Caribbean from a West Indian perspective is more than anything else what prompts critics to identify Kincaid as a West Indian writer despite her having built her career in the United States, where she has lived all of her adult life. Although she now considers herself an American, despite her Antiguan heritage, her writing continues to be closely linked to the problematics of rewriting a history seen until very recently from the colonizer's perspective.

The rewriting of history has been a constant endeavor of twentieth-century Caribbean writers. As the various Caribbean islands have emerged from a shared experience of colonialism and slavery, their artists and writers have found a history written by their European colonizers and reflecting their Eurocentric perspectives. After independence (which for Antigua did not come until 1981) Caribbean intellectuals faced the need to counter these "flawed" accounts of Caribbean history with narratives that reinterpreted the roles played by Caribbean peoples in their own history and, by extension, reformulated the dominant notion of Caribbean national and individual identities as grounded in a history of victimization.

From the beginning of her career as a writer, Kincaid has never shied from brandishing an angry pen in denunciation of the genocide and historical erasure that has been the historical lot of colonized peoples. In the figure of the grandmother in "Antigua Crossings," who insists on her granddaughter's joining her in spitting into the sea that brought the conquerors to their shores, she had offered her first resisting heroine, one who embodied the spirit of the Caribbean "I," the narrator of her short story "Ovando," who holds the conqueror's retribution. Recently, Kincaid's interest in history has taken a more decisive bent, perhaps as a result of her delving into issues of possession, naming, marginalization, and erasure in the courses she teaches at Harvard University.

Kincaid's thoughts on history have evolved through the years. In "Antigua Crossings," where the young narrator speaks of her joy as she realizes that her Carib grandmother has not forgotten the history of her ancestors, she posited an uncomplicated faith in ancestral history as the basis for national and personal identity. By the time she writes *A Small Place* that comforting faith has disappeared and she claims no longer to care about what the peoples of the West Indies were like before they met their European conquerors: "No periods of time over which my ancestors held sway, no documentation of complex civilisations, is any comfort to me" (37). She has come to see Caribbean history as a game of musical chairs in which no one knows in advance who will be standing and who sitting down when the music stops.

In "In History," an essay published in *Callaloo* in 1997, Kincaid questions the very notion of history, reducing it to a narrative (a fiction), perhaps a theory, but not something around which one should build a sense of self. "What should history mean to someone who looks like me?" she asks. "Should it be an idea, should it be an open wound and each breath I take in and expel healing and opening the wound again, over and over, or is it a long moment that begins anew each day since 1492?" (7).

In a key passage in *The Autobiography of My Mother* Jamaica Kincaid has Xuela, her protagonist, ask a pivotal question—"What makes the world turn?"—that Xuela refuses to answer, since she can only counter the narrative of West Indian colonial history with her furious condemnation of the litany of evils produced by domination. Her question prompts another question, that of whether Kincaid is indeed interested in engaging with, countering, or otherwise challenging prevalent notions of Caribbean history or whether she and her characters are still not quite ready to move beyond the accusatory stage in which the victim's energy is consumed by the anger and frustration of ranting against the evils of the past. It is undeniable that Kincaid's prose, beginning with "Antigua Crossings" and "Girl," has been moving progressively toward a frontal assault on "History"; it is also true that she is still struggling with the parameters of the representation of history in her texts.

Jamaica Kincaid's prose offers an approach to the representation of history grounded in the use of salient historical figures (or of autobiographical characters whose very anonymity is depicted as representative of their victimization by history) as symbols of the Caribbean historical process. Christopher Columbus, Nicolás de Ovando, Xuela, Kincaid's brother Devon Drew are just a few among the many such figures through which Kincaid emplots a historical narrative that relies on the depiction of the vicissitudes visited on the flesh-and-blood body as representative of the accidents of history. From "Columbus in Chains" through Xuela's abortion to Devon Drew's death from AIDS in *My Brother* ("characters,"

if we can call them that, who are historical, fictional, and autobiographical, respectively), Kincaid often builds her commentary on the historical
process on images of the enchained, bloodied, diseased, and mutilated
body.

In the "Columbus in Chains" chapter of *Annie John* we glimpse Kincaid's first attempt at addressing the Caribbean's historical process in a
sustained way. The episode, often reprinted and quoted, describes a history lesson on the discovery of Antigua in 1493 during which Annie is
caught having written the words "The Great Man Can No Longer Just
Get Up and Go" under an illustration depicting Columbus being taken
back to Spain in chains. This embryonic attempt at historical "thought"
already contained the salient features of Kincaid's subsequent meditations on history: the teacher using her power to impose a particular view
of history (Columbus as "one of the great men in history"); Annie's
unsophisticated, instinctive, rebellion against that notion (she takes great
pleasure in seeing him "brought so low"); and the twin images of male
emasculation or symbolic castration on which it rests (that of the chained
Columbus in his most abject humiliation, and that of Annie's mother's
triumph at hearing that her own father now requires someone's help in
order to walk, a triumph expressed in the very words Annie writes under the schoolbook illustration). Triumph at patriarchal and colonial
emasculation (expressed in both cases by the same eroticized phrase) is
framed by a narrative of historical guilt (that of Ruth the dunce, an English girl, not being able to answer correctly the question on Antiguan
history posed by the teacher. The episode leads Annie to speculate on
Ruth's possible guilt at belonging to the colonial masters' country and
race, and then to assert that if her own people had been in the masters'
place they would have behaved quite differently). There, in a nutshell,
are the notions of history that Kincaid will continuously rearticulate and
elaborate in both fiction and nonfiction.

Kincaid appears to be fascinated by the figure of Christopher Columbus, who surfaces as a constant presence in her fiction and essays. He
makes his first appearance in "Antigua Crossings," where his discovery
of the West Indies heralds an era of conquest, genocide, and cannibalism.
In "Columbus in Chains," he emerges from the pages on Annie John's
copy of *A History of the West Indies* bound in chains, "staring off into
space, looking quite dejected and miserable" (77). Annie gloried in this
picture of retribution, savoring the image of just deserts. The Columbus
who discovers Antigua in "In History" is not the triumphant Columbus
of Western accounts but an exhausted discoverer, "sick of the whole

thing," yearning for his old home and running out of names to bestow on the excess of new things his discoveries forced on him.

"Ovando," a short story published in 1989, is Kincaid's most elaborate historical allegory, one in which she returns systematically to the ideas advanced in "Columbus in Chains," again through the use of a historical character, Nicolás de Ovando. The historical Ovando (1451–1511), a pivotal figure in early West Indian colonial history, was a Spanish military leader and first royal governor of the Spanish Antilles. He is infamous for being the architect of the system of *encomiendas*, or forced Indian labor, which served as the basis for the plantation system, and was the founder of the first stable community in Santo Domingo, the model for later settlements throughout the Caribbean and Latin America.

"Ovando" is the allegorical narrative, as told by the Caribbean "I," of the conqueror's physical and moral disintegration while he, standing in representation of the many who come in his wake, ravages the Caribbean landscape and peoples. This image of the conqueror made its first appearance in Kincaid's fiction in the title story of *At the Bottom of the River*, where he blots the landscape and impedes the protagonist's journey through the "terrain" of existence. The conqueror of "At the Bottom of the River" is "an empty man, entirely cut off from nature," unable to "conceive of the union of opposites, or, for that matter, their very existence" (Simmons, 43). So is Ovando, whose very emptiness is conveyed in his shriveled appearance; he was a skeleton on whose bones no shred of flesh remained, his brain "growing smaller by the millennium" (3). Like Columbus, he will appear in the text as an emasculated or castrated figure with a "child-sized penis," and like Columbus he will be portrayed in his arrogance as unaware of the soul-destructing nature of his power. Unable to accept responsibility for the irreparable harm he has caused, Ovando will fall back on notions of fate and divine will: "A power outside and beyond me has predetermined these unalterable events. All of my actions have been made for me in eternity. All my actions are divine" (4). "Ovando" takes the historical notions explicit in "Columbus in Chains" one step further, by using the allegorized historical figure of Ovando to illustrate the narcissistic or self-obsessed nature of power. Ovando becomes intoxicated with three words—"My Sheer Might"—and the words become "like a poisonous cloud of vapor . . . swallowing up everything in their path" (8–9).

In "Ovando" Kincaid tackles the notion of the illegitimacy of possession through the text's insistence on the conquerors' documents and the incoherence of the Caribbean I's inarticulate speech of defense, "delivered in a heartfelt and sorrowful and earnest way," defeated in advance by its own self-pity and awareness of having been betrayed (10). The Caribbean's defeat is seen through its mutilation: As Spain, France, England, Belgium, the Netherlands, Germany, Portugal, and Italy join in the colonial enterprise they draw lots to distribute the spoils, but their distribution of the lands and people of the region leads only to strife and discontent, and "they fell on each other with a ferociousness that I could not have imagined possible" (11).

Many of the essays from *In the Garden* explore the relationship between gardening and the history of conquest and colonization in the West Indies. "Flowers of Empire" owes much to Kincaid's extensive readings on the history of Caribbean and Latin American conquest. She has found in the many volumes she has read on the subject—the writings of Hernán Cortez and Vasco Nuñez de Balboa, William Prescott's *The Conquest of Mexico*, among others—numerous examples of how the peoples native to the region had planted things "for no other reason than the sheer joy of it" (155) before the arrival of the Europeans. The impact of the conquest, in Kincaid's opinion, can be seen most clearly in the "erasing" of Caribbean peoples' joy in planting things, in the redefinition of planting as labor through the imposition of *encomiendas*, slavery, and the plantation economy. In "Alien Soil," the fourth installment of *In the Garden*, she writes of the imposition of alien foodstuffs as a means of providing cheap food for feeding slaves. Of the breadfruit, imported into the West Indies by Joseph Banks, an English naturalist and the head of Kew Gardens in London, she writes that it has been the cause of endless disagreements between children and their parents since the Antiguan child "senses intuitively the part this food has played in the history of injustice and so will not eat it" (48). The people of the West Indies, in Kincaid's account, have what can only be called "a wretched historical relationship to growing things" and have difficulty describing it as "poetic (botany) or pleasurable (gardening)" (50).

Kincaid had addressed the central themes of *In the Garden* earlier in *The Autobiography of My Mother*, where Xuela's English husband, Philip, is portrayed as obsessed with controlling nature. Kincaid has Xuela describe this obsession as a reflection of his people's urge to conquer, of their "obsessive interest in rearranging the landscape." His gardening is not of the type she recognizes as natural and right, that of gardening out of necessity, for the growing of food and, as a result, his pleasure in gardening is shown as an aberration, because when he does grow something edible like tropical fruits, he only forced them to become what they were not meant by nature to become—either larger than they appeared in nature or turned into miniatures. Philip is another of Kincaid's emasculated male figures, an unremarkable, ordinary man, devoid of self-confidence, with skin that Xuela describes as "thin and pink and transparent." Being British, he was burdened by things over which he and his kind no longer had any control. He was "empty of real life and energy, used up," and did not look, Xuela asserts, like anyone she could or should love. And indeed their eventual marriage—which she acknowledges as a defeat—will be rooted less in love than in an apparent desire for mutual self-punishment and expiation, not a desire for masochistic suffering but as penance for the ravages of history of which they have been both victim and unwitting inflictors.

In *My Brother* Kincaid returns to gardening imagery to convey the relentless destruction of her brother's body by the virus inside him. Kincaid uses the figure of her brother's HIV-infected body as "death with a small patch of life attached to it"—as she did with the figure of Ovando—as "not yet part of history" but on its way to historical significance, a symbol of the myriad defeats endured in "a place like Antigua, with its history of subjugation, leaving in its wake humiliation and inferiority" (186). Devon was not unaware of his own place in that history, as he was "obsessed with the great thieves who had inhabited his part of the world—the great hero-thieves of English maritime history: Horatio Nelson, John Hawkins, Francis Drake" (95). He saw "the thing called history," as Kincaid herself does, as a narrative of theft and murder presented as "inevitable and even fun." Devon's naiveté about the fiction of history is evident only in his continuing to like these stories—as Kincaid does not—even when understanding that he was "among the things that had been won" (95).

Given Kincaid's predilection for autobiography or autobiographical fiction, and given a style build on spare, meticulously wrought sentences and first-person narratives, her work does not lend itself easily to the discursive articulation of history but works best with symbolic or metaphorical representations. These representations, in turn, since they are built on images of the accidents of history embodied in specific textual bodies, depend on the body's "performance" as self-dramatizing, at times self-flagellating, textual entity—the body as "symbolic construct." Kincaid has argued that in the Caribbean, where the colonizer's historical narrative has silenced the vanquished's version of events, the only defense against historylessness is to articulate the wounds of forced silence through eloquent, deafening denunciation of the evils sustained in the name of colonial expansion. These evils, as visited on the body, are displayed in her works through the humiliations (Columbus in chains), bloody abortions (Xuela's embracing of childlessness in repudiation of the legacy of lovelessness and colonial oppression that has been her only inheritance), and illnesses (the rapid spread of AIDS in a country where the corruption and mismanagement of post-independence governments has left the population unprotected and exposed) that constitute the legacy of Caribbean history. These denunciations, built on a style of writing that since *A Small Place* has been characterized by its unrelenting tone of bitterness and anger—prompting one reviewer to describe *The Autobiography of My Mother* as "a brilliant fable of willed nihilism"—constitute a stage in the development of Kincaid's historical thought, paving the way for new texts willing to answer the question, "What makes the world turn?" with a more sustained meditation on history, such as that occasionally glimpsed in some of her gardening pieces, which pointed to a more reflective, lightly ironic, sometimes even humorous approach to issues of colonialism, power, and empire.

In "Ovando" Kincaid had already announced the futility and self-destructiveness of that enterprise: "I have exhausted myself laying out before him his transgressions," the Caribbean I asserts, "I am exhausted from shielding myself so that his sins do not obsess and so possess me." Kincaid the Caribbean writer is poised at a crossroads—thematically as well as stylistically—from which she could embark on a new exploration of the Caribbean historical narrative. Kincaid the postmodern transcultural writer, on the other hand, could very well choose to focus on cultivating her Vermont garden, leaving the vicissitudes of Caribbean history behind.

3

At the Bottom of the River
(1983)

At the Bottom of the River, Kincaid's first book, gathers most of the fiction she had published in various magazines from 1978 to 1982. Of the ten stories in the collection, seven had appeared in the *New Yorker*; one ("What I Have Been Doing Lately") had been published in the *Paris Review*; another ("My Mother") echoes material included in a segment of "Antigua Crossings" in *Rolling Stone*. Of these stories only one, "Blackness," was previously unpublished.

Kincaid's "prodigal use of wildly imaginative metaphors" makes the stories of *At the Bottom of the River* dense, sometimes difficult texts for the reader to decipher (CBY 1991, 332). Barney Bardsley, writing for the *New Statesman*, argued that it was not a book "to read straight through," but rather to delve into slowly in order to "unlock a piece of yourself you did not even know existed" (33). Other critics have not been so generous; Anne Tyler, writing for the *New Republic*, called the stories "insultingly obscure" (33), perhaps because of the cryptic dreamlike quality of many of the texts.

The ten pieces that compose *At the Bottom of the River* are generally described by reviewers and critics as short stories—this despite the fact that they do not resemble traditional examples of this genre (or literary form). The tales differ from the traditional short story in essential ways; in fact, they seem to openly defy such categorization. Although they are short fictional texts written in prose, as in the traditional short story, the

tales lack the unity of plot and consistency of characterization that readers expect from short fictional prose. Whereas the traditional short story
is expected to offer a tightly structured narrative with one single plot
line and sharply etched characters, Kincaid's "stories" are fragmented
texts full of voices rarely fleshed out as plausible characters. Her aim
does not appear to be to create believable, lifelike characters, but to evoke
mood and atmosphere in the service of unfolding the trials and tribu-
lations in the relationship between mother and daughter, the central
theme of the book.

In style as well as in form the stories do not conform to the rules of
the genre. They are said by critics and readers to be closer to poetry than
prose. The language is brilliantly simple and lucid, but often it is in the
service of a poetic lyricism that conjures the surrealistic attributes of
everyday things and events. It fluctuates between the commonplace and
the mysterious and fantastic. It is a style built on the use of recurrent
motifs and reiterations, such as we find in musical refrains. Kincaid em-
ploys the Caribbean setting to great effect, evoking elements taken from
folk tales, Obeah, and West Indian rhythms. She also borrows elements
from some of her extensive readings of John Milton and the Bible, particularly those of the gospels.

In *At the Bottom of the River* Kincaid presents the most ordinary everyday events as if they were unfolding in a dream. In an interview with
Selwym Cudjoe she has described her primary objective in the book as
that of recreating the blurring of the lines between the dreaming and
waking worlds of her childhood, when she believed that dreams could
tell you things about your waking life, often things you did not want to
know (230). In the stories collected in *At the Bottom of the River* she seeks
to recreate that childhood perception of reality as not entirely to be
trusted, not necessarily what it seemed. "I think that at some point I
became obsessed with things being not that unclear, that things could
not just vanish, that there could be some light that would show the
reality of a thing, that this was false and this was right," she told Cudjoe
(231). The stories of *At the Bottom of the River* captured that "yearning
for something" that characterized Kincaid's early work, a time when she
was experimenting with the most suitable styles, language, and voices
to recreate the Antigua she carried within her despite her voluntary exile.
The collection shows the various styles, structures, and themes through
which Kincaid searches for her own voice as a writer and marks the
process of her literary apprenticeship.

"GIRL"

"Girl," the first story of the collection, was Kincaid's first work of fiction. The one-sentence story was written on a Sunday afternoon in February 1978, when Kincaid sat at the typewriter in her Hudson Street apartment and attempted to recreate her mother's voice in its first fictionalized incarnation. That afternoon she knew she had found her voice as a writer—a voice that turned out to be that of her mother (Simmons, 15). The story consists almost entirely of a mother's litany of instructions to her adolescent daughter, delivered in a preachy monologue interrupted twice by the daughter's own voice (clearly marked by italics in the text). The piece is written in the simplest of languages and describes the most mundane daily chores and circumstances; but it nonetheless succeeds in creating two vivid characters, with two distinct voices and two contending personalities.

In "Girl," Kincaid uses the mother's exhortations to her daughter to outline the limitations the latter must accept if she is to become the imitation of a proper English lady her mother desires her to be. These involve correct gender roles (such as not squatting down to play marbles) that link the child to domesticity and an acceptance of the patriarchal parameters under which her life must unfold (domesticity is often in the service of assuring the comforts of the males of the family). The struggle between the two characters—the rebelliousness implied by the daughter's two interruptions to the mother's monologue—is both familial and political. The mother's injunctions stem from a need to guide the daughter's behavior toward conforming to social and sexual patterns she has imbued from Antigua's English colonizers; the daughter's resistance is both part of her maturation process and necessary for her own decolonization (her breaking away from patterns of behavior copied from a dominant but not native culture).

The story opens interestingly enough with the reminder that Monday is the day for washing the white clothes—a "whitewashing" of sorts—with everything the image holds of sexual and racial symbolism. The West Indian setting of the story is promptly evoked through the many seemingly insignificant details of food (pumpkin fritters, salt fish, and dasheen), weather (hot sun), and culture (singing benna, setting the table for tea, blackbirds that may be something else altogether). In this particular setting two races and two sets of cultural presuppositions are at work. For the girl in "Girl," a black girl in a Caribbean colony, social success requires a mimicry of "white" ways as well as sexual "whiteness" or purity.

The mother's message, as internalized by the daughter in this incantatory repetition that is the text of "Girl," focuses most particularly on matters of propriety (the "soaking her little cloths" that indicates that the girl has reached puberty and is now a sexual being, not singing benna in Sunday school, not walking "like the slut you are so bent on becoming," [3]). This very concept of propriety interweaves cultural and sexual themes. Singing benna (a folk song) in Sunday school juxtaposes local folk culture as an element of resistance against Sunday (Church of England) school. Walking "like a lady" and not speaking to wharf-rat boys opposes notions of (British) ladylike behavior to local or native (i.e., natural) interest in sexuality. Her mother's injunctions against what comes seemingly naturally underscore the borrowed nature of her principles and her role as an agent in the imposition of foreign values on her daughter, thus linking the tensions between mother and daughter to the tensions between the colonizer and the colonized.

The mother's admonitions are also indicative of her society's notions of class. Her voice betrays her awareness of the connections between propriety of behavior and the possibilities of class mobility. The daughter for whom she craves the attributes of "a lady" must first learn to behave as such. She must not speak to those who are socially beneath her (wharf-rat boys) and must learn to recognize and respect social hierarchies (even such an insignificant act as setting the table has social repercussions, and she must learn to perform this task differently when it involves an important guest). In this context clothes emerge as a social text with deep significance. From the quality of its materials (cotton fabric should have no gum on it) to its cleanliness, neatness (the girl is taught how to iron a shirt so it does not have a crease), and state of disrepair (a hem coming down is indicative of potential sluttiness), clothing becomes a symbol of class status and moral superiority. Clothes, like manners, have the power to hide the girl's "natural" impulse to become a slut.

The importance of appearances—the hiding of the true nature of things—is a central theme of this story, where the mother feels charged with the task of teaching her daughter the need for hypocrisy as a tool of survival. Her detailed instructions about how to regulate her smiles to give the receiver the proper message of acceptance or disdain, or setting the table in a way that indicates the importance of the guest, are elements in an understanding of the social landscape that has little to do with true feeling or a recognition of human rather than social value. Late in the story the mother will instruct the daughter on matters of transgression. She teaches her how to make a medicine to abort a fetus (a theme that resonates throughout Kincaid's fiction and is linked to her mother's unsuccessful attempt to abort her brother Devon). She also teaches her how to spit up into the air if she feels like it without suffering any consequences. Transgressions, if we follow the text, are acceptable only if they are in the service of concealing violations of the sexual rules that could result in social or class ostracism.

The one element of the native culture the mother openly embraces is Obeah, the African-based system of beliefs that involves the supernatural, witchcraft, sorcery, and magic and acknowledges the power of spells to inflict harm or help in healing. The presence and power of Obeah surfaces in the text through warnings about catching "something" if the girl picks up someone else's flowers or against throwing stones at blackbirds that may not be blackbirds at all but spirits in disguise. The making of medicines (a healing function of the Obeah practitioner) can be used to cure disease (e.g., a cold) or "throw away a child" (5). Other harmful, or at the very least manipulative, aspects of Obeah are hinted at when the mother speaks of ways of loving a man. Although validated by the mother's acceptance, Obeah is nonetheless presented as a system that is of value to aid in teaching the child hypocrisy and manipulation, not as a positive cultural force that can work toward the overall good despite its potentially harmful aspects.

Underlying these detailed teachings and admonitions is the mother's sense of responsibility for what her child will become, an important factor contributing to the tensions between mother and daughter. It points to the need for separation between the two, for the daughter to establish her own set of rules and expectations. The only potential for resistance in the story is embodied in the girl's two interruptions. Early in the text she breaks the mother's text to deny that she ever sings benna, and never in Sunday school. To this the mother does not reply. The second rupture to the mother's harangue is a question—*but what if the baker won't let me feel the bread?*—that draws an angry remonstration from the mother. Is she to understand that after all her admonitions and instructions the girl will grow into the sort of woman whom the baker will not allow to touch the bread? Has she after all become the slut her mother has warned her against becoming? The character of these interruptions implies the daughter's siding with the local or native culture. The suspicion of her singing benna and the mother's perceived need to repeat her warnings against sluttiness of behavior indicate the daughter's tendency (despite her denial that she ever sings benna) to behave in a way that is native to her surroundings, an implied rejection of the colonizers' mores.

"Girl" announces the themes and concerns that will dominate Kincaid's subsequent fiction. The mother's voice and presence represent the social and familial forces against which the daughter must battle in order to grow into her own power and maturity. The link between the mother's power and colonial authority and mores, a theme Kincaid will develop more fully and openly in later fiction, is articulated here in a symbolic yet eloquent way. The story evokes the beauty and vigor of the world of Kincaid's childhood as well as its menacing elements, symbolized here by the power of Obeah, but it also points to the girl's need to leave that world if she is to escape the domination of the mother's all-powerful voice. Above all, in "Girl," Kincaid builds on autobiographical episodes to posit sexual awakening as the moment of rupture of the previously harmonious relationship between mother and daughter. The moment of approaching independence is the moment the mother's benevolence turns into aggression, when the battle for continued control of the daughter is fully engaged and the daughter must find her own voice to articulate her resistance if she is to survive.

"IN THE NIGHT"

"In the Night," the second story of *At the Bottom of the River*, plunges the reader into the mystery of a West Indian night, recreating its haunting and menacing beauty. The story is divided into five short sections, each with its own individual focus, although all connected by the voice of the adolescent girl through whose perspective we glimpse the life of the Antiguan night.

The language of "In the Night" differs markedly from that of "Girl," which precedes it in the collection. Whereas "Girl" was written in the simplest of languages, "In the Night" is filled with poetic resonances, rhythmic repetitions, and symbolic references as the narrative voice takes us "behind the daylight facade of rationality" (Simmons, 77) into a world where the mundane joins the world of ghosts and wandering souls. The first section of the text, for example, opens with a description of the night as divisible, fragmented, not as time but as a space, with deep holes, edges, roundnesses—"flat in some places, and in some places like a deep hole, blue at the edge, black inside" (6). This space opens to allow the night-soil men to come in.

Kincaid plays on the reader's lack of familiarity with West Indian types and expressions to turn what is commonplace in Antigua—the night-soil men who come to empty the pails in those places where there is no sewer system—into mysterious figures who provide a link to the world of Obeah, magic, and apparitions. She describes these men as shuffling figures moving rhythmically, as in a dance, making a scratchy sound with their straw shoes. They have the ability—the power—to see a *jablesse*, a figure of folklore who has the power to assume any animal or human form.

In this first section of "In the Night" the narrative voice itself seems to wander the neighborhood, disembodied like a ghost, listening to the sounds of the nights. These sounds, in turn, merge what can be heard by the human ear (a cricket, a church bell, a house creaking, a man groaning, music played on the radio) with what is soundless by nature (the sound of a woman's disgust at the man groaning, the murdered woman's spirit back from the dead, the sound of a woman's head aching). Here there is a marked division between the male world of sound and the woman's world of soundlessness, underscored by the violence of the man as he stabs the woman, the undertaker's complicity in taking her away, and the reality of the woman having to resort to haunting the man from beyond the grave ("he is running a fever forever," [7]) as the only form of justice open to her.

This first section of "In the Night" underscores the power of Obeah, as both a major force in Caribbean culture and an important element in fostering Kincaid's creativity. The evocation of Obeah gives Kincaid access to a world where the boundaries between the mundane and the surreal are blurred, allowing her to use language and poetic imagery to convey the in-betweenness of Caribbean reality. In the narratives of *At the Bottom of the River* the commonplace and the fantastic merge and separate, giving Kincaid's style its characteristic poetic quality. This quality is particularly evident in the final paragraph of the first section of the story, where the narrator "sees" Mr. Gishard, a *duppy* or spirit, standing quite nonchalantly under the tree in front of the house where he lived when alive. The living accept his presence just as casually, acknowledging it as a natural element in the landscape, a continuation of the world of the living. In just the same casual way, Kincaid blends the real and otherwordly in her prose, giving the narratives in this collection their surreal quality, which comes from the use of commonplace language for what is for her American readers uncommon realities.

In the second section of the story the narrator abandons the third-person voice of the first part and speaks in the first person, assuming a more personal, more immediate perspective. This brief section focuses on the harmonious relationship between mother and daughter before other children were born. This is a recurring theme in Kincaid's fiction, linked to her own devastation when the first of her three brothers was born, a subject about which she has written repeatedly. The section describes a dream in which the narrator hears a baby being born, breathing and bleating. The image metamorphoses into that of the narrator and the baby as lambs eating grass in a pasture. The narrator awakens from her dream, having wet her bed, to find her "still" young and beautiful mother tending to her.

The use of the word "still" marks the significant shift between the time when the mother could "change everything" and the darkness that follows (8). In her dream, the narrator is "in the night," the only light being that which she glimpses in the far-off mountains. Kincaid often plays with images of darkness and light in her fiction to signal transformations (see, e.g., the use of light imagery in "At Last"); the lights herald the presence of a *jablesse*, described here as "a person who can turn into anything," with eyes that shine as brightly as lamps and usually appearing as beautiful women (9). It offers the first instance in Kincaid's fiction of equating the figure of the still young and beautiful mother, who transforms herself into a shrew once the daughter reaches adolescence and other children are born, with the transforming qualities of the frightening figure of the *jablesse*.

In the third section of "In the Night" Kincaid once again draws from autobiographical material, this time focusing on a sharply drawn character modeled on her own stepfather. The section opens with a somewhat enigmatic technical device, which appears to put into question the truth or validity of the descriptive segment that follows it. The segment consists of a long paragraph completely enclosed in quotation marks except for the opening phrase: "No one has ever said to me" (9). Whether this puzzling phrase is meant to indicate that the quite straightforward description of the narrator's relationship with her father that follows is something that, although true, no one has ever said to her before, or whether it means that it is a fabrication because no one could ever say such things of her father, is left completely to the reader's discretion. As a device it may strike the reader as overly obscure, even unnecessary.

The rest of the segment is one of the most straightforward of the book. In it Kincaid paints a somewhat idealized picture of a kind and thoughtful man whose happiness centers on his family and whose daily habits, commonplace and conventional as they are, are marked with a dignified solemnity. The segment focuses particularly on his selection of clothes, as if the small vanities and renunciations that go into obeying the social conventions as to dress—he would like to wear pink but knows "it isn't becoming to a man"—were indicative of the solid respectability whose very dullness is endearing to his daughter (9). This tender portrait of a modest man living in a small colony, who orders the clothes for special days from England, is made particularly poignant by his dependence on books to escape the humdrum predictability of his life. His reading about rubber plantations and the circus, things he has read about but never seen, frame the limitations of his desires.

The fourth section of "In the Night" opens with a catalog of the many flowers that "close up and thicken" in the darkness of the West Indian night. This list of tropical blooms underscores the Caribbean setting of the story. Familiar as they are to the West Indian reader, with commonplace names like daggerbush, turtleberry, and stinking-toe, they appear as exotic and mysterious to the reader not familiar with the tropical landscape. The otherwise unremarkable listing closes with a surprising personification of the flowers—"the flowers are vexed"—that marks the transition between the evocation of the flora and the series of activities, both harmless and harmful, that go on under the cover of night: basket-making, sewing, a carpenter crafting a beautiful mahogany chest for his wife, someone "sprinkling a colorless powder outside a door" to cause the birth of a stillborn child (11). Once again, Kincaid juxtaposes the natural and supernatural elements of the West Indian landscape in the aid of developing a style that, in *At the Bottom of the River*, still rests somewhat heavily on highlighting the exotic elements of Caribbean natural and cultural reality for the unfamiliar reader.

The fifth and final section of "In the Night" returns to the relationship between the girl and the mother, here presented as a couple delighting in their domesticity—the mother/daughter bond having replaced the husband/wife connection. The segment outlines the daughter's fantasy of growing up and marrying "a red-skin woman with black bramblebush hair and brown eyes," drawn as an idealized portrait of the mother figure (11). She imagines a life of great simplicity and self-sufficiency, in which the two would be complete unto themselves, living in a West Indian version of the enchanted cottage, harmonious and fulfilled. To accentuate the image of completion, Kincaid relies in part on what in other texts will become a symbol of rupture, the presence of two women standing on a jetty. Often in her fiction, most notably in *Annie John*, Kincaid will use the autobiographical episode of the daughter's departure from a jetty, as the mother waves goodbye, as the most absolute image of rupture and separation. In the fantasy of concord that closes "In the Night," however, the two women stand embracing on a jetty, undivided and whole. The portrait of their happiness that closes the story, the daughter's assertion that once she marries a woman like this she will be "completely happy" every night, counterbalances the many images in this story of the night as dark and menacing.

"AT LAST"

In "At Last"—as in "Girl"—Kincaid offers another dialogue between a mother and daughter. In the story, which is divided into two sections— "The House" and "The Yard"—the two voices probe the past they shared before the harmony between them was broken by the birth of other children. The two voices in the story are often undifferentiated, blurring the identity of the precise speaker, so as to underscore how much still remains of the closeness and intimacy they once shared despite their estrangement. As they dissect their joint lives, their tone grows increasingly sorrowful, as if the past they were summoning held something extremely precious and now lost. The reader perceives these voices as corresponding and merging but remote, as if coming from behind a closed door, or as if they belonged to disembodied ghosts coming back to the house they used to share when alive.

The first section of the story, "The House," follows the two characters/ voices as they tour their former home, noting the impact of the time past on the objects once so familiar: the wood shingles are weather-beaten, the paint fraying, the unplayed piano now just collects dust. The emphasis in the opening paragraph is on loss and death: dead flowers, dead hair still left on the brush, letters that brought bad news. The mother's question ("What are you now?") and the daughter's answer ("A young woman.") hint at a period of separation between them or at two ghosts traveling back in time and observing their former selves as in a film (13). The longing to retrieve lost memories—expressed, for examples, in the characters' wish that "everything would talk"—points to their effort at recovering their past and examining it again in the light of the present, seeking a new understanding.

The series of questions and answers around which the first section of the story is structured involve episodes in their past that the daughter has misremembered or misinterpreted or things the mother now regrets having done. They provide a path through the significant moments of their relationship and offer clues as to the possibility of their recovering their former closeness. The first of these questions—"What was that light?"—becomes a leit-motif (a repeated element, like a refrain)—reiterated throughout the story, symbolizing the clarity the voices would like to shed over the past (13). Throughout the first section of the story the voices will follow the light, wondering where it comes from, watching it flash, making one of the voices wish she could shine in the dark. The emphasis on the light underscores the importance of "seeing" for the two voices, as seeing is linked to understanding the past. Their failure to see their joint history with clarity is announced by the appearance, in the final paragraphs of the first section, of a blind bird dashing its head against a closed window. Kincaid will use the bird image repeatedly to symbolize the frustration of a young woman struggling against her mother and her colonial environment, but here she has added blindness as an extra and meaningful element linked to the mother and daughter's tragic inability to see. (The image of the blind bird complements that of a caged hummingbird, appearing some paragraphs before, that dies after a few days, "homesick for the jungle," [16].) The women's defeat is underscored by the answer to the final question of this section—"What of the light?"—to which the answer is a dejected "Splintered. Died" (19).

Kincaid's technique of building her story around a series of questions allows her to present the tensions in the mother/daughter relationship in a dynamic manner; they are displayed before the reader rather than described, albeit enigmatically, their meaning veiled by metaphor. The way the questions are presented on the page—most often isolated as separate, one-line paragraphs—underscores their role in marking significant moments in their relationship. The first of the questions thus isolated, for example, shows the mother/daughter figures at their most harmonious, when one can still act as the mirror for the other. One of the voices remarks of the other that her lips are "soft and parted." The reply—"Are they?"—implies an acceptance of this self-reflectiveness, a validation of the other's gaze. The reply to the second of these stand-alone questions—an inquiry as to why the doors had been shut so

tightly—draws a response that articulates the distance that has developed in the way they perceive the reality around them: the doors,
according to the other voice, "weren't closed" at all. This is followed by
the acknowledgment that once they had held hands and been beautiful
together, but that was before the birth of other children brought pain
and sleepless nights.

In "At Last," Kincaid builds an atmosphere of dread around a series
of images of menace and apprehension. They follow on the images of
death and decay of the first paragraph, but become increasingly important in the text after the articulation of the growing estrangement between the mother and the daughter. The daughter then emerges as a
young woman standing near the dead flowers, the light turning the image into that of a carcass, a skeleton on which the mother lives and feeds.
Although the two pray to be blessed and "to see the morning light,"
they live through a hurricane that shakes the house to its foundation,
mirroring the shocks that jolt their relationship (17). Once these differences surface in the text, moreover, the two voices become less ambiguous, the two figures grow more easily identifiable by the reader. The
mother's voice emerges with particular clarity, speaking to the daughter
about the time when she was an infant and she had wished to feed her
but her milk had soured, reiterating how much she had been loved, how
she had been dry and warm. Then they had possessed the light, and the
mother "would shine in the dark." As the first section draws to a close,
Kincaid addresses more directly the birth of "the children," linking them
to the transformation of the mother into the frightening figure of a *jablesse*
who appears sometimes as a man, sometimes as a hoofed animal, having
accomplished her metamorphosis from loving mother to figure of fear.

The second section of the story, "The Yard," is narrated by a different
voice, that of a third-person narrator, objective and detached, who
evokes the timelessness of the yard. This mythical yard contains all there
is of childhood mirth, beauty, and promise; but it also contains everything there could be of menace in such a symbolic setting, one that provides a transition between the world of nature and the world of home
and domesticity. Everything that the yard could contain that would hold
fascination for a child (a sparrow's nest, a pirate's treasure, trees bearing
fruit, marbles, a small garden full of bluebells) is counterbalanced by
what the yard could contain of threat (an old treasure broken, a sharp
quick blow, a duck's bill, hard and sharp, the oppressive heat). Kincaid
thus prepares the terrain for a meditation on the permanence and significance of life and the physical world. "At Last," the title of the story,

is the phrase that introduces the pivotal question—"To whom will this view belong?"—which is followed by an inquiry as to what becomes of things after they are dead and gone (16). The question appears to point to the repetitive nature and meaninglessness of life, to days following upon each other, identical and unchanging. But the final images of the narrative seek meaning in the hopeful sound of a child's voice (the daughter of the first section) again inquiring about the past. The question—"What was the song they used to sing and made fists and pretended to be Romans?"—seeks a link, a connection, albeit through a game, between an individual's life, however humble and obscure, and a historical consciousness (19).

In "At Last" Kincaid includes thematic and autobiographical elements that she will explore more fully in other writings, both fictional and nonfictional. One of the voices recalls having forgotten something under the bed, which, as it decayed, became covered with white moss; the episode will reappear in *Annie John*. The oft-narrated attack by red ants on her brother Devon appears here for the first time, although parts of that tale (the dangers of planting okra, which harbors red ants, too close to the house had already appeared in "Girl"). References to "the rain that time" anticipate the "Long Rain" chapter of *Annie John*. The allusion to an illness that caused a worm to crawl out of man's leg refers to the death of Kincaid's young half-uncle, which she narrates in several fictional and nonfictional texts, particularly in *The Autobiography of My Mother*. Kincaid, moreover, will experiment in this tale—as in many of the narratives that constitute *At the Bottom of the River*—with imagery that will recur in subsequent writings: a young woman crossing the open sea alone at night on a steamer, changes in the texture of skin as symbolic of profound emotional change, the image of the young bird dashing itself against a closed window described above, the hard prolonged rain of *Annie John*, the birth of other children as rupturing the harmony between mother and daughter. "At Last," as many of the stories in the collection, reveals Kincaid's apprenticeship as a writer. The stories illustrate how Kincaid, at this very early stage of her career, experiments with forms, symbols, imagery, and the creation of character, looking for the most appropriate vehicles for her narrative material.

"WINGLESS"

"Wingless" explores the world of the child as she grows into an awareness of herself. The story, divided into six sections of uneven length,
opens with a recollection of the routine of the schoolhouse, where a
group of children chant rhymes to learn how many pennies in a shilling,
how many shillings in a pound. In "Wingless," Kincaid returns to the
use of light as symbol of self-knowledge and self-awareness that she had
elaborated in "At Last," although here it is more explicitly connected to
the notion of self-discovery. The narrator distances herself from the children reciting their lessons, as if to indicate that she has surpassed that
stage in her own development, before declaring that she swims "in a
shaft of light" and can see herself clearly.

In this first section of "Wingless," the narrator, a young woman on
the threshold of womanhood, ponders her forthcoming adulthood, wondering what kind of woman she will become. She describes herself—in
a brief sequence that foreshadows the "Columbus in Chains" chapter of
Annie John—as perhaps standing on the brink of a great discovery after
which, like Columbus himself, she may be sent home in chains. Looming
above her is the figure of the mother, about whose love the narrator is
not certain, whose love is fraught with strain, conflict, and ambiguity.
She seeks to define herself against the mother, attempting to elucidate
how much power she can wield against her once she becomes a tall,
graceful, and beautiful woman capable of imposing her will on people.

The recurring motif in this segment of the story is that of the narrator
seeking to see herself clearly. The process of attaining self-knowledge is
inextricably linked to separation from the mother. The daughter must
find another object for the "love like no other" that she bestowed on the
mother before their relationship soured. She describes her mother's smile
as the repository of her goodness, but later in the story that same smile
will turn "red" and kill a man. The daughter, "a defenseless and pitiful
child," must find a path away from a life reduced to an apprenticeship
in dressmaking, a life that follows the pattern of the mother's life. (Kincaid's mother once apprenticed her to a dressmaker, in an episode that
became to her symbolic of her family's inability to recognize her talent
and promise.)

In this opening section of the story, the narrator of "Wingless" stresses
her adolescent unhappiness and frustration. Powerlessness emerges as a
dominant theme. She lacks the commanding understanding of the world

that adulthood requires, and her life (and this segment of the narrative) is filled with questions: she doesn't understand the gradations of manners and cloth color; is she horrid now and will she ever be so?; her charm is limited and she has not learned yet how to smile; she has cried big tears as a result of her disappointments. She dwells on these disappointments, as Kincaid herself will do in her fiction, holding them close to her breast, "because they are so important to me" (24). The answers to her questions are not forthcoming, since she is not yet a woman but a "primitive and wingless" creature on the threshold of maturity.

The second section of "Wingless," a brief dialogue between mother and daughter, shows the mother as mocking and cruel, delighting in frightening the daughter and oblivious to any lasting harm she may cause her. The relationship between them is thus defined, as in so many of Kincaid's tales, as one of power, and the mother is depicted as utilizing any means at hand to maintain her supremacy. Kincaid builds on the common perception of the heart as the repository of love to develop the image of its being strangled as symbolic of the mother's willful destruction of her daughter's love for her.

Section three, which follows in a thematic progression, underscores Kincaid's notion of childhood as a state of complete powerlessness before the omnipotent mother. Here, the mother's power extends to being able to walk across a carpet of pond lilies, eating pond-lily black nuts. Having created this fairy-tale, miraculous setting (with its symbolic reminder of Christ walking on water), Kincaid then describes an encounter between the mother and a man dressed in clothes made of tree bark, a meeting full of physical and sexual threat (he speaks so forcefully that "drops of brown water sprang from his mouth"; he blew himself up "until in the bright sun he looked like a boil," 25). The mother, after initially attempting to shield herself, instead of using her cutlass to cut the man in two, kills him with her "red, red smile" (25). Kincaid uses the episode to emphasize the nature of the mother's power—she is not only able to make a man drop dead, but she does it effortlessly. Her weapon, a red smile, is linked by its effectiveness and mystery to Obeah and magic and by its color and implied treachery to the female arts of coquetry and seduction that the mother has sought to teach the daughter elsewhere in the stories of *At the Bottom of the River*.

In part four of the story the narrator dwells on the power of the sea, with its blinding storms "shaking everything up like a bottle with sediment," its sharp-toothed eels and its mystery, and on the seashore, full of noisy birds and noisier families. The sea follows her all the way home to "the woman" (26). In this new rendition of the mother, she appears as a power comparable to that of the sea, more frightening to the daughter than its mysteries. The section ends with a brief dialogue between the narrator (the daughter) and "the woman" (the mother) centering on the question of fear itself. The daughter's acknowledgment (in answer to a question) that she is very frightened of the mother figure is greeted by the mother's mockery and laughter.

Part five of "Wingless" offers a brief recitation of the narrator's fears, listed as if they were the frightening dreams of childhood. Cows, hurricanes, the lack of light, unfamiliar noises, boxes that must be handled with care, a big white building with curving corridors, a dead person. Ending the list, as the most frightening thing of all, is the woman she loves "who is so much bigger than me" (27). Here, as in other stories in the collection, most notably "My Mother," Kincaid uses the mother's hyperbolized size as metaphor for the daughter's perception of her limitless power.

The sixth and final section of "Wingless" evokes the stillness of the night and the peacefulness of the child falling asleep. It is the most poetic and lyrical segment of the story, built on refrain-like repetitions of the phrase "now so still" as animals and insects subside into sleep. The natural world thus surrendering to sleep is viewed subjectively, from the narrator/child's perspective, as the various creatures relinquish the activities that impacted on the narrator during the day (as they revolted her, pleased her, stole from her, gratified her). Kincaid returns here to the metaphoric use of light of the beginning of the story to describe how sleep leads to self-oblivion. Initially, the narrator swims in a shaft of light and can see herself clearly; here, as she falls asleep, she stands against the light, casting a shadow of which in her sleeping state she will be unaware. Her hands, which are made to stand for her entire body, her entire self, recede from the memory of her daily activities (touching, caressing, dressing, holding a cone of ice cream, praying) into a still, dreamless sleep.

"HOLIDAYS"

"Holidays" is one of only three stories in *At the Bottom of the River* not set in the West Indies. The various locales of the seven brief sections (the mountains, a lake in Michigan, the seashore) recall the places where Kincaid vacationed during the four years she spent as an au pair with the

Arlen family in the late 1960s. They will also feature prominently in several chapters of *Lucy*. These settings, however, are the only openly autobiographical elements in the story, which does not explicitly address any of Kincaid's known experiences during those years.

The first section of "Holidays" is the only one in the story in which the narrator assumes the first-person "I," identifying herself as a person on holiday, whiling her days away in a house from whose porch she can face the mountains. The cadences and rhythms of this segment of the narrative mark the voice as West Indian, an identification corroborated by details such as the calypso about a man from British Guiana that runs through her mind, the memory of a superstition about killing your mother, and her dream about not being on the porch facing the mountains. There is an underlying tone of wonder in this segment of "Holidays," as if the narrator marvels at finding herself in such a place, occupying such a space, surrounded by objects, books, landscapes that are unfamiliar and somewhat alien to her life. As she idly contemplates her surroundings and surrenders to sleep, her West Indianness looms larger, she attempts to write a letter (a symbol in Kincaid's fiction of an attempt to establish a link with her home), she asserts her belief in superstitions as if in affirmation of her origins, and she drifts into sleep and dreams of home (or, more precisely, of a place like Kincaid's own home in Antigua, where you cannot sit on the porch facing the mountains because the topography is marked by nothing much higher than a big hill).

In this first section of "Holidays" Kincaid builds a metaphor of budding creativity through a series of images (symbols) of artistic energy ready to burst. The narrator's idleness—her apparent listlessness, her walking aimlessly around the house, her poking the fireplace ashes with her toes, her solitary presence, the undisturbed silence, her efforts to look at herself—is depicted as necessary to the process of introspection and self-awareness that will eventually lead to writing. From the opening sentence, when she walks into a room where an artist has left some empty canvases (blank spaces providing the materials for art), to her abandoning her subconscious to the song from home, the reader is presented with a series of images of emerging creativity. She looks through the encyclopedia of butterflies and moths with beautiful pictures of the beauty that emerges from the chrysalis, she tries to write her name on the dead ashes of the fireplace but it is too impermanent a medium, she leaves a dark spot when she cleans her toe on the royal-blue rug (a veiled reminder of Kincaid's colonial roots), she attempts to write a letter in another failed creative effort, she surrenders to the lure of the rhythms from home and falls into a dream. If *At the Bottom of the River* marks Kincaid's apprenticeship as a writer, this section of "Holidays" illustrates her consciousness of that apprenticeship as she depicts the budding artist as a young woman in search of a medium.

The second segment of the story consists exclusively of dialogue, not of conversation necessarily, but of various disconnected utterances presented out of context. The speakers are not identified, and the fragments appear as if overheard by a narrator vacationing at the seaside. The link between them is precisely their being scraps of chit-chat typical of vacationers: things they have back home; comments on the sunset, the pebbles, the houses, their plans for dinner; descriptions of new friends. Altogether they help define an atmosphere of holiday-making, where new superficial acquaintances are made, and people pursue amusement as their main goal. The phrase that closes the segment, however, deflates the levity and merry-making of the vacation, by recalling how later, on thinking back on the holiday, "we will be so pained, so unsettled" (33).

Section three of the story catalogs a series of vacation disasters, offering a perceptively amusing list of the many cheery catastrophes that can mar a middle-class vacation. The narrator offers no commentary; there is no speaking "I" to place the list in a subjective context. Yet its cumulative impact is that of mockery. Deerflies, skunks eating garbage, a camera forgotten in the sun, stepping on dry brambles, sunstroke, a skirt hem caught in barbed-wire—the list of trivial melodramas plays against the expected vacationer's reaction to them, highlighting their insignificance and mocking the vacationer in the process.

The fourth segment of "Holidays" strikes the reader as out of place in the story. Unlike the other parts of the narrative, this one seems at best only tangentially related to the holiday theme of the other segments. The focus is on a young blind man walking out in the midday sun, observed from inside a house (by vacationers perhaps—hence the possible tangential connection to the central theme of the story). The narrator—again an objective, depersonalized voice—describes the tragedy of the lovesick man who lost his sight in an attempted suicide after killing a man he saw kissing the woman he loved. He is surrounded by the indifference of all around him; even the dogs shun him, as if to underscore that a vacationing spot is not an appropriate place for such a reminder of pain, passion, and intense drama.

Part five, like part two, consists exclusively of dialogue. It follows a conversation between a vacationer and a native at a tropical holiday spot.

Its recurring motif—"things are funny here" (34)—seems intent on establishing the locals' inability or unwillingness to follow European custom: they are holding a May fair, but it is July; they swim in the warm seawater just before their Christmas dinner. The juxtaposition of perspectives—the vacationer's and the local resident's—together with their agreement that "things are funny here"—temporarily bridges the cultural gap between them, creating the kind of temporary alliance possible only while the vacation lasts.

The sixth segment of "Holidays" follows two young middle-class American boys from vacation to vacation as they grow up into gentlemen looking for "large-breasted women" (35). The theme that threads its way through the various vacations briefly evoked in the story—fishing in Michigan, visiting the Mark Twain museum in Missouri, milking cows in Wyoming, changing a car tire somewhere—is that of the loss of innocence and wonder that is the lot of male American adolescence. They are shown as moving from guilelessness as they fish together, needing none of the comforts of domesticity and position, to limited horizons as they get trapped in the expectations of their gender and class. Their lives, as vacation follows vacation, become impoverished, reduced to a cliché of male success. What was promise and purity in their childhood disintegrates into a false notion of gentlemanliness and a caricature of lust.

The seventh and final segment of "Holidays" works as a counterpart to section three. There, the catalog of insignificant disasters made a mockery of middle-class holiday-making; here, Kincaid outlines the ideal holiday for the ideal American happy family, a holiday so perfect as to be almost a parody or hyperbolized version of a vacation. Its very perfection distorts its reality. In section three, all the little mini-disasters pointed to the vulnerability of a middle-class holiday, one that could be marred by the tiniest of mishaps; here every detail—the beautiful family, the fields covered with flowers, the constant laughter, the lack of anxiety, the funny postcards—points to the mindlessness of such pleasurable pursuits. The description of this idealized perfect vacation contains within it the seeds of the bitter irony that Kincaid will pour on the figure of the tourist in *A Small Place*.

"THE LETTER FROM HOME"

"The Letter from Home" is, like "Girl," a brief one-paragraph, one-sentence story. And, like "Girl," it uses the incantatory recitation of a woman's daily chores—the mundane description of the restrictions of the female world—to accentuate the menace that lurks behind everydayness and domesticity. The story, although structured as one long, unbroken paragraph, can nonetheless be separated into two distinct voices and two clearly defined styles. Given the autobiographical subtext of Kincaid's writing in *At the Bottom of the River*, the reader is justified in assuming that the story focuses on a letter from the mother at home received by the daughter abroad.

Kincaid seeks to differentiate the voices stylistically in the text. The sections of the narrative that constitute the letter from home, for example, are characterized by simple declarative statements almost invariably beginning with "I"—"I milked the cow, I churned the butter..."—that seem to float above the surface of reality, not breaking through its superficial layer to communicate to its addressee (the daughter) anything of the emotions and thoughts of the writer (37). They can be readily distinguished from those sentences focusing on the receiver of the letter, which are longer and more complex in structure and describe her as engaging with her surroundings in a more vital way. These sentences rarely begin with "I," and are not centered on the daughter's own self, seeking instead to describe her environment, the objects surrounding her, the weather, her emotions and responses. It is as if the daughter, confronted with the mother's "I," could not bring herself to assert her own voice.

Kincaid offers subtle clues in the story as to the setting for these two voices, placing one in the Caribbean, the other somewhere in the snowy north. The sections focusing on the mother, for example, focus on domestic activity in a place where she must light candles at night (implying a lack of electricity) and where things moving in the shadows may be menacing spirits. The sections focusing on the daughter, on the other hand, speak of tree branches "heavy with snow," humming refrigerators, a goldfish living in a bowl, hats on hat stands, and coats hanging from pegs. The complexity of the daughter's new environment—with its appliances, houses with many rooms, dripping faucets, hissing gas, books, and rugs—contrasts sharply with the simplicity of the mother's surroundings, evident in the uncomplicated nature of her daily chores and the simple syntax of the sentences of her letter to her daughter.

"The Letter from Home" contains two brief sections clearly differentiated by punctuation from the rest of the text. The first, in quotation marks, offers bits of ambiguous dialogue spoken by an unidentified man.

Some of this dialogue—an inquiry as to the children being ready, for example—could belong to the daughter's world (an autobiographical element perhaps, given Kincaid's work as an au pair on her arrival in the United States, when letters from home were most painful to receive). Some could belong to the world of the mother, as in the inquiry as to whether the children will bear their mother's name (Kincaid, an illegitimate child herself, bore her mother's maiden name).

The second of these sections, enclosed in parentheses, introduces the first of several biblical references in the story. The parenthetical segment consists of six questions about heaven and hell, the meek lamb, the roaring lion, and the streams running clear. Their combined purpose is that of ascertaining whether the worlds that the mother and daughter live in conform to the rules spelled out by Euro-Christian logic. These questions emphasize Christian geographical hierarchies—heaven *above*, hell *below*—and the power hierarchies of colonial relationships—the lamb lies meek, the lion roars. The allusion to colonial relationships is stressed in the line that follows the parenthetical segment, which alludes to ancient (conquering) ships still anchored in the peninsula.

"The Letter from Home" ends with two biblical images that accentuate the gospel-like resonances of the brief narrative and underscore the narrator's rejection of the God-fearing "home" she has left behind, a home that occasionally intrudes in her new life when she receives a letter from her mother. The first follows the daughter's description of a universe created by divine wisdom, a universe in which the earth spins on an imaginary axis whose existence is accepted as a matter of religious and scientific faith, a universe where valleys correspond to mountains that in turn correspond to the sea, which corresponds to dry land. This image of perfect harmony and symmetry, however, masks the ultimate menacing correspondence, that of the earth to the snake after the Fall. The snake, having lost its limbs as punishment for drawing Eve into sin, must forever lurk in the shadows awaiting its prey. This image of the snake as a menace is linked in the story to the figure of the mother, who early in the narrative had described herself as having shed her skin. This final correspondence frees the daughter's voice, for in the second and final biblical image she assumes the "I" she had avoided until now, assuming her own declarative voice to describe the figure of the shrouded Christ (identified by the capitalized "He") beckoning to her and whistling softly. She slyly rows her boat away, "as if I didn't know what I was doing," showing through that pretense of ignorance (and the implied

acknowledgment to the reader that she knows precisely what she is doing) her determination to leave behind the world of her mother and her
willingness to challenge divinity itself (39).

"WHAT I HAVE BEEN DOING LATELY"

Of the stories collected in *At the Bottom of the River*, "What I Have Been
Doing Lately" is the most lighthearted and playful. Kincaid is not known
for giving in to whimsy in her writing; on the contrary, she has often
been taken to task for prose whose tone is too steeped in anger, particularly in her fictional and nonfictional portraits of her mother. In her
early prose, her surreal fantasies lean heavily toward the menacing and
frightening. In "What I Have Been Doing Lately," however, we find
Kincaid at her most whimsical. The story—a narrative whose structure
loops on itself twice like an amusement-park roller coaster—blends the
nonsensical elements characteristic of children's narratives with the for-
malistic and thematic experimentation we have come to associate with
the work of writers such as French "New Novelist" Alain Robbe-Grillet,
whose writings Kincaid admires, and Julio Cortázar, short-story master
of the 1960s Latin American "Boom."

Like a modern-day Alice in her darker and more foreboding Wonderland, the narrator of "What I Have Been Doing Lately" sets out on reluctant adventures when she gets up from bed to answer the door, only
to find no one there. She starts walking north through an ever-changing
landscape, encountering wondrous and sometimes menacing things,
tumbling down a deep hole, returning to the surface, running into a
woman who asks her what she's been doing lately, to which she replies
with the tale of how she was lying in bed when the doorbell rang—thus
starting the tale from the beginning again. The second telling of the story
reworks significant elements of the narrative, adding details, redirecting
incidents, refocusing themes, only to end with the narrators going back
to lying in bed, "just before the doorbell rang" (45). This looping of the
narrative, which has us return twice to the beginning to start anew, results in a self-reflective text, what is known in literary criticism as a meta-
narrative (a text that calls attention to the techniques and devices on
which the author relies for effect).

In style, "What I Have Been Doing Lately" is built around simple
declarative sentences that describe a landscape often absurd and nonsensical, where contradictory realities merge, as in dreams. As the nar-

rator steps outside, it is either drizzling or there is a lot of damp dust in the air; she walks down a path, past a boy tossing a ball, but when she looks back the path has been replaced by hills and instead of a boy there are flowering trees. She sits for years by the banks of a big body of water before taking a boat across. From the opening lines, the style signals an entrance into a world of childlike bewilderment, where disbelief is suspended and little is anchored in reality. From the moment the narrator steps out of the door, the writing revolves around itself. Kincaid, in the double retelling of her story, explores various modes of narrating her tale, showing the process through which narrative material becomes art. It is a story of apprenticeship, conscious of its artificiality, of its presentation of writing as an evolving process.

Thematically, "What I Have Been Doing Lately" returns to the notion of the voyage as a separation from loved ones, the mother particularly, and explores the narrator's yearning for home. The cyclical structure of the story, which keeps bringing the narrator back to her present, away from the home she yearns for, underscores the permanence of that separation and accounts for the note of sadness with which the story ends. "I felt so sad," the narrator tells us, "I couldn't imagine feeling any other way again" (45). Here, as in almost all her narratives, Kincaid draws on autobiographical materials familiar to her readers, albeit in an elliptical way, placing these elements in an incongruous Wonderland setting. When she sets out on her voyage she looks south (toward her Caribbean home), but decides to walk north. She comes to a big body of water, but it takes her years to get across. She looks behind her, but everything familiar has vanished; a deep hole opens before her and she plunges in. She resurfaces because she misses all the people she had loved, only to run into a woman whom she mistakes for her mother and whose question sends her back to that bed in which she is lying when the doorbell rings. To the reader familiar with Kincaid's personal story, it is easy to read in these details the correspondences with her own experiences, glimpsing, in the process, how she has turned them from autobiographical fact into the materials for fiction. They help her create a system of symbols that guide the reader through her writing, like a key that opens the path to understanding her literary universe.

Kincaid provides such keys in "What I Have Been Doing Lately" through the differences between the telling of the story and its retelling as the tale loops on itself. Whereas the first telling dwells more extensively on the Wonderland elements of the narrative landscape, the second part is more solidly grounded in reality, more focused on elucidating the themes of voyage, separation, and longing. Now, coming across the great body of water is as easy as paying her fare, but the reality found in her new environment is not the beautiful world she expected, but one in which she is surrounded by black mud, where people whom she thought would be laughing and chatting and beautiful are no such thing at all. Thus, with great narrative economy, Kincaid articulates the themes of disappointed expectations and sadness and regret for what the narrator has left behind, expressed in the dreamlike vision of the bend leading to her home, where she would find her freshly made bed, her mother, and those she loved—only to discover herself back in bed just as the bell is about to ring.

"BLACKNESS"

"Blackness" is one of the most lyrical stories in *At the Bottom of the River*. The narrative, divided in four separate sections, draws on the incantatory rhythms of prayers and the psalms for its poetic resonances. Yet, unlike its biblical rhetorical models, which aspire to lead toward God's light and salvation, "Blackness" moves the narrator toward darkness and oblivion. The narrator of "Blackness"—unlike the many narrative voices in *At the Bottom of the River*, who seek clarity and self-knowledge through swimming in shafts of light—seeks self-erasure in the darkness.

The first section of the story evokes the paradox (or contradictions) of the blackness in which the narrator would like to be engulfed. The blackness, which descends like a heavy fog onto her world, is all things: silence and deafening sound, visible and invisible, not her blood but something that flows through her veins. The enigma of blackness, its perplexing incongruities, is meant to mirror the narrator's despair, her inability to keep herself out in the light.

In those instances in the story when the narrative voice surfaces from the darkness, moving toward the light, it revels in the joy the light brings. Most of the images of joy in the story are directly or indirectly related to the light: faces turned toward the sky, a "sliver of orange on the horizon," the last vestiges of the setting sun, a rolling green meadow, a spring of clear water. The narrator, however, when questioning her own nature, acknowledges the fascination of the blackness. Her lamp remains unlit, and she recognizes the darkness as buried deeply and permanently in the human breast, while the glimmering light is shallow, impermanent. Through this first section, Kincaid will develop the image of the mine and of the narrator as a miner seeking "veins of treasure" (48). The image that closes the opening segment of the story is precisely that of the heart as a mine holding a treasure of love, joy, and pain, buried in darkness but penetrated here and there by shafts of light.

In the second section of the story the narrator falls into a dream that plays on images of light and darkness, thus picking up the thematic thread of the first part. She dreams of bands of men returning from battle, exhausted, the chambers of their weapons empty. As they pass her house they obliterate the light, "and night fell immediately and permanently," blotting out everything that she found pleasurable, all the beauty and safety of her world.

In the third section, the narrator identifies herself as a mother watching her daughter, who is transparent in the light. As in many other renditions of motherhood in Kincaid's fiction, this one is tinged with a note of cruelty, although in this case it is the daughter, not the mother, on whom cruelty and pitilessness have taken hold. The mother is all sacrifice, going to great lengths for her daughter's joy and comfort (she chewed her food for her when she was small, she carries a cool liquid in her flattened breasts to quench her thirst, she creates moments of joy for her); the daughter is all greediness and self-absorption in her eagerness to take what is offered. For the portrait of the daughter, Kincaid borrows elements usually associated in her fiction with mother figures, chief among them the qualities of the *jablesse* who is able to mutate her body into frightening forms: revolving eyes burning like coals, teeth that suddenly grow pointed and spark, arms that grow to "incredible lengths" (50). She feels no pity for the hunchback boy whom she renders deaf and incapable of direction and whom she leaves in a hut built on the edge of a steep cliff. In her preternatural wisdom—her knowledge of things beyond the physical world that is akin to clairvoyance—the narrator of "Blackness" prefigures the characterization of Xuela, the protagonist of Kincaid's third novel, *The Autobiography of My Mother*.

The daughter in this section of "Blackness" stands "one foot in the dark, the other in the light" (51), bridging the gap between the two worlds, one threatening to engulf the narrator, the other offering fleeting glimpses of joy. She has the ability to move from one to the other, rushing "from death to death" (51). As someone who has mastered the powers of the *jablesse*, with her connections to the underworld and the darkness, and as someone enamored of "great beauty and ancestral history," the daughter is, unlike the narrator, self-affirming and beyond despair. She can always return to the light.

In the last section of "Blackness," the narrator hears "the silent voice" of self-erasure and oblivion calling to her, obliterating the blackness. The brief segment recalls an image familiar to moviegoers: that of the hero or heroine walking in acceptance toward death, embracing the mist that brings an end to disease and despair. Following the familiar choreography of such scenes, almost a cliché in the Hollywood filmmaking of the thirties and forties, we follow the figure of the narrator as it moves slowly toward the voice, shrugging despair and hatred like a mantle, embracing the mist that drowns her, erasing her image from the screen.

"MY MOTHER"

"My Mother" is considered by many critics to be the second most successful story in *At the Bottom of the River*, after "Girl." It offers Kincaid's most sustained rendition of the theme of the love-hate relationship between mother and daughter in this collection. The story, which is divided into nine brief sections and narrated in the first person, chronicles a young girl's struggle to gain emotional independence from her mother. It focuses on the interconnected themes of power and powerlessness to which Kincaid will return so often in her stories and novels.

The first section of "My Mother" opens with a statement of the devastating burden that anger at her mother places on the daughter, expressed in a hyperbolic, exaggerated note that sets the tone for the rest of the story: immediately after wishing her mother dead, the daughter cries enough tears to drench the earth around her. This use of rhetorical overstatement as a stylistic device will aid Kincaid in the portrayal of the mother as a larger-than-life figure and of the emotional connection between them as deeper and more binding than such connections normally are. She will also establish the themes around which the tale will revolve, themes she has elaborated in earlier work: the immeasurable closeness that linked mother and daughter, a suffocating, overwhelming love; and the devastation of the separation between them when puberty sets in and the daughter must grow a bosom of her own on which to rest her head. The flood of tears that opened the story then becomes a small pond of "thick and black and poisonous" water, and the relationship between mother and daughter becomes one of pretense and hypocrisy.

In the second section of the story, Kincaid plays with images of light and shadow to depict a ritualized dance of broken harmony between mother and daughter. The sequence, unfolding like a dream, opens with a familiar image in Kincaid's writing—that of the young woman seeking her reflection in the mirror as symbolic of the search for an identity independent of the mother. The effort is fruitless because the room is submerged in darkness and the mother controls the light. The play of shadows in the glow of the candles lit by the mother is depicted as a dance that mirrors their conflictive relationship, reversing the established balance of power, where the all-powerful mother reigns supreme. The shadows make a space between them "as if they were making room for someone else," displacing the daughter. But then the mother's shadow is shown dancing to the daughter's tune, giving her a fleeting sense of control before the mother blows out the candles. The daughter's brief and illusory taste of power underscores the mother's strength and authority and returns the daughter to her initial posture, still sitting on the bed, "trying to get a good look at myself" (55).

In the third section of the story, mother and daughter transform themselves into lizards by means of an oil rendered from reptile livers. The mother's transformation is described in great detail; the daughter's is presented as a secondary, imitative gesture that disallows any possibility of her own independent metamorphosis. The mother's mutation into a reptile, usually a snake, is familiar to Kincaid's readers. It is often linked to the representation of the mother as a *jablesse*, a creature of evil that can transform herself into anything she wishes. The details used to describe the mother's new form are frightening, even revolting: teeth arranged into rows reaching back to her throat, hairlessness, a flattened head with blazing, revolving eyeballs. The daughter's mimicry of the mother is poignantly described as having reduced her to traveling on her underbelly, with a darting and flickering tongue.

In the fourth section, mother and daughter are standing on the seabed in a perfect mimicry of harmony, both aware of the hypocrisy and pretense needed to sustain their hapless relationship. The daughter sighs— "the kind of sigh she had long ago taught me could evoke sympathy" (56)—and the mother receives her sighs as her due, in a wordless play of appearances. Once again, Kincaid elaborates a symbolic representation of the mother/daughter relationship as one fraught with tensions that arise as the daughter grows into adulthood and must establish a relationship of equality with her mother. The process of maturation, presented in this section as a physical transformation that gives the daughter an impregnable carapace and makes her feel invincible, shakes their wordless arrangement to its foundation. Their relationship requires the mother's dominance and the daughter's submission; hence the daughter's ire when her hopes to see the mother "permanently cemented to the seabed" are disappointed and the mother looms above her, still bigger and more powerful. The daughter's struggle and frustration against this imposed powerlessness leads her to a rejection of her mother's caresses, followed by "a horrible roar, then a self-pitying whine" (56). Kincaid recreates the daughter's bitterness through images of repulsion: as the daughter becomes a woman (like her mother) her skin blackens, cracks, and falls away; like the mother, she grows rows of teeth in retractable trays; as they walk out of the Garden of Fruits they leave in their trail small colonies of worms. These images are meant to evoke for the reader the festering anger that poisons the daughter's life.

In the fifth section, Kincaid continues to build on the daughter's festering bitterness as a developing theme. Here, after establishing the mother's contemptuous mimicry of the daughter, the daughter attempts to defy and destroy the mother by building a house for her over a deep hole. As in the preceding section, Kincaid portrays the daughter's growth into womanhood as a series of physical transformations undergone in symbolic spaces; here, the mother and daughter find themselves in a cold and dark cave where the daughter grows special adaptive features (lenses that allow her to see in the darkness, a special coat to protect her from the cold) only to find the mother mocking her achievements and laughing at her. The daughter then builds a beautiful house with all the features that would please her mother—her own mockery of perfection and happy domesticity as it conceals a menacing hole, symbol of the emptiness of their own domestic felicity. She hopes that the mother will fall into the hole and thereby into her power, but the mother once again proves her omnipotence by walking on air once she enters the house and praising its excellence. The daughter is left to her admission of defeat (she fills up the hole) and venting of her rage (she burns the house to the ground).

The sixth section returns to an earlier theme—that of the mother as a colossal physical presence that overwhelms the daughter, leaving her glowing red with anger. The daughter's attempt at separation is at best only partially successful: she lives on an island with eight moons, but covers their surface with expressions she has seen on her mother's face; she builds a house across a dead pond from her mother's, but cries constantly for the latter's company. Here, Kincaid expands on an image she had used in the first section of the story—namely, that of the poisoned pond (which earlier had been formed out of the daughter's tears of bitterness and regrets) as the symbol of strains that lead to a separation between mother and daughter, strains linked to the daughter's desire for an independent existence. The section ends with the daughter's crying herself into a deep dreamless sleep.

The seventh section returns to a pivotal moment in Kincaid's personal history, one she has used as symbol of separation before and after the writing of "My Mother": the mother walking the daughter to the jetty from which she will board the boat that will take her away from her home island. But here she reverses the by-now-familiar elements of the anecdote so that what begins as a ritual of separation ends as a rite of reconciliation and oneness. She returns to the sleep motif of the previous section—where the daughter, worn out by her burning anger at the mother, falls into a dreamless sleep—although here the daughter's sleep in the cocoon of a boat encased in a large green bottle and the dream takes her back home. Like a film being rewound, mother and daughter move from separation to recognition, from caution and politeness to walking in step, from talking to a merging of voices, until the daughter could no longer see "where she left off and I began" (60).

The eighth section returns to the image of the house as the idealized space where mother and daughter can live in perfect harmony, merging and separating as creatures about to enter "the final stage of our evolution" (60). Here, in order to set the mood of continuity and permanence for the section, Kincaid relies on elements drawn from her own mother's autobiography (which she will develop more fully in *The Autobiography of My Mother*), in particular that of the young woman crippled in a bicycle accident, an episode linked to the experiences of Kincaid's maternal aunt. The idealized home in which mother and daughter can live in perfect unison—the mother's house—contains within it the past, encapsulated in the memories it holds of things and events that have passed in and through it. The rooms open into each other, in an image familiar to moviegoers (see, e.g., the dream sequences designed by Salvador Dalí for Alfred Hitchcock's *Spellbound*) to signal the opening of doors to the past or the deeper recesses of the unconscious. Mother and daughter are represented as walking through the rooms as if one, an image preceded by that of the daughter lying in the hollow of the mother's stomach, as if she had returned to the womb.

In the ninth and final section, the daughter is depicted as having fully embraced her submission to the mother and is rewarded by being allowed to merge with her. In the last of her mother's many transformations, she becomes Yemaya, Afro-Caribbean deity of the seas, who sees to it that the fishermen return to land with a bountiful catch. Drawing from one of the salient images of the previous section, the daughter appears ensconced in the mother's "enormous lap." Images of paradise abound as the story comes to its close, underscoring the notion of the daughter's perfect happiness now that she and the mother are one: a bower made from flowers, a hummingbird that nests on the daughter's stomach ("a sign of my fertileness," 61), warm rain, and lambs (which she uses in the story as a symbol of childlike innocence and vulnerability).

"AT THE BOTTOM OF THE RIVER"

"At the Bottom of the River," the story that gives the book its title, is the longest of the volume. The six sections that compose the narrative revisit the central themes of the collection, from the allure of the void and nothingness of "Blackness," through the evocation of the dignity and integrity of the father in "In the Night," to the lost idyllic relationship with the mother of "Girl," "The Mother," and "Wingless."

"At the Bottom of the River" opens with a meditation on man's responsibility to interpret and give meaning to nature. The opening paragraph is but a description of a wondrous natural landscape of steep mountains, powerful streams, plains and ridges, gorges and glittering pools, all awaiting "the eye, the hand, the foot that shall then give all this a meaning" (63). There is a faint trace of mockery in this description of man as the measure of all things, a note of slight derision, as if to indicate that the narrator is not quite sure that man is up to the task of interpreting a nature more powerful and lasting than he is. The second paragraph of the segment underscores this notion, as it depicts a man living in a small room, existing in a world "bereft of its very nature," unaware that there is a task of great magnitude open to him if he could stir and embrace it. Kincaid builds this section on repetitions of the phrase "he cannot conceive," underscoring his poverty of spirit and imagination, his very incapacity to take stock of his world. Unlike the many young female narrators struggling between darkness and light and the search for knowledge and identity in *At the Bottom of the River*, this man "sits in nothing" (64) and cannot be the measure of anything.

The second segment of the story returns to the image of the father figure Kincaid had developed in "In the Night," a figure that owes much to that of her own stepfather. This portrait of the father, like the previous one, underscores an ordinary man's delight in the habitual and commonplace. He is a man who, unlike the solitary man of the first segment of the story, has embraced his life of work and domesticity and glories in his routine. His work as a carpenter offers meaning and pleasure; the placidity of his domestic arrangements is a source of joy. He is contented and satisfied, and just a bit vain. This portrait, however, differs from the one Kincaid offers in "In the Night" in significant ways. In "At the Bottom of the River," the father figure is shaken out of his complacency when one day, seemingly out of the blue, he glimpses the immensity of the Earth's magnitude—represented here by fossils, layers of geological strata, veins of gold in stone, mountains covered with hot lava—and realizes his own paltriness and insignificance. The realization destroys his self-satisfaction and contentment, as now he finds himself confronting death and nothingness, imagining that "in one hand he holds emptiness and yearning and in the other desire fulfilled" (67). The loss of innocence embodied in this man's confrontation with the potential meaninglessness of life is poignantly counterpoised against the theme of the young woman's loss of innocence that runs through the stories of *At the Bottom of the River*. Unlike the naive, unquestioning father figure she has created in her stories, only occasionally dreaming of things beyond his limited horizons, Kincaid's young women narrators are without illusions. Their struggle against their mothers, their refusal to yield to the many transformations that would have made them like their mothers, has left them without that capacity for wonder the father possesses; but it has also left them with a shield of protection against the naiveté that blights the father's life after his realization of his own inconsequence in the large scale of things. They are keenly aware of the futility of many human struggles and, unlike the father, know that before them there is "a silence so dreadful, a vastness, its length and breadth and depth immeasurable. Nothing" (68).

The third part of "At the Bottom of the River" further develops the theme of death and nothingness of the previous section. In this segment, however, there is the narrator's own voice, a narrative "I," confronting the void. The meditation on death with which the section opens under-scores the narrator's existentialist perspective: the inevitability of death can strip life of all meaning and she struggles to hold on to some significance through the contemplation of her own place in the cycle of life. She wishes she could reach out with her hand to make the earth stand still, but is forced to accept "the death in life" (73). If in the previous segment Kincaid juxtaposed the father's efforts to find meaning in life against the magnitude of the geological cycles the Earth has undergone, here the cycles of plant and animal life are presented as the unstoppable force making a mockery of the narrator's attempts to defy death and oblivion. "Death is natural," someone says to her, and she feels mocked.

In part four of the narrative Kincaid returns to a theme that readers have come to associate with her fiction—that of the estrangement that develops between mother and daughter when the latter enters puberty and must begin to separate from the mother and establish her own independent identity. This theme, as revisited in "At the Bottom of the River," opens with an invocation to the light, Kincaid's favorite metaphor for the quest for maturity and self-knowledge. In a direct reference to the figure of the daughter in "Blackness," the narrator of "At the Bottom of the River" struggles to exist "between the day and the night" (73), between light and darkness. She sees herself as a child, when she lived in perfect harmony with her mother and regarded her face as one of "wondrous beauty." In a rare reference to the colonial background of her childhood in *At the Bottom of the River*, Kincaid links the unqualified love and harmony she felt for her mother then to her period of blindness to the realities of Antigua's colonial situation. (The theme will become one of increasing importance in her writing after the publication of this collection.) Here, Kincaid offers an image of false concord in her description of the rows of dark-skinned colonial girls mindlessly singing an English hymn. The narrator's process of maturation involves shedding both her illusion of blissful unity with her mother and her delusion about glorious moments of contentment and joy being possible with "wanton hues of red and gold and blue" (an allusion to the Union Jack) swaying in the breeze.

The fifth section of "At the Bottom of the River" accounts for the title of the story; here, the narrator stands by the mouth of the river, staring through the clear and still water at the world that unfolds at the bottom. What she sees are pictures of idealized domesticity: a house of rough heavy planks surrounded by a wide stretch of perfectly mowed green grass, a flower garden, everything imbued with a supernatural light that fills everything and holds some profound but as yet unknown meaning.

A naked woman appears (yet another rendition of the mother figure) who directs the narrator's gaze toward a world stripped down to the bare essentials, where all the familiar elements of the landscape—sun, moon, mountains, seas—are distilled to their very essence.

Kincaid returns in this segment of the story to her use of the light as a metaphor for clarity of vision. The light that fell on everything made all things transparent, "so that nothing could be hidden" (77). The narrator (the daughter), as most of Kincaid's narrators in the tales collected in *At the Bottom of the River*, takes advantage of the light to look at herself and within herself. The description of the physical characteristics she sees—as if for the first time—culminate in her description of her skin as red—"the red of flames when a fire is properly fed" (79)—a characteristic Kincaid often evokes to represent female beauty and fulfillment. Above all, the narrator uses the light to recognize her complete dominion over her will—her having attained maturity and independence. She is now ready to enter the water and allow her physical body to dissolve into it, to penetrate that supernatural space created by the light at the bottom of the river. As she fuses with the light she becomes like a prism, "refracting and reflecting light," and finally attains beauty.

In the sixth and final segment of the story the narrator emerges from the light in which she had plunged in the preceding section to ponder the power of a small glowing thing surrounded by darkness to help her emerge from her pit and lure her toward life. Here, Kincaid responds to the despair she had described as belonging to the two men of the first and second parts by underscoring her narrator's desire to struggle against the blackness and nothingness that lead to such despair. She then moves her character toward the light, reentering the everyday domestic sphere, reencountering commonplace objects. She asserts the strength of her connections to "all that is human endeavor," and feels herself growing "solid and complete," her name "filling up [her] mount" (82). Kincaid closes the story—and the book—with an affirmation of the daughter's identity and her determination to embrace life, thus bringing the process of maturation and separation from the mother—the thematic focus of the book—to its logical and most satisfying conclusion.

A FEMINIST READING OF *AT THE BOTTOM OF THE RIVER*

The work of Nancy Chodorow, author of *The Reproduction of Mothering* (1978), is notable among American feminists for its emphasis on the importance of mothering in the formation of gendered identities and its pioneering consideration of class and race issues as crucial elements in children's acquisition of notions of appropriate gender behavior. Mothering, Chodorow has argued, is a process geared to producing female children who will fit comfortably in the private, domestic world, leaving male children to the public, social world (Chodorow, 174). It is Chodorow's contention that growing into womanhood means coming to terms with "the ideology, meanings, and expectations that go into being a gendered member of our society" (98). Girls, Chodorow points out, are expected to be "more like and continuous with" the mother than boys, making the process of separation from the mother a more distressing process for girls, who are not expected to "individuate themselves, to see themselves as distinct from their mothers" (166). In her analysis of Chodorow's work, Elizabeth V. Spellman takes her theories one step further, arguing that "what one learns when one learns one's gender identity is the gender identity appropriate to one's ethnic, class, national, and racial identity" (88).

Chodorow's theories can be extremely useful in helping us understand Kincaid's depiction of the tensions between mother and daughter as stemming from the clash between the mother's desire to mold the daughter into a copy of herself and the daughter's determination to develop her own independent personality and ideas. In *At the Bottom of the River*, Kincaid uses the figure of the mother as the main conduit for the myriad limitations that a patriarchal society imposes on young women. The mother's efforts to channel the daughter's activities, interests, and behavior into patterns that the mother perceives as socially acceptable lead to the daughter's perceiving her as a *jablesse* calling on the daughter to transform herself into disgusting things—lizards, snakes, monsters.

The tensions between mother and daughter are aggravated in *At the Bottom of the River* by Kincaid's insistence on establishing links between the mother and colonial culture and mores. As complicated as the stresses between mother and daughter are in her fiction, they are further problematized by the mother having formed her notions of the proper ideas and behavior for her daughter from British colonial models. The mother's admonitions stem from her perceived need to form the daughter into a proper colonial subject, one who does not give in to local or native ways but must imitate colonial patterns of behavior. In "Girl," for example, we see the mother functioning as such an agent of colonial assimilation, teaching her daughter what she perceives as behavior necessary to "whiten" herself. In that story, as in many others in the collection, the daughter's resistance stresses her preference for native ways as an affirmation of the native culture. The strains between mother and daughter thus acquire symbolic meaning, as they are made to stand in representation of the struggles for supremacy between colonial empire and the colonized. The mother's efforts to adapt and embrace colonial culture must be seen as representative of her acceptance of the status quo, of her own colonized mentality; the daughter's efforts to establish her own separate identity, in turn, stand as representative of Antigua's attempts to nurture its own political and cultural independence.

4

Annie John
(1985)

Although *At the Bottom of the River* was a great success with critics, its complexities of theme and style did not make the text readily accessible to the general reader. *Annie John*, Kincaid's fictionalized account of her experiences growing up in Antigua in the 1950s, was to be her first popular success. Acclaimed by critics and readers alike for "the honesty, lyrical beauty, and richness of detail" of its prose (Perry, 492), *Annie John* made Kincaid's writing accessible to an unprecedented number of readers.

All eight chapters of *Annie John* had appeared as stories in the *New Yorker* prior to their publication in book form in 1985. (This pattern of publishing chapters of her novels-in-progress as independent prose pieces in the *New Yorker* continued through the writing of *The Autobiography of My Mother*, after which Kincaid severed her relationship with the magazine.) The earliest chapter of *Annie John* to be thus published, "The Circling Hand," appeared in November 1983; the last, "The Long Rain," appeared in July 1984.

GENRE

The pattern of serialized publication that initially brought *Annie John* to the attention of readers led to some early confusion on the part of reviewers as to what literary genre—the novel or the short story—the text belonged to. The writing of the various chapters as self-contained texts—"stories" that could be read and enjoyed by readers of the *New Yorker* as independent pieces—meant that when brought together as a book they produced an episodic story with a somewhat disjointed plot. These episodes were linked as a "novel" by the strong presence and unmistakable voice of the young narrator through whom Kincaid fictionalizes her experiences growing up in the small Anglo-Caribbean colony of Antigua. However, unlike the traditional novel, which is characterized by a tightly woven plot where episodes, characters, and themes are closely interlaced to produce a seamless whole, the various narratives that make up *Annie John* come together as fragmented moments in a young girl's life. They owe their coherence as a "novel" to the centrality of Annie's voice and presence.

Annie John fits perfectly into the subgenre of the novel known as *bildungsroman* or novel of development, which chronicles the moral, psychological, and intellectual development of a young man or woman. The bildungsroman has been a favorite genre of Caribbean writers, who have used its focus on the central character's growth and formation to establish parallels between their experiences and those of the small West Indian colonies in which their characters' lives unfold. Among the many excellent examples of Caribbean bildungsroman we find George Lamming's *In the Castle of My Skin* (1954), Merle Hodge's *Crick Crack, Monkey* (1970), Erna Brodber's *Jane and Louisa Will Soon Come Home* (1981), Zee Edgell's *Beka Lamb* (1982), Magali García Ramis' *Felices días, tío Sergio* (1986), and Michelle Cliff's *Abeng* (1984). Like *Annie John*, these novels are anti-colonial narratives that chronicle the protagonist's growth toward maturity and independence as a mirror to his or her society's progress from colonialism to independence. Kincaid's impressionistic, richly nuanced story of young Annie John's uneasy relationship to Antiguan society is presented chiefly through her problematic relationship with her mother, allowing Kincaid to build thematic parallels between Annie's ambivalence toward her often domineering mother and the ambiguities of Antigua's history of subordination to British colonialism.

PLOT DEVELOPMENT

The text of *Annie John* consists of eight chapters, arranged chronologically, that chronicle the salient episodes of the protagonist's life from the age of ten until she prepares to leave Antigua for England at the age of seventeen.

"Figures in the Distance"

The first of these chapters, "Figures in the Distance," finds Annie and her family in temporary exile from their home in St. John's, the capital of Antigua, while the house is under repair. Living temporarily in the outskirts of town, within sight of the cemetery, young Annie develops a growing fascination with death. The "sticklike figures" of mourners she sees in the distance (and which give title to this chapter) awaken her to an awareness of both the reality of death (particularly that of children) and the body of spiritual and religious beliefs connected to Obeah that make of death such a threatening presence in her society. The four parts into which the chapter is divided offer four distinct instances of Annie's increasing fascination with the death of young children.

The first section chronicles her discovery that children can indeed die, and that she is as a result vulnerable to a fatal illness or accident, or that she could fall victim to a persistent evil spirit. In this first section, Annie's mother emerges as a powerful figure who can seemingly tower over death itself. She is the repository of intricate knowledge about death and spirits as well as about the most mundane, everyday details surrounding death (undertakers, bathing the corpse, the timing of funerals and its meaning). The section introduces the notion of Obeah as a powerful element of the native culture that will be pitted against colonial domination, signaling this early in the text Annie's commitment to Antiguan cultural beliefs as the foundation of her image of herself and her society.

The second segment, which takes place after Annie's return to her house in town, tells of the death of a girl younger than Annie herself. Although Annie did not know this bony, red-haired girl—whose death was caused by a disease that prompted her to eat mud—the death strikes close to home because the girl not only dies in Annie's mother's arms but is prepared for burial by Annie's mother. Although Annie's father is also linked indirectly to the death by being charged with building the coffin, it is her mother's more active participation that profoundly impacts Annie, marking the first instance of distancing between Annie and her mother: after having bathed, stroked, and dressed the dead child, Annie is temporarily repulsed by her mother's hands and cannot bear to have her caress her, touch her food, or help her bathe. Annie's proximity to this death, however, confers on her a certain fleeting importance at school, where in return for her many retellings of the salient details of the story she receives countless descriptions of other probable and improbable deaths.

The third segment of this first chapter offers three examples of the social and spiritual understanding of death in Annie's world. The first concerns a girl at school, a dunce whom Annie alternately patronizes and torments, whose mother dies in childbirth, thus turning her into a pariah, a "shameful thing" left alone in the world by her mother. The second—the death of a neighbor across the street with whom Annie is intimately familiar—provides an example of a "natural" death that produces no anxiety or fear. The third invokes the world of superstition and folklore—a young girl is induced to stop sucking her thumb by her mother's dipping it into water in which a dead person had been bathed. The segment ends with a discussion of what mothers are capable or not capable of doing to their daughters to make them conform.

The final section, the longest of the opening chapter, describes Annie's obsession with going to funerals and visiting funeral parlors and private homes where the dead are laid out for viewing. Despite the fact that those whose deaths are being mourned are complete strangers to her, she feels progressively emboldened to take an active part in the rituals as a mourner. When she is finally afforded the opportunity of attending the funeral of a humpbacked girl her own age whom she knew (although only by sight), the experience is narrated in painstaking detail—every memory of the dead girl is recalled, the number of people in attendance is detailed, the girl's appearance is minutely dissected, the hymns sung are evoked. The segment, however, ends with an episode that announces what will be the central theme of Chapter Two, and indeed of the book as a whole—that of the appearance of the first fissures on the till-then smooth surface of Annie's relationship with her mother. Having returned home from the funeral of the humpbacked girl to lie to her mother about not having picked up the fish for dinner, she is confronted with the truth and punished. However, her mother, who had announced she would not be kissing her goodnight, finally relents; but the seeds and anxiety of separation, thematically connected in the chapter to the notion of the death of a child, are firmly planted here to be developed in subsequent chapters.

"The Circling Hand"

Chapter Two, "The Circling Hand," consists of five sections of various lengths that focus on events unfolding during the summer of the year when Annie was twelve, two years after Annie lived through her obsession with death and funerals. Its central theme, anticipated at the end of the previous chapter, is the growing strain in the relationship between Annie and her mother. In this chapter the stresses are compounded by Annie's growing awareness of her mother's sexuality. In many of the episodes narrated in this chapter, the father hovers guilelessly in the background, his presence a constant reminder to Annie that the blissful image of the inseparable couple she and her mother represent can at any time be shattered by his exercising his claims on the mother as his wife. In fact, the title of the chapter, "The Circling Hand," refers to a pivotal episode in which Annie walks into the house unexpectedly to find her parents making love. Unable or unwilling to grasp the truth of what is taking place, her gaze becomes fixated on her mother's hand as it goes around and around in a circular motion on the small of her father's back. She stared at the "circling hand" as if she would "never see anything else in my life again" (31).

The first section of the chapter opens with the image of Annie awake in her child's bed listening to her parents as they go through their morning routine. After her father's departure for work, Annie and her mother follow their own school-holiday routine, which primarily involves Annie's introduction to the many details of organizing and running a household: selecting bread at the baker's, choosing fruit and vegetables at the market, discussing the provenance of fish and crabs with the fishmonger, preparing lunch, doing the laundry. Annie's apprenticeship in the domestic arts—her preparation for marriage and household economy—includes her learning about the perils of the social world in which she lives. The women her father had loved and had children with before marrying Annie's mother loom as menacing figures in this social landscape, threatening figures from which her mother must protect her since in their hatred they are capable of causing Annie physical harm, either directly or through the agency of an Obeah curse. The protective baths that Annie and her mother take together underscore the theme of water as purifying and revitalizing element that will be found throughout the book (see, e.g., the chapter entitled "The Long Rain"). The section ends with a description of her family at lunch during which Annie observes with interest her mother's coquettish behavior toward her father and the impact her beauty and seductiveness have on him. Early in the narrative Kincaid establishes the position of the father as the dominant pater familias who receives preferential treatment in the family and who can command the mother's attention away from Annie whenever he desires.

The second segment of the chapter offers a brief history of Annie's parents' childhood. Her mother, who was born in Dominica, had left the island for Antigua after a quarrel with her father. The boat in which she traveled to Antigua was lost at sea for five days during a hurricane, but she arrived safely with an enormous wooden trunk that now contained many mementos of Annie's own childhood: handmade clothing and baby blankets, her christening outfit, baby bottles, photographs, birthday dresses, report cards, and certificates of merit from Sunday school. The occasional airing out of these things gave mother and daughter the opportunity to tell and retell the family stories that would serve as the foundation for Annie's personal history. These occasions fostered their closeness and intimacy, and Annie cherished their physical proximity, reveling in her mother's beauty and smells, feeling enveloped in her mother's love. Her father's story, in contrast, was one of lovelessness. Abandoned by his parents, and having lost the grandmother who brought him up when he was young, he evoked Annie's pity. From her own state of bliss in her mother's unqualified love, her father's lovelessness loomed like an unfillable void. This segment of the chapter closes with a vivid image of Annie's "paradise": sometimes when she helped her mother tend their herb garden, her mother would stoop down and kiss Annie on the lips and neck.

The third part of the chapter focuses on the process of physical maturation Annie undergoes during the summer of her twelfth year and the emotional stress it leads to as she feels her oneness with her mother fast evaporating. As her legs become more "spindlelike," her hair more unruly, the smell of her perspiration more unfamiliar, her mother announces that she is too old to continue to look "like a little me," plunging Annie into a morass of "bitterness and hatred" that threatens to consume her (26). Annie's physical changes mark her readiness to become "a young lady," and the process of turning her into her mother's notion of what a proper young woman must be only widens the gap between them. Gone are the days in which they would sit in harmony going over the things in their trunk, gone were the showers of "kisses and affection and attention"; they are replaced by distrust and disapproval, and Annie is faced for the first time with the sight of her mother's back "turned on me in disgust"'(28).

In the fourth and pivotal section of this chapter, Annie describes her preparations for beginning at a new school in September as a preamble to her fateful early return home from Sunday school to find her parents making love. Returning home in a rush with the Bible-school prize with which she hoped to recapture her mother's love, she finds her parents in their bed, consumed with each other and completely oblivious to her presence. Annie's reaction is one of unmitigated hostility to both her parents, but particularly to her mother, whom she suspects of having been aware of her presence in the house before she noisily began to set the table for lunch. She considers all marks of affection as finished between her and her mother—she was sure that she could "never let those hands touch me again"—and speaks to her mother in a challenging tone she had never dared use with her before (32). Disgusted, and determined to treat her parents from then on with veiled contempt, she puts her happy past behind her, believing that she would never "think of it again with fondness" (32).

The brief segment that closes the chapter tells of Annie's return to school after the summer holiday and of her falling in love with a classmate named Gwen. Having transferred the overwhelming love she once felt toward her mother to her new friend, she keeps the friendship a secret from her mother. Her secret gives her a quasi-malicious power over her mother, who remains as unaware of having lost her daughter's fervent love as of Annie's deep feelings of betrayal at feeling herself shut out of her parents relationship.

"Gwen"

Chapter Three, which bears the simple title of "Gwen" and is divided into four sections, focuses on Annie's successes at her new school while developing further the description of her physical maturation, which culminates here with her first menstruation. In the first section, Annie takes us through her first day at her new school, where her teachers bear the names of English generals (Nelson) and infamous prisons (Newgate) as reminders of their exalted hierarchical positions as English teachers in a colonial school. Annie's fears about social acceptance and intellectual recognition are quickly allayed by the success of her first in-class assignment—an autobiographical essay that Annie reads aloud to the class with stunning success. In contrast with the work of her classmates—which seems overly concerned with relatives living abroad, hopes of emigration, or fleeting contacts with those who themselves have had fleeting contacts with English aristocrats—Annie produces a heartrending exploration of the growing gap between her and her mother, illustrated through a correspondence between water and the loss of the mother. The story is rendered metaphorically through Annie's description of how she, unable to swim despite her mother's repeated attempts at instruction, is separated from her mother (a strong swimmer) while they are bathing in the sea. Annie, powerless to join her mother, is forced to wait until her mother returns to shore, but not before she dissolves into tears of fear and frustration. The episode, as described by Annie in her essay, leads to a recurring dream in which her mother has swum away and sits remote and unapproachable on a rock, sometimes by herself, sometimes joined by her father. Showing that she has already learned to manipulate her "autobiographical" text to suit her audience, Annie invents a fictional ending in which her mother, deeply distressed at being told of the recurring dream, cries and holds Annie in her arms, erasing the nightmare. Her mother's actual reaction when told of the dream, however, had been quite different: she had turned her back on Annie indifferently and advised her somewhat callously not to eat certain kinds of unripe fruit before going to bed.

In the second segment of the story Annie is rewarded for her triumph with Gwen's admiration and love. Annie's infatuation with Gwen is described in the vivid but conventional terms of a deep adolescent love affair, from which Gwen emerges as the idealized love object pampered by the light and the soft breeze. Their growing intimacy is punctuated by their sharing their likes, dislikes, dreams, and feelings. But even with Gwen Annie is reluctant to divulge the sad state of her relationship with her mother, fearing her friend's misunderstanding and condemnation.

In the third segment of the chapter Annie describes how her intellectual achievements in school earn her the friendship of the brightest and most interesting of her classmates (with whom she forms a pack of sorts) and the appreciation and trust of her teachers, who often leave her in charge of the class during their absences. Her height and strength—until then considered as unwelcome developments that had propelled her into an unwanted path toward young womanhood—now make it possible for her to excel at sports and assume a leadership position. Her position as a leader among her classmates brings up the thematic link between

Annie's rebellion against her mother's power and her wishing to develop a powerful position of her own. She practices at being alternately kind and cruel to her friends and classmates, exercising the kind of arbitrary power she has seen displayed by both her mother and the colonial elite the mother emulates. As rebellious as Annie wishes to be, she is still bound by a colonial education, as is made evident by Kincaid's reference to her admiration of Enid Blyton, author of "the first books I had discovered on my own and liked" (52). (Blyton is a controversial English writer of children's books widely read in the first part of the twentieth century in England and its colonies despite their reactionary and racist characterization of blacks.) As Annie reconciles herself to her growth and maturation she begins to separate from the world of home and from her mother, seeking information, comfort, and affection from her peers. The thought of home with her mother and father as the ideal space is replaced with the dream of a gray house of many rooms on a lane with high and well-trimmed hedges that she would share with Gwen.

In the fourth and last segment of "Gwen" Annie describes the first day she began to menstruate, contrasting her fear and physical distress with her mother's nonchalance and half-mocking reminiscences of her own first day. Annie alternates between discomfort and shame (the cloth between her legs felt heavier and heavier and she was sure everyone knew what was happening to her) and a cool apathy as she shows everything to her friends (none of whom had begun menstruating) "without the least bit of flourish, since my heart wasn't in it" (52). Feeling inexorably pulled toward an adulthood she neither wants nor is prepared for, she sits among her friends wishing she could transcend their world and live in a place where there was no future "full of ridiculous demands," no hindrance to desire, only their love for each other. She is sent home from school early after fainting, and confronts her mother's solicitude with a bitterness born of the death of her love.

"The Red Girl"

The first part of "The Red Girl" recounts how Annie learned how to deceive her mother and get away with behavior her mother had absolutely forbidden. The overall theme of the chapter, indeed, is that of Annie's triumph over maternal surveillance. She made an art of looking like the very picture of innocence while stealing books, playing marbles, and befriending the Red Girl, a playmate who represented the antithesis of what her mother considered proper behavior for a young girl. The Red Girl climbed trees, played marbles with the Skerritt boys, bathed and changed her clothes only once a week, kept her hair dirty and matted, her fingernails filled with dirt. Their secret friendship posed a direct challenge to Annie's mother, and Annie therefore "worshipped the ground her unwashed feet walked on" (59). They would escape together to the lighthouse, from whose balcony they had a vantage point on both land and sea, as if to show that their friendship shed a clearer light on those aspects of life that Annie's mother had tried to keep her sheltered from.

The second section of "The Red Girl" describes how Annie's new friendship leads her to an obsession with playing marbles, one in the "new series of betrayals of people and things" that Annie embarks on as a challenge to her mother's authority. As her relationship with the Red Girl develops, it takes precedence over Annie's love for Gwen, and the marble playing replaces all the other games and amusements Annie had previously enjoyed. In the process Annie amassed an impressive collection of marbles that she was hard-pressed to keep secret from her mother's inquisitive eyes.

In the third segment of this chapter, Annie perfects her deceitful practices so as to be able to continue to meet the Red Girl in secret. Taking advantage of her mother's desire to see her excel in her academic work, she invents school projects that purportedly take her to the hills to collect specimens, draw from nature, observe the landscape. Her relationship with the Red Girl moves into a new phase as they fall into a pattern of alternately inflicting pain and caresses. In a quasi-ritualistic play, the Red Girl pinches Annie fiercely until she cannot control her tears and her chest began to heave, at which point she would stop pinching and begin to kiss the painful spots. Annie describes the sensation as "delicious" and ponders the impact that her own mistreatment of other girls had in their continuing adoration of her.

In the fourth section, Annie moves from deceit to theft in order to buy small trinkets to offer the Red Girl as presents. She steals mostly from her parents, rejoicing in betraying their trust. In the pivotal scene of the chapter, Annie is discovered by her mother as she emerges from the special place under the house where she hides her marbles. Discovering in Annie's hand an unusually beautiful marble she had won after a great effort and which she intended to offer to the Red Girl, the mother becomes obsessed with discovering Annie's hiding place. Her failure to do so only contributes to Annie's growing contempt for her; Annie delights in her description of how her mother rants and raves while unbeknownst to her her foot is touching the very place where the marbles are hidden. The section ends with Annie in suspense, barely able to swallow her supper while she wonders if her mother's vigilance will now increase to the point that she will have to abandon her secret life of pain-and-pleasure encounters with the Red Girl and games of marbles with companions her mother would find unsuitable.

In the fifth part of the chapter Annie's mother, obsessed with finding the offending marbles, uses the narrative of her past as bait to seduce Annie into revealing their hiding place. She weaves tales of how once a basket of figs she was carrying on her head turned out to also contain a long black snake or of how she had worshipped her brother but he had died of "something the Obeah woman knew everything about" (69). The stories are offered as if they could cast a spell that would lure Annie into a state of rapture or sympathy that would lead her to lower her guard and give away the location of the hiding place. She is about to give in when she awakens from her daydream to hear her mother's voice, "warm and soft and treacherous," asking where the marbles are. She can respond with her own warm, soft, "and newly acquired treacherous voice" that she does not have any marbles and has never played with any.

The sixth and final section of Chapter Four explains how three simultaneous events close the "Red Girl" chapter of Annie's adolescent rebellion: she begins to menstruate, stops playing marbles, and the Red Girl moves to Anguilla to live with her grandparents. Annie ends the narrative of the Red Girl interlude with a dream that once again imagines an alternative "home" where she could live with the object of her love and outside the power and influence of her parents: an island where she and the Red Girl would live, feeding on wild pigs and sea grapes, and from which they would send confusing signals to boats cruising by, causing them to crash onto the rocks.

"Columbus in Chains"

Chapter Five of *Annie John*, "Columbus in Chains," is one of the most reprinted and discussed sections from the novel. This is so because of the political and historical content of the chapter, which addresses directly for the first time in the book the colonial condition of Annie John's home island and her latent resistance to it. Although previous chapters of *Annie John* contained allusions to colonialism and cultural domination (see, e.g., the concern with England and migration in the girls' autobiographical essays and the discussion of the English people's inadequate notions of bathing in "Gwen"), "Columbus in Chains" tackles these cultural and political issues from Annie's personal vantage point.

The chapter, which is divided into two parts, opens with a reference to the permanence of things outside the classroom, where Annie, prefect of her class, sits reflecting on her book, *A History of the West Indies*. Outside, the daily routine continues apace—the baker is baking her buns, her mother shoos the hens, her father complains about his partner; inside, Annie daydreams about her unsuitability for the position of prefect, given that she is the "worst-behaved" girl in her class, and reflects on her rivalry with second-place Hilarene and on her sympathy for yellow-haired Ruth, the English minister's daughter and the class dunce. Ruth's lack of familiarity with the history of the West Indies, for which she is often made to wear the glittering dunce cap, allows Annie to ruminate on the legacy of slavery and colonialism, offering several ideas that will resonate throughout Kincaid's fiction. Annie sees Ruth's predicament— that of being forced to live in a colony where everything reminded her of the harm her ancestors had done—as worse than the situation of the former slaves, who could take comfort in the notion that if they had been in the same situation they would have behaved better. Annie claims that if her ancestors had traveled from Africa to Europe, they would have taken "a proper interest" in the Europeans, said "How nice," and returned home "to tell their friends about it" (76).

Annie's ruminations on West Indian history take her ahead of her classmates in her West Indian history text, to an illustration of Christopher Columbus being sent to Spain fettered in chains attached to the bottom of a ship. The sight of the great man being brought so low affords Annie a somewhat perverse pleasure; she savors the irony of seeing the man credited with having brought enslavement to her people and colonial control to her island humiliated in his turn as a result of his own quarrelsome nature. "[J]ust deserts," she calls it, and takes it one step further by linking the illustration to an episode in her own family history. The words Annie writes under the picture, defacing the book and bringing the wrath of her teacher on her—"The Great Man Can No Longer Just Get Up and Go"—are the very same words that Annie's mother had used in triumph on hearing that her own father, with whom she had quarreled before leaving Dominica, now required help in order to walk.

The second part of the chapter describes the teacher's ire at the discovery of Annie's impertinence and how her anger leads to Annie's own punishment and humiliation. Miss Edward's wrath stems from her own reverential notion of Columbus as an imperial icon juxtaposed with Annie's instinctive resistance to a distorted colonial narrative. As a result, she was sent to the headmistress, who removed her from her position as prefect and ordered her to copy John Milton's *Paradise Lost*. Although Annie's description of Miss Edward, the teacher, is charged with mocking irony—her pimples are depicted as ballooning into huge boils, her bottom seems to rise so high it could almost touch the ceiling—she nonetheless retains the power to punish Annie's blasphemous defamation of "one of the great men in history," and her subsequent lack of remorse, by forcing her to endorse the power of Milton's narrative (as representative of English cultural domination).

A direct consequence of Annie's own humiliation—of her being brought so low herself—is that despite her worsening estrangement from her mother she yearns for her mother's embrace and words of comfort. The final episode of the chapter narrates how Annie's hopes are dashed, further widening the gap between her and her mother. Her parents, deeply engrossed in their own conversation, take little notice of her and seem oblivious to her misery. Her mother, furthermore, tricks her into eating breadfruit by pretending it is a new type of rice imported from Belgium. Confronted with her deceit, her mother laughs, her mouth open to "show off big, shiny, sharp white teeth," prompting Annie to think that her mother had suddenly turned into a crocodile (84). This imagined transformation, reminiscent of the many metamorphoses into animals or monsters that the mother figure undergoes in *At the Bottom of the River*, underscores the deterioration of Annie's relationship with her mother and her need to develop different avenues for affection and comfort.

"Somewhere, Belgium"

In the three sections of "Somewhere, Belgium," Chapter Six of *Annie John*, Kincaid has Annie describe in poignant detail how she faced the devastation of the final and decisive rift between herself and her mother. The climactic confrontation between them that will lead to Annie's collapse in "The Long Rain" and her departure from Antigua in "A Walk to the Jetty" unfolds when Annie is fifteen and imagines her deep unhappiness as a small black ball wrapped in cobwebs, like a tumor within her, no bigger than a thimble, but weighty and mighty, blighting her life. In her description of such an acute state of adolescent anger and depression, Kincaid walks a fine line between the imaginative language needed to describe something as intangible yet real as despair and the need to keep the narrative firmly within her character's voice and personality. She achieves this by having Annie give form to her despondency through images of balls wrapped in cobwebs, thimbles, and black "things" standing between her and her mother, and by having Annie relate her dispiritedness through comparisons with books she had read and the contrast between her inner feelings and the radiant sunshine and blooming flowers surrounding her.

In the first section of the chapter, after describing her unhappiness, Annie focuses on the hypocrisy into which the tensions between her and her mother have forced her. They continue to play their established roles of doting mother and adoring daughter to the world while engaging privately in a fierce battle fueled by that "something I could not name" that was akin to hatred and that Annie projects into a dream in which the words "My mother would kill me if she got the chance. I would kill my mother if I had the courage" would go around in her head (89). The recurrent dream takes on a heightened reality, leading Annie to scrutinize the events in her life in terms of whether they pointed to her mother's having her chance or to Annie herself acquiring the necessary courage.

In the second segment of the chapter, Annie offers the details of the deterioration of her relationship with her friend Gwen. Having demonstrated exceptional intellectual ability, Annie had been moved to a higher form with girls older than herself from whom she felt alienated. Self-absorbed and vain—they carry mirrors in their school bags—they cannot offer true companionship to someone like Annie, who is yet unable to see herself clearly. Annie had tried to maintain the intensity of her connection to Gwen, but their paths were quickly diverging. While Annie seemed increasingly concerned with books and dreams of escape—her reading of a biographical sketch of Charlotte Brontë made her yearn to escape to "Somewhere, Belgium"—Gwen appeared preoccupied with conventional, more ordinary things. Gwen's concern with gossip, for example, or her engrossment in matters of love and matrimony, lead Annie to conclude that "something terrible had happened, and I couldn't tell what it was" (93). Her suggestion that Annie marry her brother Rowan— a suggestion so removed from Annie's as yet unfocused but definitely different hopes and aspirations—shows the extent of the gap that has opened between them, and Annie begins to avoid Gwen with pretexts of academic work and other obligations.

The section ends with the detailed narrative of an episode that reveals the complexities of Annie's changing image of herself. One afternoon, having taken a route home through Market Street in order to avoid Gwen, Annie stops before a store window, examining her reflection in the glass. She cannot recognize herself—what she sees reminds her, not of her familiar image of herself, but of a painting she had seen recently of *The Young Lucifer* wearing the kind of smile that tells everyone the person "is just putting up a good front" (95). The comparison Annie establishes between herself and Satan as a lonely and vulnerable figure cast away from paradise underscores her belief that she herself has been cast out, that, given her alienation from her mother, the loss of her friendship with Gwen, and her disaffection with everything around her, she, like Satan, should sit down on the sidewalk and weep tears of bitterness.

Her miserable reverie is interrupted by her becoming the object of the mocking attention of several boys somewhat older than herself who greet her with exaggerated and malicious courtesy. Her recognition of one of the boys as a childhood playmate leads to bittersweet memories of how he had taken advantage of her gratification at having an older boy as a playmate to abuse her. The mockery, and the memory of the indignities she had suffered at his hand as a child (not only had he insisted on having the upper hand in all the games they played, but once had made her take off all her clothes and sit on a nest of red ants), are connected thematically to Annie's present quandary—the fact that she is on her way to becoming a young woman and that the indignities of sexist gender relationships loom ahead of her. Her defiance of the restricted roles open to her as a girl is seen both in her dismay at realizing that Gwen has taken for granted that she wishes more than anything else to marry and in her recollection of a game she used to play with the mocking boy—a recreation of the trial and execution of a man found guilty of killing his girlfriend and the man with whom he had found her drinking in a bar. During one of their recreations of that drama the boy had found himself hanging by the neck from the front gate, unable to extricate himself, and Annie had been too petrified to summon help, shaming her mother by her inability to act. Although Annie displays remarkable maturity and poise in greeting the boy politely despite her obvious embarrassment, the encounter reminds her of a time when her relationship with her mother was still harmonious; her mother had come fiercely to her defense when the boy had made her sit on the ants' nest.

The third and final section of the chapter narrates Annie's crushing encounter with her mother when she returns home after the incident with the mocking boys. In the opening sentences of this segment Kincaid returns Annie to the image of the thimble of unhappiness within her, described here as spinning inside her, bumping against her heart, chest, and stomach, scorching from within. Having pleaded extra studies at school as the reason for her lateness, she is confronted by her mother's claim that she had been inside a store on Market Street and had seen her "making a spectacle" of herself by acting like a "slut" in front of the boys (102). Annie, drowning in her fury, feels the word "slut" overwhelming her and replies ("as if to save myself") "like mother like daughter" (102). Annie's response resounds like an earthshattering blow between them, pitting against each other the "two black things" that stand as representative of their mutual hostility. But her mother's reply— "Until this moment, in my whole life I knew without a doubt that, without any exception, I loved you best"—deals Annie a more devastating blow as it seems to withdraw her mother's love from her with splintering finality, opening "a deep and wide split" between them and turning Annie's world upside down.

Sitting in her bedroom, surrounded by the furniture her father had lovingly made for her, Annie finds, stored under her bed, the trunk in which her mother had put all her belongings after quarreling with her father and leaving his house forever. The memory of her mother's quarrel with her father is thereby connected to Annie's own quarrel with her mother, linking them as natural progressions in their family history. Her mother's trunk now contains Annie's things—the mementos of her own past that she once enjoyed perusing with her mother—and the thought of it splits Annie's heart. Part of her wants to retreat into a safe and beautiful space with her mother; the other part wants to see her dead and coffined at her feet. Her decision is rendered when her father, sensing the tension at home, offers to make his wife the set of furniture she has been wanting for a long time and in turn asks Annie what she would want him to make for her. Her immediate response, "a trunk," signals her desire to make the quarrel stand and her need to ultimately leave home, like her mother before her. Whether her departure would mean freedom from her mother remains questionable at the end of this chapter, which closes with Annie's uncertainty as to whether she would find her mother's shadow standing between her and the rest of the world.

"The Long Rain"

Chapter Seven of *Annie John*, "The Long Rain," is divided into seven brief sections and tells the story of the prolonged illness that follows Annie's frightful quarrel with her mother in Chapter Six. During this illness Annie retreats into a semblance of her childhood, a time during which she was completely dependent on her parents and could count on their unqualified love and support. It is as if, having felt deprived of maternal care, she wills herself into a state of infantilism where she must be coaxed into eating and, like a baby, wets her bed. Ultimately she must reemerge into the turmoil of her adolescent world, but not before, cocooned by her grandmother back into health and strength, she finds the resolve to carve a persona and a future separate from her mother.

In the opening section of the chapter, Annie describes the mysterious illness that slowly overtakes her after the disastrous confrontation with her mother and the symbolic request for a trunk of her own that follows. Kincaid weaves Annie's narrative around a series of thematic threads, chief among them the images of rain and drought around which the chapter revolves. Her illness is preceded by a prodigious drought lasting for over a year and develops during a "long rain" pouring continuously for three and a half months. The torrent makes the sea rise, permanently covering what used to be dry land; in much the same way Annie will grow taller, outgrowing her clothes and shoes and coming out of her illness towering over her mother and father and having gained a remarkable degree of inner personal strength. In this first section, however, Kincaid limits Annie's narrative to her parents' bewildered reaction to this mystifying illness while Annie seeks to describe the condition akin to a nervous breakdown from which she is suffering. She seems to be floating in a state of semiconsciousness, weightless, detached but aware of her surroundings, hearing conversations as if through a thick fog. Words flew across the air toward her, but "just as they reached my ears they would fall to the floor, suddenly dead" (109).

In this opening section of Chapter Seven, Kincaid has Annie return to the image of the black thing lying inside her head that she had developed in the previous chapter, the thimble blotting out the memory of everything that had happened to her in her fifteen years. To this image she adds that of the sound of the rain on the galvanized roof as something pressing her down, bolting her to the bed. Kincaid relies heavily on wa-

ter imagery to convey Annie's sense of disconnectedness: the rain anchors her to the bed; the sea mirrors her growth in the cocoon of illness
Annie builds around her like a protective shell; sounds rock in her ears
like a large wave dashing against a seawall; in a dream she drinks in
the sea in huge great gulps leaving only the dry seabed; when she starts
to leak out the seawater through little cracks in her body, she wets her
bed and must be changed by her parents as if she were still an infant.
Her awareness of her father's near-nakedness as he holds her comes as
a jolting reminder of the sexuality that she seems partly to be trying to
avoid by her refuge in sickness. It underscores the source of her illness
in her grief at losing her mother at the moment of puberty, a moment
when her fear of growing up coincides with her mother's rejection.

In the second part of the chapter, Annie is propelled by her mother's
offer of chocolate milk into a hallucination. As she feels part of the black
thing inside her head break away, replaced by a yellow light, she sees
herself as a small toy Brownie, dressed in the regalia of the First Division
troop to which she belonged. The vision centers on the hierarchical and
ceremonial character of the Brownies, emphasized through the many in-
signias, emblems, badges, and citations that are part and parcel of the
rituals of the organization. These are most clearly connected in Annie's
waking dream to colonial control as the girls begin their ceremonies by
following the rising of the Union Jack with their eyes, pledging allegiance
to "our country, by which was meant England," and doing "all sort of
Brownie things" (115). The Brownie trance ends with Annie's minuscule
figure trying to return home along a road that remained its normal size;
she is drawn back to reality by her mother's voice uttering words that
reach Annie's ears incoherently but nonetheless restore her to the reality
of her sickbed and lull her to sleep.

In the third segment of "The Long Rain" Annie's mother res rts to
Obeah in her attempts to heal her daughter. The father, disapproving of
Obeah practices, arranges to leave the house before Ma Jolie comes to
cleanse Annie's body and bedroom of any potential evil lurking men-
acingly over her. The rituals of anointing Annie with special oil and
lighting special candles leave an impression of beauty on Annie but otherwise fail to draw her out of her weakened condition. The segment
closes with a reminder of cultural hierarchies as the father's obvious
disapproval of Obeah practices forces the mother to rearrange the medicine shelf in Annie's room, placing the medicines prescribed by the doctor (which had been just as ineffective in curing Annie) in front and the
remedies prescribed by Ma Jolie in the back.

In the fourth section of the chapter Annie's parents try to resume their normal routine when her illness goes into its third week only to have to rearrange their lives again when Annie, left unsupervised for a short while, destroys the family photographs. The incident sheds light on Annie's inner turmoil; its bizarreness reads like her effort to obliterate the stresses and tensions that have led her to illness and derangement. In her delirium-ridden mind, the photos blew themselves up until they touched the ceiling, keeping beat to a music Annie could not hear, perspiring until their smell was unbearable to her. They seem to move as in a parody of sexual intercourse, falling back on the table limp with exhaustion when their strange dance is finished. Annie, faced with this row of photographs of people dressed in white in a travesty of purity— Annie in her white dress uniform and her Communion dress, her Aunt Mary in her wedding dress, her father in his white cricket uniform— rises from her bed to give them all a good wash in a sort of purification ritual. She washes them thoroughly, cleaning crevices, trying to straighten creases, removing the dirt from her father's trousers before dusting them with talcum powder and covering them with a blanket so they can sleep. In the process she eliminates the faces from all the people in the wedding picture, except for herself, in a gesture of self-affirmation and alienation; in a photo of her mother and father, she had erased them from the waist down, obliterating the sexuality Annie found so problematic; in a picture of herself in her Confirmation dress she had erased everything except a pair of shoes with decorative cutouts on the sides that her mother had found inappropriate and over which they had quarreled bitterly. The shoes, a memento of a time when she had told her mother she wished her dead, remain as an affirmation of her right to her own sexual identity.

In the fifth part of the chapter there are indications that Annie is beginning to emerge from her self-imposed illness. Having forced the household to organize itself around her needs and assured herself of her mother's constant attendance (the neighbors do the shopping for her, the fisherman delivers the fish), she begins to respond, albeit in somewhat bizarre ways, to the stimuli around her. When Mr. Nigel, the fisherman, comes in to see her after bringing the fish, she is responsive enough to comment that he is just like her father. He laughs in response, and his laughter "filled up my nostrils, my throat, my lungs, and it went all the way down until every empty space in me was just filled up with Mr. Nigel's laugh" (121). The joyous moment is anchored in Annie's approval of Mr. Nigel's satisfaction with his life in all its unconventionality:

he loves his work and enjoys a harmonious relationship with his partner (with whom he shares a boat, a house, and a wife). At the sound of his laughter Annie leaps out of bed and throws herself at him, knocking him to the ground in a caricature of sexual attack, telling him all that rushed into her mind about him, her mother's disapproval of the wife he shared with Mr. Earl, her great-grandfather's failure as a fisherman, while he listens in placid nonchalance.

In the sixth section of the chapter Annie's grandmother, Ma Chess, arrives unexpectedly from Dominica on a day when the steamer was not due. Ma Chess, a more knowledgeable Obeah woman than Ma Jolie and a Carib woman, coaxes Annie back into health, not through remedies, but through her willingness to nurture Annie from her symbolic infancy by accepting the stages through which her granddaughter must progress back to health. She curls up with her in a fetal position, providing a womblike space for Annie's healing. She feeds her and bathes her, in the way Annie's mother used to do, replacing the mother who now turns increasingly to the father for companionship. Ma Chess links Annie to the island's pre-Columbian past and to African cultural practices that the father negates and the mother can only practice secondhand. Ma Chess offers a primordial maternality. Her success is an affirmation of Annie's much needed connection to a past other than the one Miss Nelson and her other schoolteachers have tried to impose on her and of the validity of native cultural roots and traditions connected to precolonial history.

In the seventh and final part of "The Long Rain" the rain stops and Annie's illness mysteriously goes away. The rain-soaked island begins miraculously to restore itself, and Annie starts the slow process of re-covering her strength. Annie's post-illness resolve is to never see any of the things familiar to her ever again—not to see the sun shine day in and day out, not to see her mother bending over the cooking pot, never to hear her voice again. She longs "to be in a place where nobody knew a thing about me" (128). Her home island having become "an unbearable burden," she wishes she could hold it under water until it died. Her return to school is punctuated by her efforts to reinvent herself through her eccentric clothes, her new and strange accent, her newfound power. Her self-dramatization is stamped by her relentless efforts to differentiate herself from her surroundings, to present herself outwardly as different from anybody her fellow students have ever met, as the new persona she will need when she leaves everything behind and goes to the new dreamed-of space for which she longs. The period of her illness has given birth to a freer and more independent self.

"A Walk to the Jetty"

The final chapter of *Annie John* opens with an affirmation of identity— "My name is Annie John" (130). The five parts into which the chapter is divided follow the progression of Annie's last day at home, as she prepares to board the boat that will take her to England to train as a nurse. The chapter is marked by the duality of Annie's position: at seventeen she is at once still firmly planted in her old world while already distanced from her past, looking into a future she is already refashioning into something different from what her mother planned for her.

The first segment finds Annie still in bed taking stock of her room, disconnecting herself from everything she is determined never to look at again. Her summing up of her life underscores the emotional distance from her parents that has widened in her perception since she began to regard them as sexual beings in their own right—"Now they are together and here I am apart," she says. Lying in the bed her father had made for her, for what she is sure will be the last time, she relishes the thought of every act of the day being one she will perform for the last time. The room, where everything—furniture, clothing—was made by her mother or father, leaves no space for the expression of Annie's own subjectivity. Her strong desire to leave this space forever is a reflection of her desire to define a space of her own where she can no longer feel that "the two of them made me with their own hands" (133). She glories in the thought that she will forever be away from people who can recall her past history, acknowledging the feeling of gratification as "the strongest thing in my life" (134).

The second segment of the story opens with Annie's announcement that the Anglican church bell had struck seven. The tolling bell—a reminder of Antigua's colonial history—signals the start of Annie's preparations for departure. With ceremonial studiousness, Annie dons clothes and jewelry doctored by the Obeah woman, has her hair pressed, shares a Sunday-style breakfast with her parents, and receives the many friends of her mother who come to show the appropriate amount of joy and sorrow at her departure. Throughout these ceremonial farewells, Annie's public and private selves play out conflicting roles: she looks at her parents at breakfast "with a smile on my face and disgust in my heart"; she says goodbye to Gwen affectionately while wondering why she continues to behave like a monkey. In her description of the morning's events Annie returns to the image of her parents as a unit that excludes her;

their festive mood strikes her as proof of their relief at her leaving. The brief section contains two instances of Annie's rejection of the notion of marriage: she replies to her parents' suggestion that in due time she will write to announce that she is getting married with a contemptuous "How absurd!"; Gwen's parting announcement that she was more or less engaged to a boy from Nevis is met with a "Good luck" that manages to conceal her disdain for the way in which Gwen had degenerated into "complete silliness" (137).

The third segment of the chapter follows Annie's actual "Walk to the Jetty," for which she leaves with her parents at precisely ten o'clock. The description of their half-hour walk reads like that of a ceremonial procession through the salient moments of Annie's past. "I was passing through most of the years of my life," Annie asserts as she walks past the house of the seamstress to whom she was once miserably apprenticed, past the road she had taken to school, church, Brownie and Girl Guide meetings, past the road down which she walked in her first unaccompanied errand at age five, past the bank and the shop where she chose the doll she wanted for Christmas, past the shop with the porcelain dog that enthralled her as a child. The bittersweet procession marks the last time in which Annie and her parents will walk "in the old way," with Annie between her mother and father, and the details Annie offers of this dreamlike walk read like her effort to encapsulate the idealized memories she intends to treasure. As a result she presents them in her text as part of a dream in which she saw these places "as if they were hanging in the air" (143). The dreamlike sequence ends with their arrival at the jetty.

In the fourth section of the final chapter, Annie chronicles her feelings as she boards the launch that will take her and her parents to the boat anchored in the bay. As she reaches the bay, Kincaid returns Annie's narrative to the water symbolism she had used so effectively before, evoked here through Annie's old fear of "slipping between the boards of the jetty and falling into the dark-green water where the dark-green eels lived" (143). The jetty conjures negative associations of her walks there with her father, during which he would become engrossed in conversations with the watchman about subjects beyond her interest. Annie, in turn, will invoke images of self-obliteration as the means of conveying her feelings of loss as she leaves the island—she feels held down against her will, as if she were burning from head to toe, she imagines that someone is tearing her up into little pieces that will float down to nothing in the deep sea. In this section Annie's narrative voice uses the phrase

"I shall never see this again" like a mantra that makes her heart alternately swell with gladness and shrivel inside her. Once in the launch, however, as they move away from the jetty, the haunting quality of her surroundings vanishes, the familiar sights resume their ordinary non-evocative aspect, the sea regains its habitual blue. Gripping her parents' hands tightly, Annie has a fleeting feeling that "it had all been a mistake," that she can still remain in the comforting security of the world she knows; but in a moment of epiphany remembers that she was no longer a child and that "now when I made up my mind about something I had to see it through" (146). The section ends with the launch arriving at the ship, "and that was that" (146).

The final section of "A Walk to the Jetty" completes the process of Annie's severance from her parents and her past. The awkward farewells from her parents in her small cabin are punctuated by Annie's now familiar duality—they smile at each other, "but I know the opposite was in my heart"—and the contrast between Annie's desire to flee and the performance of sorrow expected from her (147). She has to remember, for example, that it was expected of her to stand on deck and wave the red handkerchief given to her by her mother for that purpose and to continue to do so until the launch bearing her mother disappears in the distance. The book—which had opened with Annie's obsession with death in "Figure in the Distance"—closes with an evocation of water and rebirth. After the figure of the mother vanishes, Annie returns to her cabin, from which she hears the waves lapping around the ship, sounding as if a vessel full of liquid was "slowly emptying out" (148). The image, juxtaposed as it is in the text to that of the water vessel emptying out, invokes the flow of the amniotic fluid that precedes birth, signaling Annie's emergence from the womb into an independent self.

SETTING

In *At the Bottom of the River* Kincaid relies on an exoticized Caribbean setting to convey the foreignness of her characters' environment. The various narrative voices that people her first collection of short stories evoke elements from folk tales, rituals and beliefs drawn from Obeah, and familiar West Indian rhythms to create a setting that the reader can recognize as enigmatically Caribbean. In *Annie John*, given the different genre and the style requirements of a *bildungsroman* or novel of development, Kincaid must invoke for the reader a more nuanced natural and social landscape against which Annie's life can unfold. This means that in *Annie John* Kincaid must flesh out the specificities of the Caribbean landscape to present a convincing background for Annie's movement from childhood to young adulthood.

The tale of Annie John's growth into maturity is set in the island of Antigua, Kincaid's birthplace. This is established in the opening pages of the text through the use of specific place names (streets, neighborhoods, buildings) and other geographical markers (hills, bay, seashore) that paint a panoramic picture of the capital city of St. John's, Annie's hometown. Details of weather, flora, and fauna contribute to establishing a distinct sense of place early in the narrative. In Chapter One, "Figures in the Distance," for example, Kincaid situates her story in the West Indian context through the summoning of the farm animals, specific varieties of flowers and fish, and materials for building that are native to the region.

Because the tale is presented through the eyes of Annie John, Kincaid faces some limitations in conveying the social landscape on which her protagonist's story rests. Since Annie begins her tale by describing events that happened when she was still a child, her early social connections are naturally filtered through her mother. In the early chapters of the narrative, particularly in "Figures in the Distance," Annie is literally removed from social contacts. She has no playmates and has frequent interaction only with a neighbor who gives them table scraps to feed the pigs; her first descriptions of people are those of the figures of mourners she sees at a distance. Indeed, an intrinsic part of Kincaid's narrative is that of describing how Annie's social connections broaden as the tale develops. Her world, which is confined to the home and immediate neighbors at the beginning of the story, grows progressively wider—the scope of Annie's friendships and acquaintances, as well as the geographical space she occupies, broadens as the story progresses, until at the end she has turned her back on Antigua and looks ahead at a seemingly limitless and foreign social horizon.

The town of St. John's, as it emerges from the pages of *Annie John*, is characteristic of Anglo-colonial West Indian capitals of the mid-twentieth century. Divided along class and race lines, the Afro-Caribbean population of Annie's Antigua has been accustomed to the presence of British expatriates in positions of authority for centuries. As a child of urban working-class parents, Annie has little occasion for direct contact with the British officials in Antigua; the English who come into her sphere are minor officials, doctors, Anglican ministers, or teachers from whom she experiences directly the patronizing solicitude that is the most common face of colonial racism in the Caribbean. As her experiences with teachers in the "Columbus in Chains" chapter demonstrates, the role of such expatriates is that of preserving a pattern of deculturation whose object is to keep present in the minds of the colonial subjects the superiority of British culture and the concomitant inferiority of native cultural practices. Her teachers' admiration for Columbus as one of the great men in history—when contrasted to Annie's view of Columbus as a mean-spirited man who unchained a series of disastrous events on the Caribbean region—is emblematic of the imposition of particular cultural perspectives that results from the presence of British officials in colonial settings.

Since Annie's contact with such officials is limited, her experience of colonialism is filtered through the adults whose view of themselves and their island has been formed through an acceptance of the superiority of things English. Annie's parents are examples of such conformity. Her father, for example, rejects Obeah practices in favor of Western-style doctors; her mother seeks to emulate the mores and practices of the English middle class, using those standards as her guide in socializing Annie. Examples of such devaluation of local culture abound in the text and Kincaid makes clear her own position in favor of local cultural practices by having Annie's recovery from her pivotal illness rest on the practices and knowledge of her Carib grandmother, a powerful Obeah woman.

Obeah as a set of African-derived religious and curative practices is a repository of resistance in the text. It is one of the salient elements used by Kincaid to establish her cultural and geographical setting in the novel. It informs the notions of death and mourning practices in "Figures in the Distance," provides the baths that protect Annie from the evil unleashed on her by the women her father had loved before marrying her mother, restores Annie's physical and emotional health in "The Long Rain." As one of the most distinctive elements of Antiguan culture, Obeah provides a key element in defining the culture that informs Annie's resistance in the text.

CHARACTER DEVELOPMENT

As the narrator and central character of the novel, Annie dominates the text of *Annie John*. Her voice controls both her own characterization and that of all other figures in the text, making her the filter through which we as reader encounter her reality. Annie is a complex figure. As she moves through her adolescence, a trying period of discovery and loss, she must harden herself against her mother's efforts to recreate herself in her daughter and against the colonial myths that have informed her mother's notion of what both she and her daughter should be.

One of the most important elements in Annie's characterization is the acknowledged autobiographical nature of the text. Kincaid, through the many different versions of the episodes of her life she has told in her writings and interviews, has invited readers and critics to identify her with Annie John. Given her constant weaving and reweaving of the by-now-familiar narrative through her various books, Kincaid's readers have come to equate her narrative voices with her own, making it difficult to separate author from narrator. Her characterization of Annie John, as a result, is a complex balance between the fictional and the autobiographical, filtered through Kincaid's extratextual commentary on the "truth" value of her fictionalized narrative. Critics are indeed invited through this commentary to rework for themselves the significance of Kincaid's deletions and additions in her characterization of Annie, making of her an open, fluid figure.

As a character, Annie must be seen in connection with her mother, particularly since the character's hard edge develops as a result of her mother's grating presence in her life. Annie's perception of the world, as it grows increasingly complex throughout the text, has at its core the identification between her mother and everything she feels she must reject in her world. Her growing bitterness against her mother, in fact, is the foundation of her character's development. Pitted against a mother who moves from idealized to hated figure, Annie must develop a bittersweet core of hardness as a protective shield.

What then, of this beloved and hated mother? What are the glaring faults that draw such anger from her daughter as to make her want to reject her and her world? The characterization of the mother is one of the least successful elements in *Annie John* when seen from the perspective of the character's development as explanation of what lies at the core of the central relationship of the novel. Annie's mother, also named Annie, appears as a beautiful figure in her daughter's eyes when the relationship is a harmonious one at the beginning of the text, and as an almost repulsive figure, reptilian and treacherous, when the relationship turns sour. Throughout the text she is seen only as Annie sees her, and the dominance of Annie's perspective makes it impossible to establish a clear picture of who the senior Annie John is.

Perhaps the most problematic aspect of the characterization of the mother in *Annie John* is what is absent from the text that could help explain to the reader the foundations of Annie's burning anger. When confronted with Annie's overpowering anger, some readers have been struck by the absence of convincing evidence of the mother's iniquities. The mother's sins—her conventionality, her efforts to make a proper young lady of her daughter, her fuzziness, her consciousness of class hierarchies, her unquestioning acceptance of colonial notions—pale before the grievous offense of her sexual presence, the evidence of her sensual connection with her father seen in their shared laughter, the constant awareness of each other from which Annie feels excluded. There are no other children in *Annie John*—the birth of the half-brothers that sparks the burning animosity between Annie and her mother in other works is missing from this text. So is the reader's awareness that the model for the father figure in *Annie John* is Kincaid's stepfather, whose entrance into the author's life, bringing with him not only the awakening of her mother's dormant sexuality but also the possibility of children to challenge the daughter's position in the mother's affections, proved to have such a devastating impact on Kincaid's life. As autobiographical fiction, the text leaves out possible explanations and interpretations that readers and critics have gleaned from Kincaid's other nonfictionalized autobiographical writing. The incompleteness of the explanation offered in *Annie John* has troubled those among readers and critics who expect greater thematic and structural coherence from a novel, leading them to "complete" the text in the light of a biographical reading.

Annie's father, Alexander John, is a silent background figure, perceived more than seen in the text of *Annie John*. Where her mother is vocal and outspoken, he is quiet and reticent. His presence is felt as he prepares for work in another room; he takes his daughter for quiet walks to the jetty; he tries to say his farewells as she boards the boat, but the words fail him and he's reduced to an eloquent gesture. His most forceful gesture in the novel is his disapproval of Obeah, and then it is expressed through his absenting himself from the house while the Obeah woman is present and frowning on seeing the Obeah remedies she has prescribed lined up on the shelf next to the doctor's prescriptions. His shadowiness makes him the perfect framework for the mother's vibrant physical presence. Indeed, in a world populated by women—Annie, the mother, Ma Chess, Ma Jolie, Gwen, the Red Girl—he stands out as the only dominant male presence.

His maleness, despite the privileges it affords him in the form of dinners prepared, baths drawn, and clothes ironed, does not equate to dominance within or outside the household. A decent man of regular habits, older than his wife by thirty-five years, he is portrayed as having outlived his philandering years to enjoy the comforts of quiet domesticity. Content to accept both the political as well as the domestic status quo, he cannot offer Annie a parental alternative to the dominant mother. Annie will emasculate him symbolically in the photograph-washing episode of the novel in punishment for both his weakness in providing a foil to her mother and for her awareness of his role in awakening her mother's sexuality and thereby helping to drive a wedge between them.

Ma Chess, Annie's Carib grandmother and a powerful Obeah woman, is Annie's link to both the pre-Columbian ancestry that lies at the foundation of Caribbean identity and to the cultural and religious syncretism characteristic of West Indian societies. This syncretism—this reconciliation or fusion of systems of belief deriving from Amerindian, African, and European cultures and practices—is a vital element in Annie's search for an individual identity that allows her to come to terms with a disjointed past. Ma Chess's willingness to return Annie to the stories from her past that the mother has silenced, her affirmation of native culture through her embracing of Obeah, her knowledge of the African and Carib healing practices that Annie's father repudiates, her embodiment of a maternality not connected to sexuality, are all crucial elements in creating the conditions for Annie to recover from her long illness and emerge strengthened and empowered.

Annie's friends Gwen and the Red Girl (to each of whom a chapter is dedicated) represent two alternatives open to Annie as she seeks to define her personality and carve out a direction for her future. They can be seen, as a result, as the two sides of Annie's duality, the two poles between which she must define herself. The fine line Annie must establish between these two alternatives still remains to be drawn at the novel's end, but the characterizations of the two friends help to flesh-out Annie's dilemma, bringing it to dramatic light.

Gwen, with whom Annie falls passionately in love as she starts a new school at age twelve, becomes her inseparable friend and confidante during most of her school years. Drawn together by Gwen's admiration of the autobiographical essay Annie writes on the first day of school, the two friends seem almost like mirror images. Gwen is the idealized object that seems to fulfill every image of goodness and neatness Annie has been taught by her mother to aspire to. The pleats of her tunic are always in place, her cotton socks fit neatly around her ankles, her ash-colored knees look as if she had just finished saying her prayers. She represents the destiny that Annie must learn to avoid—leaving school early, descending into silliness and gossip, marrying someone she has known all her life. Gwen provides a backdrop for the tensions between Annie and her mother, as her development as a character maintains her within the scope of conventionality that Annie fears her mother wants her to accept. If she is to grow into her own individuality, Annie must outgrow Gwen and everything she represents. The deterioration of their relationship can be thus seen as the outcome of Annie's movement away from the gender limitations and intellectual vacuity of her home society and into a world of possibilities as yet unknown at the end of *Annie John*.

The Red Girl's role is that of introducing Annie to the notion of transgression, to offer an example in flaunting the conventions that Gwen exemplifies all too well. Unbathed, uncombed, unrestrained, nameless except for her descriptive nickname of the Red Girl, accustomed to playing marbles with the Skerritt boys, she stands against every constraint Annie finds stifling in her own life. She schools Annie in betrayal of her mother and Gwen by offering tempting opportunities for infractions of the rules of respectability that are so intricately bound in Annie's mind with her mother's acceptance of colonial mores. Annie's life begins to revolve around her triumphs over her mother's surveillance, learning lying and deceit as weapons of resistance in the process. The Red Girl's symbolic potential is most poignantly expressed through the ritual of pain and pleasure that they perform during their meetings—the Red Girl pinches Annie until she draws tears and then kisses the painful spots—which embody the pain and pleasure that are the result of her transgressive behavior. Her betrayal of her mother and the consequent crisis it causes after she discovers Annie's marble-playing prowess leads to emotional pain while the exhilaration of her incursions into theft, unconventionality, and disobedience is a source of irreverent pleasure. Ultimately, however, the Red Girl's style of freedom is too steeped in abandon and randomness to provide an ideal model for Annie's more ambitious and goal-oriented personality and she must leave the text. Annie's apprenticeship in rebelliousness under the Red Girl, however, plants the seed of a political defiance she will display in the chapter that follows "The Red Girl" in the book, "Columbus in Chains."

A GENRE-THEORY READING OF *ANNIE JOHN*

In the field of poetics (the branch of literary criticism that deals with the nature, forms, and laws of literary texts), classification of texts according to genre categories is a time-honored mode of analysis going back to Plato's *Republic* (fourth century B.C.). Genre—an established class or category of artistic composition, such as the short story, the essay, or the novel—constitutes one of the key principles in the study of literary production. The text of *Annie John* has been variously described as a novel and a collection of short stories, with proponents of its classification as a novel dominating the discussion. A reading of the text in the light of genre theory can shed light on the various elements that help critics classify *Annie John* as a novel.

Confusion as to the genre classification of *Annie John* surfaced with the publication of the text in book form. Some critics familiar with *At the Bottom of the River*, including those who had read the various "stories" that constitute *Annie John* in the *New Yorker* prior to their publication as a book, expected Kincaid's second book to likewise be a collection of short stories and so called it in their reviews. The episodic structure and autobiographical nature of *Annie John* contributed to this early confusion since autobiography—unlike the fictional novel or short story—belongs to the nonfictional genre of the essay.

The first question that arises concerning the text of *Annie John*, then, is whether the text belongs to the category of fiction or nonfiction. It is well known that Kincaid drew on her own experiences growing up in Antigua as the basis of her book, and that Annie John is Kincaid's alter ego or other self, a textual representation of Kincaid's own persona. The author, however, has spoken frequently about her manipulation of her experiences to create the text of *Annie John*. These "manipulations," to use her own term, point to the use of the autobiographical material as the foundation of a fictionalized text or a text in which the "truth" of Kincaid's experiences has been "manipulated" or changed through distortion, additions, reinterpretations, exaggerations, and deletions. The result is not autobiography, or the true account of a person's life written by him- or herself, but fiction, a text that contains a significant degree of invention.

In literary studies, the category of fiction pertains to literary works whose contents are the products of the imagination and are not necessarily based on fact. Fictional prose, as in the case of *Annie John*, can belong to one of two genres, the novel or the short story. The two differ in length and level of plot complexity. Whereas the novel is a fictional prose narrative of considerable length with a complex plot stemming out of the actions, dialogue, and thoughts of the various characters, the short story is a short piece of prose fiction having few characters and aiming at unity of effect. The question that has preoccupied critics is whether there is enough of a complex plot uniting all the various episodes of *Annie John* for them to constitute a novel. We must also consider that within the novel there are subcategories, or subgenres, variations of long fiction among which we find the historical novel, the psychological novel, the picaresque novel, and such popular examples as the mystery and science-fiction novels. *Annie John* belongs to the subgenre of the *bildungsroman* or novel of development, which follows the development of a young person from childhood to the threshold of adulthood.

What are the elements that have led critics to agree on the designation of *Annie John* as a novel? Unlike the tales of *At the Bottom of the River*, where the different episodes are narrated by a variety of voices, *Annie John* is unified by the centrality of its narrative voice. As a first-person narrative, Annie's perspective dominates the text, giving the various chapters an integrated point of view. As a character, she grows before the reader's eyes; her development as a character provides a distinct plot line for the text. Her presence as a central consciousness in the narrative, together with that of the various characters she introduces us to, offers a unifying element; the story unfolds as a result of their interactions, and we follow the various characters as they develop through their contact with Annie and each other.

If we accept Annie's development as a character as a central plot line— as is customary in the *bildungsroman*—then we must look into character development as the source of the text's structure or organization. The story of Annie's growth into adulthood is arranged chronologically, beginning when Annie is ten and ending when she leaves Antigua at the age of seventeen. The various stages through which this tale unfolds, however episodic or loosely connected, still constitute a plot, a story line linked through what each contributes to our understanding of Annie's process of growth and maturation. Their episodic nature means that there are gaps in the narrative, that Kincaid does not attempt to provide a continuous narrative in which every stage of Annie's development is accounted for. What she does provide are the salient points in Annie's story, the moments of importance that explain the choices available to her and what she makes of them. Furthermore, in true novelistic fashion, the episodes are organized dramatically so as to lead to a climactic chapter—"The Long Rain"—in which Annie's dilemmas reach a boiling point and she suffers the equivalent of a nervous breakdown from which she must emerge as a young woman.

The novel, if so we can call it, is also unified thematically. The recurrence of a number of themes—Annie's process of maturation, the role colonialism plays in her development, the centrality of her relationship with her mother, the various modes of resistance she adopts in her search for personal autonomy—all contribute to integrate the various narrative strands of the text into one unified whole. When brought together with the centrality of Annie's voice and a narrative structure organized around the salient moment in Annie's development, they provide the necessary elements to consider *Annie John* as belonging to the genre of the novel.

5

Lucy
(1990)

Lucy, Kincaid's second novel, is the critically acclaimed story of a young West Indian woman working as an au pair to a wealthy white family in New York City. The novel, a heavily autobiographical text based on Kincaid's early experiences in the United States in the late 1960s and early 1970s, has been praised for its powerful evocation of relationships between women—mothers and daughters, rich and poor, black and white. (It has also been criticized as coming too close to actual events in the life of her second employers in the United States, but that criticism is extraliterary and, in many ways, irrelevant.) Like *At the Bottom of the River* and *Annie John* before it, *Lucy* offers yet another exploration of Kincaid's love/hate relationship with her mother; however, unlike those earlier texts, it opens new avenues for Kincaid's fiction, particularly in its examination of the narrator's search for a medium for artistic expression. *Lucy*, whose heroine closes the narrative facing an open blank book, is Kincaid's portrait of the artist as a young woman.

PLOT DEVELOPMENT

Lucy is divided into five chapters, all of them published as independent pieces in the *New Yorker* between June 1989 and September 1990 prior to their appearance in book form in late 1990. Mediated by *A Small*

Place, the essay about corruption and mismanagement in Antigua that Kincaid published in 1988—a text that in its reliance on anger as a weapon marks a thematic and stylistic breakthrough for Kincaid—*Lucy* is the first of her novels set outside her home island, and although it can be seen as another installment in Kincaid's autobiographical chronicle—a sequence to *Annie John*—it adds to the autobiographical element a new level of literary maturity. *Lucy* could be viewed as Kincaid's first truly mature work of fiction, one in which the autobiographical and novelistic elements are blended more deftly and with greater skill.

The most salient difference between *Lucy* and *Annie John* is indeed structural and organizational. Despite having been published as installments, just like the chapters of *Annie John*, the five episodes of *Lucy* work well as a continuous narrative with a well-articulated plot. Where *Annie John* remains episodic and somewhat disjointed, *Lucy* interweaves the various strands, images, metaphors, and characters of the text with greater skill. This is, above all, the result of the scope of the events narrated: *Annie John* covered a period of seven years and could not account for anything but the most significant events in Annie's life; *Lucy*, on the other hand, unfolds during Lucy's first year in the United States, and the relative shortness of the narrated time, as well as the more condensed canvas of spaces and characters, allows for greater continuity in the narrative.

"Poor Visitor"

The opening chapter of *Lucy*, "Poor Visitor," introduces the reader to the book's narrative voice as Lucy Josephine Potter (Potter is Kincaid's real surname) faces her circumstances in the first day of her new life as an au pair for a New York family. Lucy's first-person narrative opens with what will become a leit motif—or recurrent theme—for the text, that of Lucy's perception of light as indicative of mood, atmosphere, and creative possibility. Lucy, who will later strive to express her talent for artistic expression through photography, will respond visually to her surroundings, offering a series of snapshots or photographic images of how she perceives her new world. Photographs will appear throughout the text as static versions of reality whose fixedness allows Lucy to observe them at leisure. The power of light to deceive and misrepresent takes a central thematic position from the opening pages of the text.

The first of the chapter's five sections begins with a description of

Lucy's drive into Manhattan from the airport, with the skyline and famous sights delineated against the night light as a background to her unease. In order to convey the discomfort of her encounter with the new, she recalls the chafing of her new underwear. To establish the contrast between her new environment and her West Indian home, she tells of her first encounter with elevators and refrigerators. The focus of this section, however, is the lesson to be learned about the deceptions practiced by the sunlight in the north. The "pale-yellow" weak sunlight offers a reminder of home, luring her into donning a gay madras dress and venturing out into what proves to be cold January air. The realization becomes symbolic of her rupture with her past, entering her life "like a flow of water dividing formerly dry and solid ground," dividing the familiar unhappiness of her past from the "gray blank" of her future (5–6). Water as a dividing element, one that can separate a person from his or her past, is the final image of *Annie John*. *Lucy* will end similarly with a flood of tears that marks the protagonist's separation from her past.

The second section of the chapter relates Lucy's discovery of a capacity for homesickness she would not have imagined possible while at home. Her previous experience of nostalgia was confined to books whose depiction of characters who deeply missed the once-despised circumstances they had left behind she had found false. In Lucy's recollections of home, Kincaid returns us to the salient elements of Annie John's story, providing an autobiographical link between the tales of her two separate protagonists: her contempt for the relatives she left behind (embodied in the Seventh-Day Adventist cousin whose Bible she has brought to New York), the memory of her last day at home (which recalls the closing chapter of *Annie John*), and the comforting thought of her grandmother, "the person I liked best in all the world" (7) and who appears to be the same grandmotherly figure as Ma Chess in *Annie John*. These details invite the reader to identify Lucy—despite the difference in name—with Kincaid's earlier protagonist, Annie, and by extension Kincaid herself.

Lucy's discussion of her homesickness is followed by a description of the small maid's room she occupies in her employers' home, which she compares with a box for the shipment of cargo. The notion of cargo—and the emphatic denial that follows it, "But I was not cargo"—alludes to the shipment of slaves to the Americas, linking the history of slavery to Lucy's position of servitude and to her feeling boxed-in in her new situation. She will later refer to herself as having arrived cloaked in the mantle of a slave. The kindness of her employers—Mariah and Lewis—comes as a reminder that she is not one of the family, that her position falls into a class hierarchy with roots in a system of class and racial exploitation that she must take into account, although not necessarily accept. Her resistance is already coded in her rejection of the term "cargo" as applicable to herself.

The section ends with a brief passage that links the topics of homesickness and servitude—themes that will recur throughout the book—and introduces another theme of importance in the text, that of the impact that the colonial history of race and class tensions has had on relationships between women. A song about feelings of emptiness heard on the radio (echoing her homesickness) serves as an introduction to a dream about an idealized picture of Christmas and children's laughter (the idealized happy family for whom she works) printed on her nightgown, whose label indicates it was made in Australia. (Kincaid will use dreams very effectively in *Lucy* to articulate the situations that Lucy understands instinctively but has yet to find the ways to describe rationally.) Awakened by the maid, a woman who had made her dislike of Lucy clear, attributing it to "the way I talked," the word "Australia" mediates between them, with its connotations of indentured servitude and transportation of criminals. The word stands between them because Lucy's clarity of vision—one of the meanings of her name is light, although she will prefer to think of it as a shorter version of Lucifer—allows her to see the kinship between herself and the maid as belonging to a class of servants enslaved and transported, while the maid cannot truly see Lucy because her gaze is obscured by Lucy's West Indian origins ("the way I talked").

In the third segment of the chapter Lucy describes her routine with the four children for whom she cares, telescoping time to give the reader a sense of the weeks that have passed and the habits and emotions that have by now become customary in her life. As she catalogues her daily activities—walking the girls to school, feeding them lunch, going to school at night, looking at the map of the place she came from to see the ocean that separates her from it—she inserts an allusion to her unhappiness as part of the routine. The winter has frozen the environment outside her as it seems to have frozen her relationships to those she left behind. She writes letters home portraying her life as if it were unfolding in a greeting card; everyone writes back in similar platitudes about how they miss her and how they can't wait until she returns. The true communication that can sustain relationships seems to be at an end.

The fourth part narrates a showdown of sorts between Lucy and the maid who does not like her over whether Lucy can dance. In the maid's opinion, Lucy's outward nunlike appearance and seeming piety "made her at once sick to her stomach and sick with pity"; convinced Lucy can't dance, and aware of her own talent, she challenges Lucy to dance to the (to Lucy) "insincere and artificial" music of a Supremes-like group (11). Although Lucy is quick to acknowledge her amazement at the wonderful way the other woman dances and moves, she is also quick to turn the other's apparent triumph into an opportunity to counterpunch with an assertion of those very West Indian roots the maid finds so offensive. In Lucy's first gesture of resistance in the book she will turn to West Indian culture as a weapon. The melodies of the maid's song were shallow and meaningless, she tells her, bursting into a West-Indian-affirming calypso about "a girl who ran away to Port-of-Spain, Trinidad, and had a good time, with no regrets" (12). Their confrontation is only the first of a series of similar encounters between women through which Kincaid will explore the limitations of the feminist concept of sisterhood across race and class.

In the brief section that follows Lucy describes the household—husband, wife, and four children—through their photographs displayed throughout the house. Their six yellow heads, she writes, were "bunched as if they were a bouquet of flowers tied together by an unseen string" (12). They were photographed as if they existed in a state of grace, as if they found everything in the world "unbearably wonderful" (13). Their stillness in the photograph, however, also indicates the static quality of their lives and world, their insulation from reality as Lucy has experienced it at home. Kincaid will return the narrative to a critical discussion of their rose-colored view of the world in the "Mariah" chapter, where this attitude to life, which to Lucy is based on a denial of the harm done to others in the world so that families like them can maintain their supremacy, stands as an obstacle to a possible friendship between herself and her employer. Yet in their casual, open relationship they offer Lucy a view of a possible rapport between children and parents different from the one she had known at home. Mariah and Lewis—and most particularly Mariah—offer unfamiliar but embraceable notions of parenting, and Mariah will ultimately emerge as an example of the "good mother" Lucy would have liked to have.

The fifth and last section of "Poor Visitor" recalls a richly nuanced dinner conversation in which the miscommunication between Lucy and her "family" is most evident. The section is built on several examples of exchanges in which either Lucy or the family fails to understand the true meaning of what is said because their different cultural frames of reference do not allow them to place the statement in the correct context. The first of these revolves around the family's constant reminders that Lucy should treat their house as if it were her home and which Lucy interprets as an indication that she was not one of them as the statement would be unnecessary if she were truly a member of the family. The second concerns Lewis's teasing suggestion that Lucy stares at them while they eat because perhaps she has never seen anyone eating a forkful of French-cut green beans. Mariah laughs naively at the joke, but Lucy, who indeed has most probably never seen anyone eating such a thing, remains serious. Her lack of amusement prompts Lewis to call her "Poor Visitor," thus negating the family's repeated assurances that she was to look on herself as one of them and treating her with a misplaced pity born out of his feeling that anyone not like them should be an object of compassion.

Lewis follows this jest with the repetition of a story he had told her before about an uncle of his who had gone to Canada to raise monkeys and had come to prefer their company to that of human beings. Oblivious to the racist undertone of any reference to monkeys to people of African descent accustomed to such racist comparisons, aggravated here by the reference to monkeys not being human beings, Lewis is shown as embodying a number of latent notions of racial, cultural, and class superiority. To this Lucy replies by recounting a dream she had had about them in which Lewis chased her as she ran naked around the house while Mariah urged him to catch her. Lewis and Mariah respond with an allusion to Freud, placing her dream in the context of Western psychological notions of repressed sexual desire, particularly given Lucy's description of the dream ending with her falling down a hole at the bottom of which were some silver and blue snakes (snakes being a phallic symbol in Freudian theory). Lucy, who does not know Freud, feels nonetheless that they have not understood the meaning she attributed to the dream. To her it represented the fact that they had become important to her, and its symbolism, from her colonial perspective, is open to different meanings: she is chased down a yellow road reminiscent both of the myth of the streets of America being paved with gold and of Dorothy in Oz following the yellow brick road that may lead her back home; instead she falls into a pit of snakes, with its biblical resonances; and through it all she remains uncatchable, as if she had learned enough already to protect herself from becoming prey to those hunting her. This is one of the many instances in the text in which Kincaid will use the color yellow in connection with colonialism and domination (see, e.g., the emphasis she places on the family's yellow heads as a bouquet of flowers when she describes their photos earlier in this chapter or the use of the yellow daffodils in "Mariah" as symbols of colonial oppression). In subsequent chapters Kincaid will build on these types of misunderstandings to flesh-out Lucy's struggle to assert her own personal and cultural individuality as a West Indian against Lewis and Mariah's dominant discourse.

"Mariah"

The refrain that runs like a mantra through the seven brief sections that comprise "Mariah," the second chapter of *Lucy*, is "How does a person get to be that way?" The question embodies Lucy's attempts to understand the source of Mariah and her family's Pollyannaish approach to life, which she believes is rooted in a complacency born of their wealth and class status. Lucy's relationship to Mariah is the most complex of the novel, and this chapter sets the parameters for the exploration of a potential friendship threatened by forces that are outside the two women's control. Running through the chapter as a leit motif are Mariah's beloved daffodils, harbingers of spring for her but symbols of colonial oppression for Lucy.

In the opening section of the chapter Kincaid has Lucy introduce the theme of the daffodils and their different significance for Mariah and Lucy. While Mariah delights in the expectation of the daffodils pushing their way out of the ground as a sign of early spring, Lucy is reminded of an old poem on daffodils by the English Romantic poet William Wordsworth (1770–1850) that was required reading in the old British colonial system of education before independence. For children being schooled in the West Indies in the early part of the twentieth century, like George Lamming, Edward Brathwaite, Derek Walcott, and Kincaid herself, this poem glorifying flowers that were not found in the Caribbean has become emblematic of a colonial system that imposed its own values and cultural standards through a system of education that fell outside local control.

Repudiation of the daffodils has become a frequent motif in West Indian literature written in English, developing into enough of a powerful symbol to begin appearing recently in Francophone literature in the Caribbean. In "Mariah" Kincaid recalls with bitterness being made to recite the poem before a school assembly, vowing later "to erase from my mind, line by line, every word of that poem" (18). The episode had led her to dream of being chased down a narrow cobbled street by bunches of daffodils until, having dropped from exhaustion, they piled on top of her, burying her underneath, never to be seen again. This dream of being chased down, coming so close to the narrative of her similar dream about Lewis, underscores the political rather than sexual nature of Lucy's dreams about being pursued. She now tells her dream with an anger that checks Mariah's urge to take Lucy under her wing, an impulse that Lucy sees as stemming from a patronizing urge to be kind to those dependent on her. Mariah's response—"What a history you have"—correctly gauges the deep historical roots of Lucy's anger, but the "little bit of envy in her voice" that Lucy gleans in her answer points to her lack of understanding of the import of that history that had made Lucy what she is. She returns to her dreams of spring, to her elaborate plans of all the outings and holidays they will all enjoy when the new season begins. Her feeling of personal betrayal when a snowstorm arrives on the first day of spring leaves Lucy wondering how a person gets to be made miserable because the weather does not live up to expectations.

The second section of the chapter revolves around letters from home, a subject she had explored before in one of the stories of *At the Bottom of the River*. The letter motif serves as a pretext to introduce Lucy's recollections of home, now juxtaposed against the coldness of the Manhattan winter that is her new environment. The letters, which she had placed inside her brassiere, where they lay "scorching my breasts," provide the heat of angry and passionate resentment rather than the warmth of comfort. They try to instill in her fear of her new world (her mother's reminder that an immigrant girl Lucy's age had had her throat cut on the subway) and remind her of fear she had known (a schoolmate possessed by the Devil who had to be sent across the sea). Here Kincaid establishes a series of images to which she will return later in the text: her anger at her mother's dire warnings, which she perceives as attempts to continue to stifle and suffocate her from afar; the notion of possession by the Devil, with whom she will identify by accepting her mother's angry implication that she was named after Lucifer; the suggestion that exile from home is like an expulsion from paradise.

In this segment, Kincaid has Lucy dwell on snow as a theme that allows her to move from home to exile and back again. Her recollection of Bing Crosby singing "waist-deep in snow" in *White Christmas* (1954), a film she went to see every year with her parents, brings memories of her scorn for her mother and her desire to cause her pain. She tries to resist the soft loveliness of snow, feeling incapable of loving one more thing that could break her heart into a million small pieces. The quickness with which spring snow melts reminds her that she had just lived "through a bleak and cold time, and it is not the weather outside" (23). Snow stands for "something heavy and hard" that was not dispelled with the spring thaw and that symbolized her bitterness and regret. Kincaid had used similar imagery in *Annie John* to convey to the reader the distress and loss that caused Annie such unhappiness and led to the prolonged illness described in "The Long Rain." The experience of snow, moreover, gives her a sharply defined sense of having a real past of her own, over which she had "the final word," disconnected from that she had shared with her mother.

The discussion of snow—and the suggestion that her experience of snow, which leaves Lucy feeling something "heavy and hard," marks the beginning of the time that she can refer to later as "years ago, when I was young"—introduces a memory from childhood that underscores Lucy's notion that "heavy and hard" represented "the beginning of living, real living" (24). A friend of her mother's, a woman named Sylvie, had gotten into a quarrel with a rival that had resulted in the woman's biting her on the cheek, leaving her scarred. Lucy thinks of the scar as a rosette that the woman had placed on her cheek on purpose to display her love of roses until she is given a glimpse of the pain, bitterness, and self-consciousness that gives the woman's voice a "heavy and hard" resonance. She concludes that although she herself may not end up with a scar on her face, "I had no doubt that I would end up with a mark somewhere" (25). The quarrel between the two women that leads to Sylvie's scar is yet another example of the complexities of relationships between women to which Kincaid plays particular attention in *Lucy*.

The third section of "Mariah" places Sylvie's scarred face in contraposition to Mariah's unblemished cheek to underscore the charm and grace of life for those with wealth, connections, pale-yellow skin and yellow hair, and pleasant smells. Mariah—who unlike Sylvie had never quarreled with anyone or gone to jail or done anything but satisfy her whims—can sing, twirl wildly around the room without knocking over anything, and look graceful and beautiful while sincerely telling Lucy that she loves her, prompting Lucy to ask herself again how a person gets to be that way. The answer, if yet unspoken, is clearly to be found in the privileges of class and race that Kincaid begins to concretize in this chapter and which stand in the way of her accepting Mariah's love and patronage despite her belief in the latter's sincerity and her own susceptibility to her graceful charm. In part, Lucy seeks to define herself against Mariah, since she represents what Lucy cannot and does not want to become. In her position as parental figure or mother substitute, Mariah becomes Lucy's oppositional figure.

The fourth segment of the chapter opens with a description of Mariah's plans for a train journey to the family's house in the Great Lakes. Her complicated arrangements, announced on the day it becomes clear that the winter season is over, precedes Mariah's orchestration of Lucy's first encounter with daffodils, an episode described in great detail. Oblivious to Lucy's prior explanation of the link between daffodils and her experience of colonial oppression, Mariah blindfolds Lucy and guides her to a clump of daffodils, literally forcing her to stare at the flowers. Mariah's impulse is to benevolently correct Lucy's "false" notions about flowers she herself loves so much, but in her enthusiasm she is blind to the ritual of control to which she submits Lucy, who must be led by the hand, blindfolded, to confront something she would prefer not to have seen, in a mimicry of colonial control. Lucy's reaction is instinctively resisting; before knowing what they are she wishes she could kill these flowers, however beautiful and simple, and lashes out at Mariah's insensitivity. This section of the chapter, juxtaposing as it does Mariah's loveliness and charming naiveté (the focus of the previous segment) and her unconscious urge to coax others to see the world as she sees it, illustrates the paradox in her character that makes it difficult for Lucy to embrace or reject her. Having cast Mariah's "beloved daffodils" in "a scene of conquered and conquests," Lucy feels the weight of their differing histories as a burden between them: "It wasn't her fault. It wasn't my fault. But nothing could change the fact that where she saw beautiful flowers I saw sorrow and bitterness" (30). In the next section of the chapter, Lucy will rearticulate her sense of the differences between them as she perceives that the passengers in the dining car as they travel to the Great Lakes all look like Mariah (i.e., they are white and middle or upper class) while the dignified older men waiting on them looked like relatives of hers. Counterpointing her awareness with Mariah's obliviousness to these differences, Lucy concludes that Mariah's perception of the world was that it was round and everyone agreed on that while she knows that the world is flat and she can fall off if she gets too close to the edge.

The fifth part of "Mariah" returns to the theme of the letters from home. Unsure as to whether she wants to go to the Great Lakes, Lucy receives a letter from her mother, narrating things about which she cares no longer, making her want to put as many miles between herself and her home island as possible. The section describes Lucy's train journey to the Great Lakes, their settling into their compartments as if recreating a scene she had seen only in films, their meal at the dining car, her nightmarish ride during which she dreams that thousands of people on horseback are chasing her to cut her into thousands of small pieces with a cutlass. This dream about being chased—the third such dream Lucy relates in the novel—again follows an instance of perception of racial and class differences and is articulated against Lucy's political consciousness of reality and human relations. It closes with yet another reminder of the perceptual gap between Lucy and Mariah: as Mariah comes exultantly to Lucy's compartment to ask her to admire the freshly plowed fields through which the train is traveling, Lucy replies with self-avowed cruelty, "Well, thank God I didn't have to do that," reminding Mariah in the process that the people she came from would not have the luxury of admiring plowed fields since they would have been too tired from doing the actual plowing.

In the sixth section of "Mariah," Kincaid has Lucy draw parallels between her employer and her mother, the principal links between them being their shared desire to make people see things their way and their expectation that their children would be exact replicas of them. The section serves to affirm Lucy's determination to die rather than become a small version of someone else—a determination that allows her to savor the irony of having escaped from a mother whose desire to control her had suffocated her only to find herself in the Great Lakes with a woman who benevolently hoped she would also come to see things her way. Lucy uses an episode when Mariah returns from the lake with some trout she had caught to establish a further connection between Mariah and her mother through the biblical story of the miracle of Jesus feeding fish to the multitudes. Mariah's invitation to Lucy to come feed the "minions," and Lucy's uncertainty as to whether she had said "minions" or "millions," introduces another one of Lucy's reminiscences about salient moments with her mother. This time she recalls her mother's amazement when she insisted on knowing how Jesus had served the fish, thinking that it may have mattered to the multitudes how the fish was prepared. The story points to personal and cultural differences in the preparation of food that would matter "in the place I grew up." To her mother the question seems pointless, and Mariah, after listening to the story, went on to cook the fish her way, "a way I did not like" (39).

The final segment of the chapter revolves around Mariah's hesitating announcement that she has Indian blood, a fact that she proclaims as if it meant her "possession of a trophy" (40). For Lucy, whose grandmother is a Carib Indian, this conqueror's boastful claim of also belonging to the vanquished is empty of any validity. It rests on a claim to possessing the essence of the vanquished, of having subsumed them into themselves, making their defeat irreparable. This desire to claim a connection to the aboriginal has become part of the American desire to claim the moral ascendancy of having belonged to the continent's original cultures. Lucy's response—her finally voicing to Mariah her question as to how she got to be that way—brings the chapter full circle.

"The Tongue"

The eight segments that compose the third chapter of *Lucy*, "The Tongue," narrate the momentous events of Lucy's spring and summer in the Great Lakes, which include Lucy's exploration of her sexuality, the collapse of Mariah and Lewis's marriage, and Lucy's friendship with Peggy, the woman who will become her roommate when she leaves Mariah's household shortly after the divorce.

The chapter opens with a series of images that move back and forth between Antigua and the Great Lakes and between motherhood and sexuality. Lucy, in the process of feeding one of the children a dish of yogurt she does not like to eat, finds herself recreating the very gestures and producing the same arguments her own mother had used when she did not want to eat, with the same limited success. As she goes through the motions she daydreams about the sensation of sucking a boy's tongue while she was still in Antigua. An observed caress between Mariah and Lewis reveals to Lucy the emptiness of their relationship, preparing the reader for a narrative of the impact of its collapse on Mariah, whom Lucy has begun to love despite the tensions between them. The caress, however, plunges Lucy into memories of other boys she had kissed, including one she would encounter in the library and wordlessly kiss and fondle furtively. These images and events, which seem to jump without any connection other than free association in Lucy's mind (and which include word of a phone call from Mariah's best friend Dinah) set the stage for the events that follow in the chapter, where the various narrative strands introduced here will be fleshed-out.

In the second section of "The Tongue" we can perceive a development in Lucy's voice—a strength that comes from having come to terms with her by-now-familiar environment and a self-confidence that stems from her awareness of her lucidity, a clarity of vision that makes her a keen observer of those around her. This keenness of vision is in evidence here in her growing distrust of Dinah, a woman she sees as vain, envious of Mariah's life, and full of ethnic and class prejudices (she dismisses Lucy as "the girl" from "the islands" who takes care of the children). This lucidity stands in contrast to Mariah's guilelessness, which is evident in her belief in Dinah's goodness and joy in life, and in her own treatment of Lucy as a friend and equal rather than an employee whose condition is beneath her. The section also examines Lucy's routine with the children and her uncomplicated love for the youngest of the children, with whom she found herself recreating the best of her relationship with her mother. Their walks through the woods on their way to bathe at the lake conjure for Lucy the fears she had developed at home, "where there was no such thing as a 'real' thing"—she recalls her mother's frightening encounters with a monkey that injures her seriously—and ultimately her exorcism of those fears when she learns to enjoy the beauty of the woods.

In the third segment of the chapter Kincaid develops the theme of Mariah's similarities to Lucy's mother, establishing these similarities as mediators of Lucy's relationship to her employer—when she loved Mariah it was because she reminded her of her mother, when she hated her it was for the same reason. Kincaid introduces an episode concerning flowers that is meant to illustrate how far their relationship had moved toward mutual trust since the daffodil incident. Here, Mariah was arranging peonies in a vase with her usual delight in flowers when she presents them to Lucy, inviting her to declare them gorgeous. Lucy's unqualified praise and exuberant enthusiasm—she tells Mariah that their smell made her want lie down naked on their petals "so you could smell this way forever"—made them recall their previous exchange over the daffodils, leading Mariah to double up with laughter. Lucy concludes the section by wishing she could have had times like this with her own mother.

The fourth part of "The Tongue" centers on Lucy's love affair with Dinah's brother, Hugh, introduced by a description of her friendship with Peggy, a young woman Mariah disapproves of. Peggy, a young Irish girl Lucy had met in the park, has reinvented herself, assuming a toughness of dress and demeanor—she smoked cigarettes and marihuana, used slang, dressed a bit like a tart—that in its rebelliousness constitutes her chief attraction to Lucy. She had amused Lucy on first meeting her by her unconcern about race—"You're not from Ireland, are you? You talk funny" (62). The proverbial bad influence, Peggy serves as an example of the differences between Mariah and Lucy's mother; Mariah has forbidden her the house and access to the children, but relents when she realizes how important it is for Lucy to have a friend. Mariah proves herself superior to her mother in being able to see "that perhaps my needs were more important than her wishes" (65).

While at the Great Lakes, Mariah, aware that Lucy misses Peggy, gives a party for Lucy to meet people her own age. Amid a crowd of people who look like models out of a catalog, and whose notions of the West Indies were those Kincaid derides in *A Small Place*, Lucy finds Hugh, an ordinary-looking young man recently returned from Africa and Asia whose informed inquiries about the West Indies attract her attention. The relationship that ensues—which quickly leads to a sexual encounter—has the matter-of-factness of a solid friendship rather than a grand passion, and it brings back troublesome thoughts about her life at home. She recalls a piece of cloth printed with Pandora's boxes—which according to myth contained all the evils of the world—from which she had made a dress she wore when she first discovered that her body was undergoing the changes brought about by puberty. Her relationship with Hugh leads to fears of pregnancy and thoughts of her mother's hypocrisy as she taught her what herbs she needed to prepare to abort a fetus while disguising the lesson as a remedy to strengthen the womb. Thoughts of having to write to her mother for herbs that did not grow near the Great Lakes bring fear of the humiliation such a step would mean. The relationship with Hugh is destined to be short-lived as Lucy, just six months away from having freed herself from the powerful bonds of home, was determined not to make new ones.

The fifth part of the chapter centers on Mariah's ecological concerns and her work in trying to preserve some farms and marshlands being slowly destroyed by development. The episode serves as both proof of Mariah's kindness and a reminder of her unawareness of the connection between her local concerns and the conditions under which people in Lucy's home island live. Lucy would like to point out to her the connection between the destruction of what she loved and her husband's daily conversations with her stockbroker. It is evidence of the affection she has developed for Mariah that she is incapable of lashing out in this way any more, that she is ready to acknowledge that "many people in her position were not as kind and considerate as she was" (73).

The sixth section of "The Tongue" uses the death of a rabbit as a metaphor for the death of Mariah and Lewis's marriage. Lewis, whose enjoyment of the lake house was limited, had planted a vegetable garden as a way of killing time; the damages the garden sustained from a family of rabbits drove him to a fury aggravated by the rest of the family's delight in the creatures. Lucy sees the resulting tensions as harbingers of the collapse of the family, from which Lewis seems severed when, accidentally but unrepentantly, he runs over one of the rabbits with his car. Kincaid underscores the pathos of the situation by having Lewis, who is approaching the house bearing the rabbit, look up to see the children's faces framed against the window in condemnation, making Lucy feel that he might remember the day as one of the most unhappy of his life.

The seventh part of the story offers the poignant details of Lewis's betrayal of Mariah—Lucy's observations of the deterioration of their relationship being confirmed by catching him and Dinah in an embrace. These details are presented against Mariah's complete lack of suspicion, and Kincaid has Lucy's voice dwell on the snapshots of the marriage, pitting the version of happiness they portray against the pain and disillusionment awaiting Mariah. As the children, instinctively alert to signs of stress, seek reassurance from their parents and Lucy, the latter establishes parallels between their situation and her own as the child of a father who, like Lewis, "could not be trusted in certain areas" (80). Her own father's relationships with the many women with whom he had children constantly placed Lucy and her mother in danger for their lives because of the rivals' access to Obeah practitioners. The experience left Lucy with a keen awareness of the pitfalls of gender relationships, making it possible for her to read the early signs of trouble that Mariah cannot see. In her description of the heartbreak in store for Mariah, Kincaid writes some of the most poignant passages of *Lucy*. Mariah, who could imagine "the demise of the fowl of the air, fish in the sea, mankind itself," could not fathom "that the only man she had ever loved would no longer love her" (81).

The eighth and final segment of "The Tongue" returns to the theme of the first section—the sensation and taste of the various tongues Lucy has held in her mouth. Her farewells from the lake and from Hugh seem tainted by her awareness of Lewis's betrayal of Mariah, and set the tone for a sum-up of her sexual experiences, beginning with Tanner—who taught her how a man can quickly equate making love to a triumph—to kissing Peggy for comfort when a boy she had liked had proven too boring. The bittersweet tone of her last embrace with Hugh contains the grief of Mariah's approaching heartbreak.

"Cold Heart"

In "Cold Heart," the fourth chapter of the novel, Lucy prepares to leave Lewis and Mariah's house for an apartment and life of her own. In the eight sections that constitute the chapter, she seeks to reinvent herself, cutting herself off from the aspects of her past life holding her down and fashioning a path for herself that allows her room for creative reinvention.

In the first section of the chapter, Lucy returns to a meditation on her relationship with her mother. These thoughts are ushered by having seen Mariah's family, in a mimicry of the quintessential happy family, leave gleefully for the country to pick apples. Aware of the fissures that will soon bring heartbreak to Mariah and the children, Lucy ponders the nature of family relationships and the connection between wealth, protection from harm, and the possibility of happiness. The section moves back and forth between the bleakness of a Sunday afternoon in October in Manhattan and Lucy's reminiscences of the emotional drought that characterized her life in her home island. Her fears, as she stands on the threshold of an independent life away from the transitional space of Mariah's home, is that of breaking away from a past she identifies with her mother—"[m]y past is my mother" (90). The section, which centers on the theme of severing familial ties (Lucy's, Mariah's, Peggy's), returns the text to the theme of Lucy's letters from home, nineteen of which remain unopened. Lucy fantasizes with thoughts of returning them unread, of burning them at the four corners in an act of rejection, knowing that if she read them she "would die of longing" for her mother (91). Her acts of disconnection from her mother—the unopened letters, the refusal to become a nurse as her mother had wished, her recollections of the time she wished her mother dead—are instances in Lucy's process of developing the "cold heart" necessary to break from her mother and her past.

The second segment of "Cold Heart" describes Lucy's fascination with Paul Gauguin, the man as well as the paintings, because of his need to leave the place where life had become a burden and make a new life for himself in a foreign place. Gauguin serves to introduce the subject of creativity and of the chances a young black woman who had left her home wrapped "in the mantle of a servant" had to find an outlet for her own artistic endeavors. Mariah, coming on her as she is deep in thought, allows her to voice her feelings by commenting on her anger, in a textual suggestion that she could act as a mediator for Lucy's self-expression. It is her question—"You are a very angry person, aren't you"—that allows for the avowal of her anger, as it has been Mariah's blunders, questions, and occasional insights that have provided the outlet for Lucy's narrative of herself.

The third and longest part of the chapter narrates Lucy's affair with Paul, a painter she had met through Peggy. The meeting with Paul and the artists with whom he surrounded himself helps sharpen Lucy's ambition to be an artist herself, a position that allowed for irresponsibility and standing apart from the rest. Her encounter with Paul also gives her a hint that perhaps she possesses a uniqueness that should be treasured as he treasures the exotic Caribbean plants—exotic to him but commonplace, even a nuisance, to people at home—that he has planted in pots by his window. Her sexual desire for Paul—whose sparkling blue eyes remind her of her lucky marble, Annie John's marble?—gives her an opportunity to reinvent herself as the sensual woman "on whom not long ago I would have heaped scorn" (100). His hands searching for an earring in the fishtank bring to her mind a half-forgotten recollection of her envy of a neighbor who met a fisherman clandestinely and got money in return for letting him put his finger inside her. Overcome with jealousy, she had wished it had happened to her, as she would have known how to turn it into the experience of a lifetime. Her flirtatious conversation with Paul proves her now to be eager to take advantage of that opportunity when it comes—she had been warned by Peggy that he was a pervert—and her boldness is yet another example of her repudiation of her mother. She had felt, in retrospect, that she had not been chosen by the fisherman because she had behaved as a young girl so "beyond reproach" that she spoke in her mother's voice, "hardly a prospect for a secret rendezvous" (107).

The fourth segment of "Cold Heart" describes Lucy's plans for moving into an apartment with Peggy. Despite Mariah's support of her as the "good mother" she had never had, Lucy has returned to thoughts of her mother and her vow to her that at the age of nineteen she would be living at home "only if I drop dead" (112).

In the fifth section Lucy returns to the deterioration of Mariah's marriage and a frank discussion of sex during which her relationship to Mariah appears to move from that of mother/daughter to that of friends. The conversation has a leveling effect, as it displays for the reader Lucy's emotional growth since her arrival at Mariah's house, her being in a position to impart as well as receive advice.

Lucy selects an outlet for her creative impulse in the sixth part of "Cold Heart," when she buys herself a camera with which to capture her own vision of the reality around her. She had just received a letter from her mother, marked urgent, that she was determined not to read. Instead she had gone off to buy a camera, recalling how she enjoyed a book of photographs of "ordinary people in a countryside doing ordinary things" that she had received as a present from Mariah. The section also describes—in an episode of betrayal that reminds us of the betrayal implicit in her refusing to open her mother's urgent letter—her afternoon tryst with the clerk at the photo shop, a young Panamanian man of Martinican parentage named Roland with whom she makes love while Paul waits for her.

The death of Lucy's father (and the secondary "death" of Mariah's marriage) is the focus of the seventh segment of "Cold Heart." The announcement of the father's death, contained in the many letters Lucy had kept unopened, intrudes on her in the person of her detested friend from home, Maude Quick, her mother's emissary. The news leaves Lucy tottering on the brink of devastation, "dying," until Maude's laughing reminder that she is just like her mother returns her to a sense of the hated reality for which she is mourning so incongruously. Her mother returns to being the woman who should not have married and had other children, the woman who had neglected Lucy and her intelligence; her father is once again the man who, after many affairs and even more illegitimate children, married a woman decades younger than himself to have someone to care for him in his old age and then died leaving her penniless and in acute distress. The details Kincaid offers in the characterization of her parents in "Cold Heart" are identical to those offered by Annie in *Annie John*, providing yet another autobiographical link between the protagonists of Kincaid's two novels despite the difference in name.

Forced to communicate with her mother, Lucy sends "a cold letter," which "matched my heart," in which she spills out her resentment against her and her father, sends the money her mother desperately needs (all her savings as well as the money Mariah gave her to replace them), and tries to close that chapter of her past by writing that she would never come home again, "I would not come home, ever" (127, 128). The letter bringing her mother's forgiving reply, reminding her that she would always be her mother, that her home would never be anywhere but with her, she burns together with all the others she had kept unread.

Lucy's identification of Lewis and her father is underscored in the eighth and final segment of "Cold Heart," which opens with a snapshot of Mariah and Lucy as mirror images of each other, one husbandless, the other fatherless. Mariah, claiming to feel "free," beseeches Lucy to forgive her mother as a way of freeing herself from the burden of her hatred. Lucy, however—having just returned from an outing with Paul during which they had discussed freedom in terms that made clear that it can be an overrated concept that can bring death—is thrown back into the maze of disappointments that fed her resentment and make it impossible for her to free herself from a mother who embodies her past. She offers a catalog of the betrayals she suffered at the hands of her parents—their complex plans for her brothers' future education and indifference to her own superior ability; the way her brothers become the center of the attention lavished before on her; her mother's unwillingness, despite their former closeness, to stand up for her and acknowledge her potential. In this narrative of faithlessness—from which Mariah tries unsuccessfully to rescue her through the chronicles of women in society, history, and culture she offers as countertext—are embodied the anger and bitterness spawned by her parents' inability to "imagine a life for me filled with excitement and triumph" (130). Lucy poignantly concludes that freedom for her is impossible as long as she continues to mourn the end of her "love affair" with her mother, "perhaps the only true love in my whole life I would ever know" (132). Once again, the details Lucy offers in the narrative correspond not only to Annie's experiences in *Annie John* but to those autobiographical details Kincaid herself has offered in many essays and interviews.

"Lucy"

In the final chapter of *Lucy* Kincaid brings the narrative full circle, back to January and winter, the season of Lucy's arrival in New York the previous year, and back to the sort of person she had been then. The six brief segments that make up the chapter offer a coda to the novel, an assessment of where Lucy has been, what she has become, and the price she has had to pay for the degree of independence and contentment she has attained. In the opening section she takes note of the many changes she has undergone. She has reinvented herself by following her intuition—like a painter, she has remade herself to approach something near physical beauty. And she has come to terms with what the colonial history of her home island has made of her: she has memory, anger, and despair to sustain her. In this recapitulation of her new self she reviews the history of Antigua, to which so much of her own sense of identity is tied, explaining how much better they would all have been if they had been colonized by the French. In her year in New York she has learned to look at the past as something under her control, something she can leave behind: "Your past is the person you no longer are, the situations you are no longer in" (137). But she remains unable to forgive her mother and, although she finally replies to her letters, sends her a false return address.

The year she has spent with Mariah and her family must also be left behind in this last chapter, and in the second section of "Lucy" she says farewell to that part of her life. The segment is constructed around a swift review of the events of the last year in which she dwells on Lewis's iniquities, the catastrophic events at home (her father's death, her guilt at not having opened her mother's letters), Mariah's bitterness at her leaving before her full year's commitment, and the possessions she has accumulated as symbols of her new self. In this section she alludes to feeling like Lucifer, cast down and doomed, a theme she will return to later in the chapter and one she had explored in *Annie John*, where Annie comments on a painting of *The Young Lucifer* she had become fascinated by and identified with.

In the third part of the chapter Kincaid returns to Lucifer as the figure Lucy claims as symbolic of her loss of paradise and innocence. Ending her tale on the threshold of an unknown world where she must create new spaces for herself, she symbolically renames herself after Lucifer, who, cast out of paradise for his sins, created a new realm of power for himself. Remembering her mother's angry remonstrance when she had asked why she had been named Lucy—"I named you after Lucifer himself"—she embraces the name and its implication, relating them to the Western cultural tradition imposed on her as a schoolchild in Antigua (she had read *Paradise Lost* as part of her colonial education) and glorying in it as emblematic of postcolonial resistance.

In the fourth segment of the chapter Lucy turns inward, examining her new space and her relationships with Peggy and Paul as temporary landmarks in her life that she is certain will be shed when she has gained the knowledge and strength necessary for her full blossoming. This lucidity is accompanied in the text by a renewed awareness of the lights and sounds around her and by the various portraits of herself—in the mirror, in Paul's photograph—that help her see the difference between how she and others look at herself. She establishes clear differences between the ways in which Peggy and Paul see the world and her own perceptions, pointing to the uniqueness of her perspective of the world. Peggy looks out the same window, but they see different things; Paul gives her a picture of herself that has made him think that he possesses her in some way, and at that moment she grows tired of him. The segment portrays Lucy as an observer in her own life, making notes of events and storing them away for the time she is ready to break free from what holds her down and move on.

Kincaid opens the fifth segment of "Lucy" with a discussion of compromises. Lucy has started her first job, her first attempt at true financial independence, and has been schooled by Peggy into the adjustments and petty hypocrisies necessary to maintain a job in the marketplace. At work, Lucy encounters a different kind of compromise, that made by her boss, Mr. Simon, who had given up his dream of going around the world taking photographs of people who had suffered terribly because he needed an income on which to live. Lucy must confront a different kind of renunciation in acknowledging that photography is not necessarily the medium in which she will express the depth of her own creativity. She had hoped that her photographs would reveal a thing more beautiful than what she thought she had seen, "but I did not succeed" (160).

In the sixth and final section of "Lucy," Kincaid has her character confront her aloneness in a bittersweet examination of the fear of a life about to unfold. Her aloneness is the result of her having cleansed herself. She has returned to her friendship with Mariah, who was alone and, unlike Lucy, felt lonely. Mariah, who in the reverse image of Lucy's building up her new nest, is dismantling hers to move away, gives Lucy a leather blank book, a new vehicle for her creativity to replace the photographs that have let her down. Mariah had given it to her in response to Lucy's comment when they had parted that her life "stretched out ahead of me like a book of blank pages" (163). Lucy will conclude her narrative in a way similar to that with which Annie had begun her own narrative—with an assertion of her full name, a statement of being. And like *Annie John*, Lucy's tale will conclude with the cleansing and liberation image of water, here present in the flood of tears that speak of the longing for love embodied in her wish that she "could love someone so much that I would die from it," and of the blurring of vision that defines her youthful state of being in flux.

SETTING

The setting of *Lucy*—New York City and an indeterminate state by the shores of the Great Lakes—is new to Kincaid's fiction. New York City stands in the text as the metropolitan center necessary to assure the West Indies its continued marginality. Lucy's arrival at this metropolitan center means that she must define herself against metropolitan notions of where she, as a young black and female colonial subject, can find her place. The story of her quest for personal independence, a postcolonial trope, must play itself against the dominant Other's background, emerging throughout the text as a metaphor for colonial liberation.

Lucy's life in New York City unfolds primarily in interior spaces—Mariah and Lewis's apartment, the apartment she rents with Peggy, the photographic studio where she goes to work late in the text—thus the geography of the city plays a very limited role in the setting of the text. In the few instances where neighborhoods are described—such as in Lucy's first visit to her lover Paul—they are bleak and uninviting. New York becomes instead a winter landscape against which Lucy's emotional loneliness plays itself out. The city becomes a cold and empty space, dark and foreboding, that does not acquire color and light until Lucy settles into her new apartment in the spring of her second year in the United States. When Lucy and her "family" spend the summer months in the Great Lakes, on the other hand, the natural environment takes center stage, and it is the rural life of the American elite through which we experience the most restful and relaxing months of the narrative. Nature, as seen through the lake, the woods through which they must cross to go bathing, the sky full of stars, the marshlands Mariah is desperately trying to save from developers, emerges as full of nuance and symbolism, a cocoon in which Lucy develops in confidence and strength.

CHARACTER DEVELOPMENT

First and foremost, Lucy is an autobiographical character, an older version of Annie in *Annie John*. In fact, despite the difference in names, Annie and Lucy read as the same character in different dress—a character who is a fictionalized version of the author herself. The quandary of autobiographical fiction is always that of finding the place in which to draw the line between truth and fiction, and Kincaid has done her best to blur that line, to encourage the reader in his or her identification despite the various markers that appear here and there to remind us that we are reading a work of fiction. It is very easy, in fact, once we become familiar with the facts of Kincaid's life, to say with great certainty that there is very little of pure uncomplicated fiction in Jamaica Kincaid's *Annie John* and *Lucy*.

As a character, Lucy is marked by her lucidity, the keenness of her understanding of the forces that dominate her world. She is the political creature that Annie John was in the process of becoming at the end of her narrative, a character who insists on seeing herself as a continuum of history, unwilling to accept a sugar-coated version of her own place in the world. Her voice is that of resistance—resistance to being subsumed in other people's notions of what and how she should be, resistance to accepting a narrative of the past that she knows to be false, resistance to remaining in comfort when only contrariness will bring her closer to her true self.

Her resistance is focused primarily on her mother, because she symbolizes all the limitations Lucy has fought against. Her mother becomes a foil to Lucy precisely because, having lived her life within the confines of what tradition and colonial mores demanded, she was too quick to accept that those limitations would apply to her daughter. Her greatest failure, in Lucy's eyes, was her willingness to dream on behalf of her sons while reducing her daughter to the most mundane of expectations. She represents and speaks for the authorities who will keep Lucy "in her place" as a young black colonial woman of very limited means and it is in her rebellion against her that Lucy enacts her quest for the independence that will make it possible for her to write. Lucy portrays herself as the artist-in-waiting, turning her own history into the narrative of resistance with which she has filled Mariah's notebook.

In contrast to Lucy's mother, Mariah becomes both the "good mother" and Lucy's first audience. It is in trying to explain herself and her history to Mariah that Lucy first crafts her narratives since, unlike her mother, Mariah will not only listen, but learn slowly to adapt her views to incorporate Lucy's viewpoint. It is not surprising that—given Mariah's role in allowing Lucy to articulate her story orally, sometimes by serving as a foil to Lucy's anger—it will be Mariah herself who will provide the first blank notebook on which Lucy can begin to record her narrative in more permanent form. Mariah, despite her many flaws of understanding and limitations in outlook, becomes the flawed yet understanding mother that Lucy would have liked to have.

Through his abandonment of Mariah and his betrayal of the children, Lewis emerges as the villain of the piece. From his early slightly patronizing stance toward Lucy to his imposing the responsibility for their estrangement on Mariah, his portrait is the most one-sided and hostile of the novel. Although seen primarily as a secondary figure—he remains for the most part in the background, hovering somewhere behind Lucy's relationship with Mariah—his apparent marginality conceals the centrality of his position. To Lucy he is an instrument of capitalist oppression, with his conversations with stockbrokers and the legal practice that she links to the exploitative domination of island nations such as hers. He, in turn, will display a patronizing tolerance of Lucy's idiosyncracies that is rooted in a deep conviction of her inability to change the world as he knows it. When the reality of his abandonment of his family takes hold in "Cold Heart" and the focus of the narrative shifts to him, Lucy refers to him as a "swine." His faults, Lucy will argue, are in his position and upbringing as a cultivated American white male of the upper classes: "A man in his position always knew exactly what he wanted, and so everything was done for him" (119). Lucy's identification of Lewis with her father crystallizes her negative portrait of him; like her father, he is not to be trusted since the primary motivation behind his every act is to satisfy his own needs. As the rabbit episode exemplifies, he may not actively cause harm to others to accomplish his goals, but regardless of the pain it causes his wife and children, he will not be sorry things went his way.

A FEMINIST READING OF *LUCY*

Lucy has been described as Kincaid's most avowedly feminist protagonist, an apt description that rests on the character's uncompromising determination to take the world only in her own terms. In many ways, Lucy fits the traditional description of the feminist heroine: conscious of the unfairness of traditional gender relationships, aware of the exploitative nature of sexual practices, vowing to make a life for herself that does not include submission to a man, searching for some measure of equality of power in her relationships with both men and women. A reading of *Lucy* in the light of feminist theory can yield numerous instances of Lucy's acting in a way consistent with feminist expectations.

In *Lucy*, however, Kincaid goes beyond traditional feminist theory to offer a postcolonial critique of feminist thought, presenting Lucy as a protagonist who is keenly aware of the movement's limitations. Lucy, a feminist in the accepted sense of the term, is also a character whose thoughts and actions are oriented toward a critique of feminism's slowness to incorporate class and race differences in its approach. Lucy's version of feminism, born of her experiences as a young black woman from a working-class colonial background, is rooted in a profound awareness that gender relations are mediated by race and class hierarchies. The character embodies the critique of traditional middle-class feminism that we have come to associate with African-American feminist theorists such as Angela Davis and bell hooks and postcolonial critic Gayatri Spivak. In *Inessential Woman*, her study of the problems of exclusion in feminist thought, Elizabeth Spelman argues that "[w]hile it is true that images and institutions that are described as sexist affect both Black and white women, they are affected in different ways, depending upon the extent to which they are affected by other forms of oppression" (122). Or, as she quotes from Angela Davis, " 'the alleged benefits of the ideology of femininity did not accrue' to the Black female slave—she was expected to toil in the fields just as long and hard as the Black male was" (122).

The variety of feminism to which *Lucy* responds is one that incorporates as a primary element an assessment of the racial differences and conflicting class interests that separate white and black women. A significant number of the plots of novels by Caribbean women, as a matter of fact, revolve around woman versus woman conflicts, as writers bring to the fore of their texts their understanding of plantation societies as the least likely settings for the development of relationships of sisterhood between white, black, and colored women. More often than not, black, white, and mulatto women "were bound to each other in the [plantation] household, not in sisterhood, but by their specific and different relations to its master" (Fox-Genovese, 100). Hence, the depictions of relationships between women in the plantation underscore the authors' understanding that "[c]lass and racial struggles assumed priority over the gender struggle, even though class and racial struggles might have been experienced in gender-specific, and indeed sex-specific ways" (Fox-Genovese, 95).

The remnants of colonial structures that forged the historical past against which Lucy must redefine herself are exemplified in the novel by the tensions between her and Mariah, through whom Kincaid explores the conflicts of power that stem from gender and race relationships in a postcolonial world. As we have seen, the tensions in the relationship between the two—their mutual affection notwithstanding—have at their root Mariah's inability to see the connection between Lucy's anger and the power women like her held over the likes of Lucy in plantation society. Victim of Lewis's sexism and Dinah's nonexistent sisterhood as she is, lacking an occupation of her own that can sustain her as her world collapses, she nonetheless experiences sexism in very class-specific ways. Her experiences of oppression *as a woman* are worlds apart from those of Lucy, who as a black working-class woman is subjected to pressures unimaginable in Mariah's world. Mariah, good-natured and generous as she is, cannot see the links between her wealth and comfortable circumstances and the oppression of women elsewhere. Her efforts at making life pleasant and easy for Lucy can only do little to transcend a history of class and racial oppression.

Lucy, on the other hand, can only see life as a series of political struggles, many of them affecting relationships between women. She is keenly aware of the connection between what seems local—the destruction of the ecology of the marshlands around Mariah's house, for example—and the need to develop and exploit resources to maintain the level of upper-class comfort Mariah and her family enjoy. From cultural hegemony to her perception of Dinah's classist rudeness, Lucy can only imagine a world in which race and class hegemonies do not determine human relationships—they have always determined her own. Her characteristic lucidity is precisely the quality that allows her to practice a feminism that takes into account the complexities of the social and economic world in which her life must unfold.

The Autobiography of My Mother
(1997)

Through the early 1990s Kincaid had been at work on *The Autobiography of My Mother*, a novel set in the island of Dominica, her mother's birthplace. Excerpts from the much-anticipated manuscript had begun appearing in American magazines such as *Essence* and the *New Yorker* in 1993; but its publication in its final book form in February 1996 drew a decidedly mixed critical response. Although most reviewers praised the novel for the piercing honesty, elegance, and brilliance of its prose, many also found its protagonist and narrator, Xuela Claudette Potter Richardson, in her "willful hardness of heart," a difficult, unsympathetic character whose defiant tale, its lyricism notwithstanding, was profoundly disturbing.

The book drew widely varied commentary from critics and readers alike. Merle Rubin, writing for the *Christian Science Monitor*, praised "the crystalline prose, precise and serene as a knife drawn through water," through which Kincaid conveys the self-portrait of "a calm, thoughtful, utterly alienated woman who has learned to lead a life devoid of love, but not devoid of dignity" (5). Cathleen Schine, reviewing the novel for the *New York Times Book Review*, concluded that the book, though "a brilliant fable of willed nihilism," was "dull and unconvincing" in its "unrelentless rhythmic message" of the emptiness of Xuela's life (5). Readers' responses ranged from charges of Kincaid's having betrayed the cultural spirit of Dominica, a society more vibrant and productive at all levels than a narrative of victimization would indicate, to feelings that no one could be as isolated or bereft as Xuela represents herself as being, particularly not in the island of Dominica. The range and vehemence of the responses to the novel have unquestionably made it, since its publication, Kincaid's most controversial text.

Yet *The Autobiography of My Mother* builds on themes by now familiar to Kincaid's readers: the problematic relationship between mother and daughter, the correlations of sexuality and power, the legacy of colonialism and racism in the Caribbean and its impact on the relationships between women of different races and classes, and the self-loathing and self-destructiveness of the colonized so brilliantly described in Frantz Fanon's *Black Skins, White Masks*.

In *The Autobiography of My Mother*, these familiar themes are filtered through the eyes of seventy-year-old Xuela, a woman of Carib, African, and British extraction born in the island of Dominica. Like the tale of Télumée Miracle in Guadeloupean novelist Simone Schwarz-Bart's *The Bridge of Beyond* (1984), Xuela's narrative of endurance in a harsh colonial environment embodies the historical trajectory of the Caribbean region. Unlike Télumée, however, for whom a nurturing community and the healing potential of folk culture provide the antidotes to colonial anguish, Xuela's prospects are blighted by her mother's death during childbirth and by her resulting inability to find a community ready to embrace her and help her overcome her loss.

The novel that chronicles her repeated disappointments and concomitant bitterness is a paean to that primary loss. Her mother, a woman whose face she will never see, of whose feet and hem she gets glimpses in dreams, whose voice she once hears singing to her in a dream, presides over the text of Xuela's life, of the motherless and childless Xuela whose autobiography is purportedly written (if we are to trust the "My Mother" of the title) by the daughter she so adamantly refused to have. The death of the mother is the axis around which revolves this tale of the wrath and heartache of an unloved child whose plight embodies the bitterness and hopelessness of the colonized.

PLOT DEVELOPMENT

The Autobiography of My Mother chronicles Xuela Richardson's life from her birth in the early years of the twentieth century to her old age as the century draws to its close. The narrative of Xuela's life is played against that of her dead mother, an orphaned woman of Carib ancestry, also named Xuela, who had been found in a basket outside the Catholic convent where she was taken in and raised by the nuns. The elder Xuela, having grown without the care of her own mother and disconnected from her Carib past, leaves the convent to marry a young policeman, a handsome, charming, and ambitious man whose mimicry of the ways of the colonizers will lead him into greed, insensitivity, brutality, and betrayal. The elder Xuela is spared the knowledge of her husband's moral decline by her premature death as she gives birth to their first child. For her daughter Xuela, the narrator of *The Autobiography of My Mother*, the lost mother will remain the repository of the selfless love that could have saved her from a life of despair. Her father's indifference and casual cruelty she will come to associate with the ways of the British colonizers who taught him about money and greed, power and domination.

Shortly after her birth, Xuela's father leaves her—together with his soiled clothes—under the care of his laundress, Ma Eunice, an unimaginative woman of limited education or understanding incapable of doing much for Xuela beyond assuring her physical survival. In her portrayal of Ma Eunice, Kincaid underscores how the character's unconscious cruelty results from the ignorance and alienation of the colonized poor. She is incapable of understanding—as the perceptive young Xuela does—that the severe punishment she inflicts on her young charge when she breaks a plate bearing a representation of an idealized English countryside as "Heaven" is reminiscent of the brutality of slavery; she likewise fails to recognize that her acceptance of an idealized picture of the English countryside as a depiction of heaven is an ironic reminder of the devastating campaign of misinformation that is at the core of the colonial enterprise.

Xuela is removed from this home at the age of seven and brought to live with her father and new stepmother. The move brings Xuela into a second instance of motherlessness, this time accentuated by her entrance into a social milieu she had not experienced before, that of the growing Creole middle class. In her stepmother Xuela quickly recognizes an enemy who, fearful of her potential influence on her father as the child of his beloved first wife, will repeatedly attempt to kill her with the aid of Obeah. The silent battle of wills between the mature-beyond-her-years Xuela and the jealous stepmother plays itself out as an eerie fairy tale in which the death intended for Xuela, borne by the present of a poisoned necklace, reverts on the stepmother's familiar, the pet dog on whom Xuela places the suspect gift and who dies gruesomely within twenty-four hours. A truce is not reached until the stepmother's pregnancy distracts her attention from her murderous resentfulness toward the loathed stepdaughter.

Xuela will leave this affectionless home at age fifteen, when she is sent to the capital, Roseau, to continue her education. In Roseau, where she is left in the care of a childless couple, she will embark on a sexual relationship with the husband, sanctioned by the wife who hopes it will produce the child she herself has been unable to conceive. Despite her sympathy for the wife, Madame LaBatte, for whom Xuela feels a degree of affection, the latter will resort to a bloody abortion that is her conscious denial of motherhood, an embracing of childlessness in repudiation of the legacy of lovelessness that has been her only inheritance. The abortion marks a pivotal point in Xuela's life, after which she withdraws temporarily into a humble shack and a period of hard physical labor, as if in penance for her act of rejection.

Xuela agrees to return to her father's home on hearing that her half-brother is deathly ill. Her return home does not signal an acceptance of her father and his ways, but allows her nonetheless the opportunity to witness the devastation his selfishness has inflicted on his family. He has grown rich from cheating people of their property, becoming in the process the symbol of the evil and absence of pity in her world. The one thing he craves, beyond money, is precisely what his children will deny him—the progeny through which he wished to prolong his legacy in Dominican society. His son dies hideously at the age of nineteen, Xuela has rejected motherhood, and his younger daughter, after ending a pregnancy with Xuela's aid, will be crippled for life in a bicycle accident en route to meet the lover her father has forbidden her to see.

As she approaches middle age, Xuela marries the English doctor she first meets at her sister's bedside, and for whom she has gone to work as an assistant. Philip, a friend of her father's, is a white expatriate with an ambivalent relationship to his nation's past. When he and Xuela first become lovers, he is still married to an English wife whose contempt for the island world that surrounds her and for its people encapsulates for Xuela all the malice and humiliation that the British colonizers had inflicted on the colonized. After her death, the result of her addiction to an intoxicating tea to which Xuela has introduced her, a poison that turns her skin black before she dies, Philip and Xuela marry. Kincaid ponders in painstaking detail the reasons behind her protagonist's marriage to someone so thoroughly associated with those who have brought such decay and ruin on her own people. Philip offers a refuge from the hardness of her life, a measure of protection from the desolation of her existence, a love that she cannot reciprocate but for which she seems nonetheless grateful, and a certain measure of sexual gratification.

In her narrative, Xuela dwells on the pleasure she derives from her sexual relationships, three of which are described in some detail—her seduction by Monsieur LaBatte, her affair with Roland, a stevedore whom she admits to having loved but to whom she nonetheless refused to abandon herself completely, her affair with and marriage to Philip. Her relationships with all three of these men are described in sensuous yet analytical detail as instances of physical pleasure that were also displays of Xuela's personal appeal and power. Throughout the text Xuela's sexuality is depicted as having contributed greatly to her own self-knowledge and physical pleasure while failing to ensure lasting happiness or satisfaction.

The final chapters of *The Autobiography of My Mother* read like a meditation on Caribbean history from the perspective of the vanquished. The friendship that has long existed between Philip and her father lays the foundation for Xuela's reflections on the ultimate irrelevance of wealth and power. Their failures and disappointments serve as confirmation of the impossibility of the parasitic relationships stemming from "the emptiness of conquest" leading to happiness. Her father dies alone and defeated, bearing on his skin the sins he has committed, the burden of those he has ruined, his failure to leave a legacy other than the money that did not assure his happiness and for which his only remaining child does not care. Philip, for all his connection to the victors, dies with the knowledge that the empire that had assured his social superiority is a thing of the past. But Xuela herself is haunted by the children she so adamantly refused to have, by the opportunities she never enjoyed, by the possibilities for love and happiness she squandered. Death, the only power before which she is willing to bow, is the only thing before her; behind her is the void of a life without love and without history.

SETTING

The Autobiography of My Mother unfolds in the lush setting of the island of Dominica, the most unspoiled of all Caribbean islands. This island of luxuriant tropical vegetation, steep green cliffs, sulfuric springs, and boiling fountains, was the birthplace of Kincaid's own mother. But Kincaid conjures up the world of Dominica not to recreate it in its physical or social nuances, but to inscribe in it a casual cruelty, to superimpose on it a world in which the ghosts of colonialism still haunt the relationships of contemporary women and men. In her depiction of Dominican nature, Xuela refuses to endow it with any semblance of positive meaning, stripping it of anything save cruelty and desolation. This identification of Dominican nature with cruelty is not unique to Kincaid. In Dominican novelist Jean Rhys's *Wide Sargasso Sea* (1966), the island's riotous vegetation and dramatic landscape are depicted with an ominous intensity that prompts the protagonist's English husband to equate it with evil. Lally, the narrator of another Dominican classic, Phyllis Shand Allfrey's *The Orchid House* (1953), faced with the menacing power the island's nature exerts over Stella and Andrew, ruefully concludes that the island offered nothing but beauty and disease.

But it is in people, not nature, that cruelty resides. The world Kincaid creates as a setting for Xuela's tale is one where all ties of compassion and affection have been severed. Kincaid, as one of her reviewers insightfully commented, "intentionally simplifies the life around her main character, rendering it free of all everydayness, purifying it until it sparkles with hatred alone" (Schine, 5). In one of the novel's earliest episodes, after Kincaid has established the bonds of casual cruelty that mark Xuela's relationship to her unloving foster mother, the young girl falls in love with a pair of land turtles, the first things she admits to having truly loved; but she responds to what she perceives as their refusal to obey her commands by packing their necks with mud, forgetting them in the space where she has trapped them, and killing them in the process. For all the narrator's references to the cruelty in Dominica's nature, the text underscores that cruelty is the result not of an indifferent nature but of a historical process that has led to widespread moral deformity.

Kincaid has Xuela reimagine the Dominican landscape as symbolic of the island's history. After the torturous abortion that is the consequence of her affair with Monsieur LaBatte, Xuela leaves in a dreamlike voyage of possession along the periphery of the island, which she describes as her claiming of her birthright: the villages, rivers, and mountains and the people. Later in the narrative she recalls an episode from her childhood when her father had brought her to see a piece of land he had just acquired, and she instinctively held herself away from her inheritance. For her father, Xuela would muse later in the text, the beauty of the sea, the richness of the landscape of Dominica, could hold "no abundance of comfort" because it only reminded of the despair of the victor and the vanquished (191–192). For Xuela, however, nature is the one consistent source of pleasure in her life, and she will speak of the road leading from her father's house to school as the place where she spent the sweetest moments of her life: the reflection of the sun on the surface of the sea, a spot where the best cashews grew, the changes of weather—all are sources of real albeit ephemeral joy.

CHARACTER DEVELOPMENT

Reviewers of *The Autobiography of My Mother* were quick to take Kincaid to task for having created a repellent heroine, admirable for her strength of character yet unsympathetic as the angry and embittered product of an unfortunate upbringing. But of all the characters Kincaid has created, Xuela is the least autobiographical, the most nakedly literary. Xuela is meant to be read not as a faithful representation of a flesh-and-blood woman, but as an artifact of the text, as a voice that can articulate, flesh-out so to speak, the predicament of the individual and community subject to the full force of colonial oppression.

Xuela's most salient characteristic is a fearlessness that stems from her having already suffered what from a child's standpoint is arguably the most dreaded and unbearable loss. This fearlessness is both a stance of defiance and a requisite for survival. She boasts of her farsightedness, her remarkable capacity for survival, as something due her in compensation for her motherlessness. This farsightedness in turn costs her the innocence and vulnerability of childhood. Given a poisoned necklace by her stepmother, she is not dazzled by it like a true child would have been, and her resistance is her salvation. She intimates, moreover, that since she has no mother and God has given no evidence of caring whether she lives or dies, she must fend for herself.

Xuela's farsightedness emerges from the text as the source of her arrogance. She depicts herself as gifted with knowledge beyond reason, and cannot conceive of her wisdom as in any way flawed. Her instinctive knowledge manifests itself through her lack of surprise at what life has to offer her. She could sense from childhood that the knowledge she needed for survival would come to her when she needed it, that she "could trust my own instincts about things . . ." (59). The appearance of her first menstrual period—unknown and unexpected—has the force of destiny fulfilled, and provokes no fear or surprise. Her knowledge stretches beyond the bounds of the real into the realm of the supernatural. In the deep of the night, when all is still, she could hear the unhearable, the sounds of ghosts, spirit, *jablesses*. Aware that to display this foresightedness will only draw distrust and hatred toward her, she schools herself in dissimulation, cloaking herself in an "atmosphere of apology," as she calls it, to hide from others the anger on which her true self feeds.

Xuela's response to her predicament is "a distilled anger" toward anything in her world that can remind her of her many losses: her mother's death, her father's (and her people's) seduction into the ways of the colonizers, the despoiling of the landscape and its people for another nation's benefit. Her anger undermines her ability to engage with a world made meaningless by the devastation of colonization. Feeling unloved herself, she is unable to feel any love other than a twisted, grotesque self-love, and seems determined to coax out of herself no pity, no sympathy, no understanding toward her fellow human beings. She refuses to find in them anything redeemable, any possibility of understanding or compassion, any motive for their actions other than hatred, greed, and contempt.

Xuela, in her narrative, describes her social position as that of "a woman and a poor one," that being the space she chooses as the site of her narrative voice. This positioning is a statement of her choice of identities because given her father's growing wealth, her education, and intelligence, she could claim a space among the Dominican middle class. Xuela's choice of identities is indicative of her philosophical stance. Kincaid wills her to identify with the poor to better articulate the social and political polarities on which the work rests. Xuela's lack of place or status in society, an extension of her motherlessness, provides the necessary textual dislocation that can give voice to Kincaid's political/ideological stance. Xuela must choose to possess herself, to be free of any acknowledged connection to colonizer and colonized in order to best articulate the brutality of the colonizers and the meekness and acceptance of the colonized.

When she acknowledges ties to this community, it is to that of the Carib people, amid the vestiges of the vanquished but not necessarily deluded, the aboriginal. Xuela's mother, a Carib, is like her ancestors, a guessed presence, but it is nonetheless there, aboriginal, precolonial, prehistorical. Xuela's identification with her mother's people, the Caribs, gives her identity the only foundation she will acknowledge other than hatred and bitterness. It is an identification as physical as it is emotional. Because of her resemblance to her mother her teachers attribute her unusual intelligence (her prescience) to evil and possession, traits they link to her Carib heritage. Yet the Caribs, although the only segment of the Dominican population to be depicted in a consistently positive manner in Xuela's narrative, are still portrayed as defeated and almost exterminated, offering no hope or refuge from the devastation of conquest and colonization.

Xuela's self-proclaimed independence from the ravages of history, the clarity of vision that allows her to see the path of destruction left behind (manifested in her own psychic wounds), her ability to excoriate both victors and defeated, and see them become vanquished and destroyed, is pivotal to Kincaid's meditation on history in the text. From the moment in her childhood when she refuses to apologize to her foster mother for breaking her plate, Xuela asserts her independence, a self-command she exercises most decidedly in her refusal to bear children through which the chain of destruction can perpetuate itself. She speaks of herself as having become "an expert at being ruler of my own life in this one limited regard" (115).

This independent stand is crucial to Kincaid's articulation of the Caribbean historical process in the novel. Kincaid refuses to inscribe Xuela's tale in the world of romance, romance being "the refuge of the defeated," who need soothing tunes because their entire being is a wound. Instead she seeks to embody the historical process through the various heritages she receives from her parents: a Carib woman dead at the moment of her daughter's birth, representative of a race doomed to disappearance from history from the moment of the colonial encounter; and a man of mixed African and European race torn apart by his historical legacy.

Xuela's mother, Xuela Claudette Desvarieux, haunts the book as she haunts her daughter. A Carib child abandoned at the door of the convent, she is frozen in a dream, descending a ladder, only the hem of her white dress visible. Xuela's narrative poignantly underscores her being cut off from that important aspect of her personal/national history. She knows precious little about her mother, and this only through what others had told her. Lacking even a photograph, she must rely on others' memories to "remember" her mother as a tall, graceful woman with a soft, fragile beauty. On this scant information she must build an entire persona. The appalling nature of her ignorance of her mother's real self is articulated in the text through Xuela's ignorance of what language (English or French Creole) her mother spoke.

The two Xuelas share their motherlessness; they both have been deprived of "that confusion of who is who, flesh and flesh, that inseparableness which is said to exist between mother and child" (199). Kincaid's emphasis on this disconnection is both personal and historical, indicating a link between Xuela's severance from her own personal history and her people's break from their aboriginal roots. The primary connection between mother and child, people and history, has been broken at the very moment of birth, leaving hopelessness in its wake. Xuela thus imagines her mother's childhood as hers has been, a joyless period. Her mother, severed from her true self by her own disconnection from her mother, was molded by the French nuns who rename her into something she was not meant to be: a submissive colonial self, "a quiet, shy, long-suffering, unquestioning, modest, wishing-to-die-soon person" (199).

For Xuela, the loss of her mother is compounded by that of a father who is unable and unwilling to make up in any way for his daughter's immense loss. Although she identifies with him—his passions, like hers, were his own—she still faults him for what she sees as his adherence to the beliefs of the people who had subjugated him (108). What she sees in him that is positive—the fact that he is said to have loved his mother deeply and suffered bitterly when she died—only serves to underscore her loss. When her mother died, the good father, the better self who had so far forgotten himself as to love his wife, also died. Of his reported great sadness after she died, all she will conclude was that it did not make him generous, kindhearted, or unwilling to take advantage of others.

Her father's role as a policeman made him a pawn in the perpetuation of colonial oppression; he is an agent of repression of the very people whose rights he should have upheld as the representative of the law. His physical appearance functions as a controlled representation of his collusion with the oppressors. He was a handsome man whose features bore the mark of his history; the child of a Scotsman and a black woman, he had his father's red hair and gray eyes. On his face Xuela saw all those he had impoverished and abused, all the children he had fathered and refused to acknowledge. For Xuela, her father's physical presence is maplike. His back is like a land mass, arising unexpectedly out of flat land, becoming an obstacle in her way. After her abortion, and just after her assuming possession of the island of Dominica as her inheritance through her dreamlike voyage around her own private globe, she dreams of her father's face as a map of the world that encompasses continents, volcanoes, mountain ranges, horizons that lead into "the thick blackness of nothing" (91). He had used the power of his presence—a power he draws from his physical resemblance to the conquerors—to solidify his connection to them. From the former he had learned to assume the appearance of trustworthiness: his clothes were impeccable, finely tailored, well-ironed and spotless, helping him hide his true character.

The father is divided from his own people by the very wealth he has accumulated through his emulation of the colonizers. Xuela in time will come to see her father's love of money as the root of all the evils she experiences in her life. Unlike herself, who saw no value in money other than that of satisfying life's basic needs, he understood only the progressive, accumulative love of money as the essence of a happy life. In this pursuit he has been forced to assume a series of deceiving masks— masking being Xuela's favorite image for his mimicry of the English— which in time become so fixed that his true self can no longer emerge from behind them. He becomes, through his adoption of these masks, as much a mystery to his daughter Xuela as her own dead mother had become. He, Xuela argues, was "an incredible mimic," a man who above all had a talent for copying the attitudes of the powerful (139). In his daughter's eyes, he is proof that the meeting of white, African, and Carib peoples characteristic of Creole societies had resulted in profoundly disturbing racial and class hierarchies. He had learned through the echoes of this encounter to despise all those who behaved like the vanquished, "like the African people," all who were "defeated, doomed, conquered, poor, diseased, head bowed down, mind numbed by cruelty," thereby learning to hate a part of himself (187). He had deluded himself into believing that he was a just man, a religious man, brave and honest, and this belief in his own honesty—another characteristic that evidences his mimicry of his self-righteous colonial models—Xuela describes as his greatest act of self-deception.

From Xuela's perspective, however, her father's greatest failing had been his having sacrificed her, his firstborn daughter, to his pretensions to being a man of the world. To this end he had carelessly placed her in danger for her life and had lavished the love he had withheld from her onto the son through whom he expected to create a dynasty. He had failed to recognize that his true child, the one he had made most like himself through his abandonment, was not the male child on whom he had placed all his hopes, but his eldest and neglected daughter. Unlike Xuela, who had rejected motherhood, he had been incapable of making himself the measure of all things. Thus, when his son dies, his world is changed forever, and he is left feeling small again, insignificant, helpless against life, having lost the belief that his efforts had some future value.

Alfred, the oldest child of her father's second wife, the child through whom her father expected to fulfill his dream for continuity, is, however, a poor creature, when compared to Xuela. Kincaid's portrait of this weak and irresolute young man underscores the irony of his maleness and status as his father's heir. Alfred was but a pale copy of his father: he wore the same white linen suits, combed his hair in the same controlled manner. Physically he resembled his mother, but unlike his mother, whose determination to neutralize her stepdaughter had made her an enemy to be reckoned with, he could be kind and gentle, not because he possessed true goodness, but because he lacked the strength necessary for evil. He and Xuela are separated by the abyss created by his father's preference for him, and she will acknowledge him as a brother only after his untimely death from a debilitating parasitic worm that filled his body with pus and emerged from his leg just as he died.

Xuela shares her father's neglect with her sister Elizabeth, but despite the commonality of their situation vis-à-vis their father, no feeling of sisterly solidarity exists between them. Elizabeth emerges from Xuela's narrative as truly her mother's daughter: emotionally crippled, vengeful, envious, a sad, embittered woman. The crippling injuries she sustains after a bicycle accident only seem to mirror her psychic scars. Poisoned by her mother's cautions about Xuela's threat to her own inheritance, the younger sister can only regard her eldest half-sibling as an enemy. Physically, she was very much like her father, more so than their favored brother. Her skin had the same tone, she evidenced a similar mixture of peoples with her red and gold and tightly curled hair and her father's gray eyes. But her father never acknowledges this resemblance: Xuela argues that he cannot see in Elizabeth anything but the femaleness that renders her valueless in his eyes.

In her depiction of Elizabeth, Kincaid emphasizes those qualities that made her the very opposite of Xuela. Unlike Xuela, whose fury at life seethed without ever overflowing, Elizabeth was unable to contain the fury within her. Her anger overwhelmed her, making it impossible for her to keep her counsel. She was also fierce in her suspicions of others, Xuela particularly, and envious of those whose gifts were superior to her own. Xuela and Elizabeth were also different in one very important respect, one that made her tragedy worse than Xuela's—the fact that Elizabeth was not loved by her mother although her mother was alive. One of Xuela's only sources of comfort was that, although deprived of her mother's love, she felt assured that that love would have been forthcoming. Her dead mother, unlike Elizabeth's, was a loving mother.

In her characterizations of Elizabeth and her mother, Kincaid addresses the poverty of spirit and closed options facing women in the

Dominican society of the text, themes she will return to in her portrayals of Monsieur LaBatte and his wife. From the moment of his introduction into the text, Monsieur LaBatte is identified with the love of money, as befits a close friend of her father's. As Xuela's seducer, Monsieur LaBatte becomes Xuela's first source of sensual pleasure, a pleasure less rooted in his own self and body than in her own anticipation. It is not clear whether they ever spoke to each other as lovers. But Monsieur LaBatte never progresses in Xuela's estimation from his ability to provide occasional physical pleasure. He can never set aside his obsession with money—evidence of his poverty of spirit—long enough for the true communication that could lead to genuine emotion. When he makes love to Xuela she experiences for the first time the thrill of sexual pleasure and describes it as an exhilarating experience, even though she does not love him. He, however, reverts immediately to indifference, his mind on other things, which she surmises is his money, which she sees lined up on a small shelf in neat rows of coins bearing the face of a king.

If Monsieur LaBatte is identified with the love of money, Madame LaBatte is associated with resignation and loss. At her initial meeting, Xuela feels an instinctive sympathy for this rich woman whose unhappiness comes precisely from having gotten exactly what she had wanted. She had wanted very much for Mr. LaBatte to marry her, and had achieved her end with the help of Obeah. But when the effects of Obeah had worn off he had turned on her, and his rejection had made of her a prematurely aged, lifeless, and defeated woman. Her kindness to Xuela awakens the young woman's sympathy and leads to a friendship tested and eventually destroyed by Madame LaBatte's hopes that Xuela would produce a child to take the place of the one she had been unable to conceive.

There are strong parallels between Kincaid's depictions of the LaBattes and her characterizations of Philip—the Englishman who would ultimately become her husband—and of Moira, Philip's wife. Philip is described as burdened by the guilt of his association with the colonizer's injustices; but, unlike her father, he did not bear on his face the imprint of his ugly deeds—by the time of his birth all the evil to which he was heir had already been unleashed. He was an unremarkable, ordinary man, devoid of self-confidence, with skin that Xuela describes as "thin and pink and transparent." But he was British and therefore burdened by things over which he and his kind no longer had any control. As with Monsieur LaBatte, Xuela begins a sexual relationship with him, aimed at pleasing herself, seeking no emotional link. He did not look, she asserts, like anyone she could or should love. He was "empty of real life and energy, used up," Xuela writes (211–212). And indeed their eventual marriage—which she acknowledges as a defeat—will be rooted less in love than in an apparent desire for mutual self-punishment and expiation, not a desire for masochistic suffering but for penance for the ravages of history of which they have been both victim and unwitting inflictors.

In her characterization of Philip, Kincaid builds on the idea of a colonial inheritance as a burden from which there was no relief, since self-condemnation is tantamount to self-forgiveness. Through his marriage to Xuela he seeks to forget the past, a wasted effort, in her opinion, since it is as difficult for the victor as it is for the vanquished to betray memory. Philip, however, despite his stated need to forget, seems obsessed with the dead and spends his time arranging and rearranging volumes of history, geography, science, philosophy, none of which could bring him peace. He became, in the process, all the children Xuela had not allowed to be born; she mediated and translated for him, she blocked the entrance to the world he had come to know.

In the creation of Moira, Philip's wife, Kincaid returns to a theme she had explored repeatedly before, particularly in *Lucy*: that of the profound impact of colonial social mores on the relationship between women of different races and classes. Moira, being English, is portrayed as extremely pleased with who she is. Like Xuela she has a high opinion of herself; but in Xuela's eyes her positive view of her traits—she saw herself as kind, sympathetic to others, decent, full of grace—is simply evidence of her self-delusion. Xuela claims a deeper knowledge of Moira than Moira herself possesses. The truth of Moira's character is again, as with Philip, skin deep: her skin was "waxy, ghostish, without life" (156). Xuela's profound dislike for Moira is founded in the latter's condescending superiority; it is a dislike that cannot be bridged by what could have formed a bond between them—their broken wombs.

Moira is depicted as living among people she did not like, people she did not regard as human. From her superior social position, she stressed the distinction between herself as a lady and the mere women who surrounded her. This differentiation allowed her to believe that she was not associated with the ordinary, that she was linked to the victors, that the life of comfort she lived in the colony of Dominica was the result of her people's triumph, a triumph that assured her continued dominion over others. It is Xuela who provides the poison with which Moira Bailey will slowly kill herself: a hallucinatory tea made of local weeds that eventually turned her skin black. This was the ultimate irony, given Moira's contempt for the dark-skinned people among whom she had lived for so many years. As a white Englishwoman, Moira had drawn her sense of her own personal and social importance from the power of her country's extensive empire. But her death, Xuela argues vehemently, had reduced her to the level of dust, just like everyone else, the color of one's skin notwithstanding.

Of all the characters created by Kincaid in *The Autobiography of My Mother*, the only one apparently immune to the plague of colonial or postcolonial angst is Roland, a black stevedore and the only man Xuela will admit to having loved. Despite his lowly position as a manual laborer and his relatively low social status (if compared with the other men in Xuela's life), he is repeatedly described as "a man." In her portrayal of Roland, Kincaid seems again to privilege the physical laborer, the Dominican working poor, as the voice of truth in her text. Roland legitimately occupies the space Xuela appropriates as the site of her own narrative voice. He thus functions in many ways as Xuela's male mirror image. Like herself, despite his being only "a small event in someone else's history" (167), he has a "miraculous capacity for self-love" and the ability to carry himself as if convinced that he is precious. What Xuela values about him, however—his oneness with his surroundings, the joyful irresponsibility of his many infidelities, his unproblematic acceptance of things-as-they-are—is the very opposite of her tortured obsession with the myriad humiliations of colonial oppression. The happiness she experiences with him, therefore, can only be temporary: Roland, precisely because of his inability or unwillingness to understand that he is at heart the by-product of myriad colonial assaults, can never reach her soul.

THEMATIC ISSUES

At the core of *The Autobiography of My Mother* is Kincaid's portrayal of Xuela as the abstraction of the Caribbean people's history of colonial wretchedness and degradation—thus the centrality of history as a theme in the text. In *The Autobiography of My Mother* every character plays a historically assigned role and embodies specific historical archetypes, giving breath and breadth to Kincaid's meditation on the significance of history for the colonized. The theme is introduced early in the text when Xuela, on first entering the classroom, is forced to learn about the history of peoples she had never met—the Romans, Gauls, Saxons, Britons—and begins to understand the use of history as a tool of domination, an "ex-pression of vanity," a version of events imposed on the defeated "with malicious intent." The acceptance of this narrative could only lead to "a humiliation so permanent that it could replace your own skin" (79). The colonizer's historical narrative divides the peoples of the world between the victors and the vanquished, with the people of Dominica belonging most categorically to the latter.

In a society where the colonizer's historical narrative has silenced the vanquished's version of events, the tale on which a sense of positive iden-tity could be founded, the only defense against historylessness, Kincaid tells us, is to articulate the wounds of forced silence through eloquent, deafening denunciation of the evils sustained in the name of colonial ex-pansion. In *The Autobiography of My Mother* this narrative of symbolic denunciation is articulated through the interrelated themes of motherless-ness, lovelessness, miscegenation, and the differences between the lan-guages of the colonizer and the colonized.

Xuela's refusal to bear children is linked in the text to her unwilling-ness to embrace a nation that has accepted defeat: "Each month my body would swell up slightly . . . mourning my heart's and mind's decision never to bring forth a child. I refused to belong to a race, I refuse to accept a nation" (225–226). Likewise, the figure of her dead mother rep-resents more than the never-known woman who gave her life; she is a symbol of the lost past, the loss of a vital link to a history before colonial exploitation. Her mother, had she lived, would have protected her from "a world cruel beyond ordinary imagining" (210). The loss of the mother through whom Xuela could have established a link to an untroubled past of precolonial tribal wholeness is presented in the novel as having left her stunted, fixated on the past and the blighted present, unable to see the future, and consequently unable to project herself into the future through children of her own. For Xuela history was not only the past, but the past and the present: "I did not mind my defeat, I only minded that it had to last so long" (139).

Xuela's dead, unattainable Carib mother is also depicted in the text as a symbol of racial purity, underscoring, by her absence from the narra-tive, the racial mixture brought about by colonization as "a parable of moral impurity." Skin—its texture, color, changing nature—conveys the accidents of history. When Xuela speaks of her mother's skin she de-scribes it as being "only itself, an untroubled past," because she was a Carib (197). But the Caribs emerge in the book as living fossils belonging in a museum. The present is represented by her father, in whose skin the ills of miscegenation are embedded. He had inherited his distinctive red hair from his own father, a Scottish drunk who had left in his wake a stream of red-haired boys, and he had spoken of his parentage with pleasure and pride, describing without irony or bitterness the "trail of misery" that had been his father's legacy. When her father embarks on his own career as an oppressor in the service of the colonizer, Kincaid has Xuela describe his policeman's clothes as having replaced his skin, becoming his defining essence. Later, as he grew richer, his finely tailored white linen suits replace his policeman's skin, as a new layer representative of his deeper collusion with the colonial enterprise.

The depth of his collusion with the oppressor is reflected in the incapacity for love that is the very opposite of the unconditional love and care that Xuela imagines her dead mother would have lavished on her. In a world devoid of a mother's love there is no difference between love and hate, since the two often wear the same fatherly face. When her father retrieves her from the foster home, following his remarriage, he punctuates their journey toward her new home with a litany of the reasons why she is going to love every aspect of her new life, repeating the word "love" like a mantra that seeks to conjure a reality Xuela instinctively knows is not to be. The very repetition of the word "love," she argues, convinces her that the emotion itself did not exist, that he sought to conjure it through words because he could not make it real though action. But by then Xuela had learned to thrive in a loveless atmosphere, having imbued her community's message of universal distrust. Mistrust, she observes, had replaced love. The colonizers had made the colonized compete for a secret, undisclosed prize, making any expression of generosity or love suspect, leaving them convinced that genuine emotion could lead to vulnerability, thereby giving someone else an advantage.

Xuela's response to the lovelessness fostered by the island's colonizers is a fierce, obsessive self-love, a love embodying her stubborn refusal to give in to the despair of the colonial self, but one that is ultimately not the most satisfying. What she had been taught to despise—her own self, her smells, the very materiality of her body—she will come to love with a fierceness that fed on the bravado with which she tried to keep despair at bay: She came to love herself "in defiance, out of despair," knowing full well that such a love "is not the best kind" (56–57). Sexual pleasure, as a manifestation of Xuela's affirmation of self, is used in the novel to underscore the hollowness of self-love as a poor substitute for the fulfilling maternal love rooted in aboriginal wholeness. Sexual desire symbolizes that "sweet hollow feeling, an empty space yearning to be filled"

(154). Xuela's fierce self-love is offered in the text as her defense against becoming one of the "shadow people," one of the zombie-like vanquished. Kincaid evokes the figure of the zombie to describe those who "had long ago long lost any connection to wholeness," left to live their lives in a colonial trance, distrusting each other, believing in other people's ghosts, speaking other people's language (133).

The contending languages of Roseau, that "outpost of despair," stand in representation of the colonial subject's inability to relish that which is not validated by the colonizer. Kincaid weaves the theme of self-love (personal and national) with that of language by having her protagonist learn to embrace the French patois or Creole spoken by the people of Dominica. As a child, Xuela refuses to speak Creole, calling it the "made-up language" of the shadow people (30). Her foster mother Eunice only spoke patois and her father consequently speaks to her in patois while under Eunice's care because he assumes she understands nothing else. But Xuela, after a silence that had lasted until she was four, speaks her first words—"Where is my father?"—in English, the language of a people she would never like and one she had never heard before. She describes her stepmother as speaking to her in patois, the "language of the captive, the illegitimate" (74), as a thinly veiled attempt to humiliate her.

Xuela's relationship with the people's language is an ambivalent one, however, and she in time comes to associate its use with genuineness and truth. She will describe her father as speaking patois only within the family circle, or with those who had known him since childhood, and will come to value his use of the language as offering glimpses of his true self. In her middle and old age, Xuela, who had throughout her life insisted on speaking English so as not to be associated with the defeated, will speak to her husband Philip in patois, while he responds in English. They understood each other better in that way, she argued, as they were speaking in the language of their thoughts.

As with Creole, Kincaid uses Obeah as an intrinsic part of the world of the colonized that the colonizers have attempted to devalue and silence. Xuela, therefore, will put it forth in her narrative as a force of resistance, a phenomenon acknowledged by all Dominicans as a given in their lives. She recognizes its potential for evil—her stepmother sends "something she could not see" to live in a favorite place of hers to drive her away and later gives her a necklace that when placed around the dog's neck made him go mad and die—but also acknowledges its positive, curative aspects. In Xuela's presentation, a belief in Obeah is emblematic of cultural resistance. Her stepmother, for example, attempts to save her brother Albert's life by laying the ailing young man on a bed of rags perfumed with vegetable and animal oils, placed on the floor so that spirits could not get to him from underneath. His mother believed in Obeah, Xuela reminds us, while his father held the beliefs of the people who had subjugated him.

The river maiden who drives one of Xuela's classmates to disappear under the river waters is a further example of Kincaid's use of the beliefs of the victimized as the means of addressing the topic of cultural resistance in the novel. The maiden—"beautiful in a way that made sense to us"—appeared to the children as they waded the river, singing a mesmerizing song that lured the boy into the deeper water, never to be seen again. This episode addresses the disenfranchising of the truth of the colonized, who see their account of these and similar incidents held in doubt and denied. The experience, as interpreted by others, becomes a myth to be silenced, "the belief of the illegitimate, the poor, the low" (38). Xuela proudly asserts her belief in the apparition in defiance of this forced interpretation of the truth she has seen with her own eyes.

Kincaid's insistence on the validation of the colonized's systems of belief as symbol of political resistance offers a clue to the narrative's handling of the themes of punishment and atonement. Xuela rejects the possibility of atonement that is so basic to European Christianity; she asserts her belief that guilt persists through generations, as does defeat. Persons and nations, from her point of view, can never truly judge themselves, since to confess transgressions is tantamount to self-forgiveness. Silence is the only form of self-punishment, a silence occasionally broken by a crier repeating over and over a list of the bad deeds committed.

A POSTCOLONIAL READING OF *THE AUTOBIOGRAPHY OF MY MOTHER*

Postcolonial theory refers to the body of writings through which scholars, writers, and intellectuals from formerly colonized territories have sought to address the process of decolonization, of the shedding of colonial power as reflected in their institutions, political and cultural systems, languages, literatures, and religions. One of the earliest theoreticians of decolonization was Frantz Fanon, author of two classics of postcolonial theory, *The Wretched of the Earth* and *Black Skins, White Masks*. For the reader familiar with the literature of decolonization it is impossible to read *The Autobiography of My Mother* without feeling the presence of Fanon's writings as a subtext to Xuela's narrative. In his writings, Fanon strove to show the many destructive ways in which colonialism affected both the colonizer and the colonized. Colonialism, he argued, had brought together two irreconcilable social orders—the colonizer's and the colonized's—doomed to coexist in perpetual tension. These tensions, evident in all facets of daily life, produced a world in which the individual—colonizer as well as colonized—was constantly in peril of capitulating to the moral and spiritual deformity of a system based on racism, exploitation, and oppression.

A psychiatrist by training, Fanon's research focused on the implications of the division of the colonial world into native and settler, seeking to illustrate the destructive effects of the colonizer's view of the native as racially and culturally inferior. His theory of decolonization advocated the use of violence as a means of reconstructing human relations, opening the way for a new society that could give birth to a "new man." True decolonization could only occur when the colonized seized their freedom through a struggle for liberation in which violence would have the cathartic effect of cleansing the colonial heritage of inferiority and submission.

Xuela's narrative establishes a dialogue with Fanon, offering her obsessive self-love as a means of transcending the categorical opposition between colonizer and colonized that Fanon analyzes in his writings. Like Fanon, Kincaid has Xuela articulate an unequivocal division between oppressor and victim, both groups representing absolute positions that can only be bridged by one "mimicking" the other. Xuela's parentage, for example, is representative of those polarities: her mother, a Carib, was the elusive aboriginal presence from whom the colonial subject has been wrenched; her father, the "mimic," was the native who had lost his own self in a tragic imitation of the ways of the oppressor, adopting a series of "white masks" through which he himself becomes an oppressor.

In this world of polar opposites, in which the colonizer and his "mimics" are validated at the expense of the colonized, those clear-sighted enough to understand the evil impact of the process must assume the task of building a positive sense of self out of the remnants of colonial destruction. Xuela's narrative seeks, if not to build the foundations for the "new man" (or woman) that Fanon envisioned, at least to reject collusion in a process that can only result in self-hatred and self-destruction. She refuses to accept the colonizer's views of those like herself, positing her obsessive, almost grotesque self-love as an alternative to self-loathing and the pernicious effects of assimilation. It is not the best type of love, she acknowledges, but it is preferable to self-hatred.

Kincaid uses Xuela's relationships with the various characters in the novel to articulate the social categories or types that Fanon describes in his writings—from Philip and his wife Moira as instances of the distortion of behavior that results from colonial social hierarchies to the use of masking as a metaphor for her father's mimicry of the colonizers. A systematic analysis of the characterizations in *The Autobiography of My Mother* in the light of Fanon's *Black Skins, White Masks* reveals how Kincaid uses the various characters as examples of the colonial "conditions" outlined by Fanon to build Xuela's narrative of repudiation of cultural assimilation.

Xuela's narrative departs from Fanon in its rejection of political action as a path to liberation. Fanon's theories are geared to the development of psychological defenses with which to combat the negative impact of colonization. The question forever present in his writings is that of how to do away with the colonial conditions that led to the colonized's predicament. But Xuela has no interest in political activity; she rejects the very notion of identification with a nation from which such activity could stem. In a key passage in *The Autobiography of My Mother* Kincaid has her protagonist ask a pivotal question, "What makes the world turn?" It is a question she sees no need to answer, one reserved for those who feel that they have everything they can see in their grasp, for those she does not resemble—men, the British colonizers, those who mimic the latter's ways, those with special privileges in the hierarchy of things. She can ask no questions since she owns nothing and is not a man: "The luxury of an answer that will fill volumes does not stretch out before me" (132). In her most optimistic moments, Xuela yearns to be part of some force of the universe that is outside history. The only thing that would have brought her complete happiness, she muses, would have been to see the past reversed, to see her island returned to the aboriginal pre-European culture. She remains to the end obsessed by the past, unable—unwilling, perhaps—to look beyond her anger to a future of transcendence through violent revolution, prompting instead the question of whether the societies of the Caribbean, like Xuela, are damaged beyond repair.

Bibliography

WORKS BY JAMAICA KINCAID (IN CHRONOLOGICAL ORDER)

Novels

Annie John. New York: Farrar, Straus & Giroux, 1985.
Lucy. New York: Farrar, Straus & Giroux, 1990.
The Autobiography of My Mother. New York: Farrar, Straus & Giroux, 1996.

Excerpts

"Marbles." From *Annie John*. In *Her True True Name: An Anthology of Women's Writing from the Caribbean*, edited by Pamela Mordecai and Betty Wilson, 112–116. London: Heinemann, 1989.
From *Annie John*. In *A Way Out of No Way: Writing About Growing Up Black in America*, edited by Jacqueline Woodson. New York: Ballantine, 1996.

Short Stories

"Girl." *New Yorker*, 26 June 1978: 29.
"Antigua Crossing." *Rolling Stone*, 29 June 1978: 48–50.
"In the Night." *New Yorker*, 24 July 1978: 22–23.
"Wingless." *New Yorker*, 29 January 1979: 26–27.

"Holidays." *New Yorker*, 27 August 1979: 32–33.

"At Last." *New Yorker*, 17 December 1979: 40–41.

"The Letter from Home." *New Yorker*, 20 April 1981: 33.

"The Apprentice." *New Yorker*, 17 August 1981: 25.

"What I Have Been Doing Lately." *The Paris Review* 23 (1981): 129–132.

"At the Bottom of the River." *New Yorker*, 3 May 1982: 46.

"Figures in the Distance." *New Yorker*, 9 May 1983: 40–42.

"The Red Girl." *New Yorker*, 8 August 1983: 32–38.

"Columbus in Chains." *New Yorker*, 10 October 1983: 48–52.

"The Circling Hand." *New Yorker*, 21 November 1983: 50–57.

At the Bottom of the River. New York: Farrar, Straus & Giroux, 1984. Contents: Girl / In the Night / At Last / Wingless / Holidays / The Letter from Home / What I Have Been Doing Lately / Blackness / My Mother / At the Bottom of the River.

"Gwen." *New Yorker*, 16 April 1984: 46–52.

"Somewhere Belgium." *New Yorker*, 14 May 1984: 42–51.

"The Long Rain." *New Yorker*, 30 July 1984: 28–36.

"A Walk to the Jetty." *New Yorker*, 5 November 1984: 45–51.

Annie, Gwen, Lilly, Pam, and Tulip. New York: Library Fellows of the Whitney Museum of Modern Art, 1986.

"Ovando." *Conjunctions* 14 (1989): 75–83.

"Poor Visitor." *New Yorker*, 27 February 1989: 34–46.

"Mariah." *New Yorker*, 26 June 1989: 32–38.

"The Tongue." *New Yorker*, 9 October 1989: 44–54.

"My Mother." In *Caribbean New Wave: Contemporary Short Stories*, edited by Stewart Brown, 111–115. London: Heinemann, 1990.

"Cold Heart." *New Yorker* 25 June 1990: 28–40.

"Lucy." *New Yorker*, 24 September, 1990: 44–53.

"The Finishing Line." *New York Times Book Review*, 2 December 1990: 18.

"Have Yourself a Gorey Little Christmas: Nine Writers Create Stories for Edward Gorey's Christmas Illustrations." *New York Times Book Review*, 2 December 1990: 16.

"Song of Roland." *New Yorker*, 12 April 1993: 94–98.

"Xuela." *New Yorker*, 9 May 1994: 82–92.

"In Roseau." *New Yorker*, 17 April 1995: 92–99.

Essays and Other Nonfiction

"The Fourth." *New Yorker*, 19 July 1976: 23.

"Jamaica Kincaid's New York." *Rolling Stone*, 6 October 1977: 71–73.

"The Talk of the Town." *New Yorker*, 17 October 1977: 37.

"The Apprentice." *New Yorker*, 17 August 1981: 25.

"The Talk of the Town." *New Yorker*, 3 January 1983: 23.

"The Ugly Tourist." From *A Small Place*. *Harper's Magazine* 277, no. 1660 (September 1988): 32–34.

A Small Place. New York: New American Library, 1989.

Foreword to *Babouk* by Guy Endore. New York: Monthly Review Press, 1991.

"On Seeing England for the First Time." *Transition* 51 (1991): 32–40.

"Out of Kenya." With Ellen Pall. *New York Times*, 16 September 1991: A-15, A-19.

"Flowers of Evil." From "In the Garden," *New Yorker*, 5 October 1992: 154–159.

"A Fire by Ice." From "In the Garden," *New Yorker*, 22 February 1993: 64–67.

"Dear John: Five Ways to Leave a Lover." *Mademoiselle*, March 1993: 202–203.

"Just Reading." From "In the Garden," *New Yorker*, 29 March 1993: 47–51.

"Alien Soil." From "In the Garden," *New Yorker*, 21 June 1993: 47–51.

"This Other Eden." From "In the Garden," *New Yorker*, 23 and 30 August 1993: 69–73.

"Jamaica Kincaid." In *Writing Women's Lives: An Anthology of Autobiographic Narratives by Twentieth-Century American Women Writers*, edited by Susan Neunzig Cahill. New York: HarperPerennial, 1994.

"The Season Past." From "In the Garden," *New Yorker*, 7 March 1994: 57–61.

"Christmas Pictures from a Warm Climate." *Vogue*, December 1994: 314–315.

"Early Delights." From "In the Garden," *New Yorker*, 12 December 1994: 63–71.

"Putting Myself Together." *New Yorker*, 20 February 1995: 93–101.

"Plant Parenthood." From "In the Garden," *New Yorker*, 19 June 1995: 43–46.

"Homemaking." *New Yorker*, 16 October 1995: 54–59.

"Flowers of Empire." From "In the Garden," *New Yorker*, April 1996: 28–31.

My Brother. New York: Farrar, Straus & Giroux, 1997.

Interview by Kincaid

"Athol Fugard: Interview with South African Playwright." *Interview* 20 (August 1990): 64.

Broadcast

"Annie John." Radio Broadcast. First Person Feminine. Second series, Tape 12, Program no. 20. Iowa State University, Ames, Iowa, WOI-FM Radio, 1981–1982.

Translations

Annie John. Translated into French by Dominique Peters. Paris: Belfond, 1986.

Anna delle Antille. Translation into Italian of *Annie John* by Cin Calabi. Novara: Instituto Geografico De Agostini, 1987.

Annie John. Translation into Spanish. Madrid: Alfaguara, 1988.

Annie John. Translation into German by Barbara Henninges. Stuttgart: Deutsche Verlags-Anstalt, 1989.

Nur eine kleine Insel. Translation into German of *A Small Place.* Stuttgart: Deutsche Verlags-Anstalt, 1990.

Autobiographie de ma mère. Translation into French of *Autobiography of My Mother.* Paris: A. Michel, 1997.

Recordings

Jamaica Kincaid Reads Annie John. Columbia, Missouri: American Audio Prose Library, 1991.

Annie John. Read by Jamaica Kincaid. New York: Airplay Audiobooks, 1994.

Jamaica Kincaid Reads from Annie John. Milwaukee, Wisconsin: Volunteer Services for the Visually Handicapped, 1994.

At the Bottom of the River. Read by Jamaica Kincaid. Washington, D.C.: Library of Congress (Gertrude Clark Whitehall Poetry & Literary Fund), 1995.

The Autobiography of My Mother. Read by Jamaica Kincaid. New York: Airplay Audiobooks, 1996.

Edited Work

The Best American Essays, 1995. Selected by Jamaica Kincaid with Robert Atwan. Boston: Houghton Mifflin, 1995.

WORKS ABOUT JAMAICA KINCAID (IN ALPHABETICAL ORDER)

Criticism

Byerman, K. E. "Anger in *A Small Place*: Jamaica Kincaid's Cultural Critique of Antigua." *College Literature* 22, no. 1 (1995): 91–102.

Caton, Louis F. "Romantic Struggles: The Bildungsroman and Mother-Daughter Bonding in Jamaica Kincaid's *Annie John.*" *MELUS* 21, no. 3 (1996): 126–143.

———. " '... Such Was the Paradise That I Lived': Multiculturalism, Romantic Theory, and the Contemporary American Novel (Don Delillo, Jamaica Kincaid, Leslie Marmon Silko)." Ph.D. diss., University of Oregon, 1995.

Chanda, Swati. "Narratives of Nation in the Age of Diaspora (Salman Rushdie, Jamaica Kincaid, Gurinder Chadha, Linton Kwesi Johnson)." Ph.D. diss., Purdue University, 1996.

Chick, Nancy. "The Broken Clock: Time, Identity, and Autobiography in Jamaica Kincaid's *Lucy.*" *CLA Journal* 40, no. 1 (1996): 90–104.

Comfort, Susan Marguerite. "Memory, Identity, and Exile in Postcolonial Caribbean Fiction." Ph.D. diss., University of Texas at Austin, 1994.

Cousineau, Diane. "Women and Autobiography: Is There Life Beyond the Looking Glass?" *Caliban* 31 (1994): 97–105.

Covi, Giovanna. "Jamaica Kincaid and the Resistance to Canons." In *Out of the Kumbla: Caribbean Women and Literature*, edited by Carol Boyce Davis and Elaine Savory Fido, 345–354. Trenton, N.J.: Africa World Press, 1990.

DiMarco, Danette. "Taking Their Word: Twentieth-Century Women Reinvent the Victorian." Ph.D. diss., Duquesne University, 1995.

Donnell, Alison. "Dreaming of Daffodils: Cultural Resistance in the Narratives of Theory." *Kunapipi* 14, no. 2 (1993): 45–52.

———. "She Ties Her Tongue: The Problems of Cultural Paralysis in Postcolonial Criticism." *Ariel* 26, no. 1 (1995): 101–116.

———. "When Daughters Defy: Jamaica Kincaid's Fiction." *Women: A Cultural Review* 4, no. 1 (1993): 18–26.

Dutton, Wendy. "Merge and Separate: Jamaica Kincaid's Fiction." *World Literature Today* 63, no. 3 (Summer 1989): 406–410.

Ferguson, Moira. *Colonialism and Gender Relations from Mary Wollstonecraft to Jamaica Kincaid: Eastern Caribbean Connections.* New York: Columbia University Press, 1994.

———. *Jamaica Kincaid: Where the Land Meets the Body.* Charlottesville: University Press of Virginia, 1994.

———. "*Lucy* and the Mark of the Colonizer." *Modern Fiction Studies* 39, no. 2 (1993): 237–259.

George, Rosemary Marangoly. "Home-Countries and the Politics of Location: Home, Nationalism, Feminist Subjecthood." Ph.D. diss., Brown University, 1992.

Gilkes, Michael. "The Madonna Pool: Woman as 'Muse of Identity.' " *Journal of West Indian Literature* 1, no. 2 (June 1987): 1–19.

Harkins, Patricia. "Family Magic: Invisibility in Jamaica Kincaid's *Lucy*." *Journal of the Fantastic in the Arts* 4, no. 3 (1991): 53–68.

Herndon, Crystal Gerise. "Gendered Fictions of Self and Community: Autobiography and Autoethnography in Caribbean Women's Writing." Ph.D. diss., University of Texas at Austin, 1993.

Holcomb, Gary Edward. "Writing Travel in Anglophone Caribbean Literature: Claude McKay, Shiva Naipaul, and Jamaica Kincaid." Ph.D. diss., Washington State University, 1995.

Insanally, Annette. "Contemporary Female Writing in the Caribbean." *The Caribbean Novel in Comparison: Proceedings of the Ninth Conference of Hispanists,* edited by Ena V. Thomas, 115–141. St. Augustine, Trinidad: University of the West Indies, Department of French and Spanish Literatures, 1986.

———. "Sexual Politics in Contemporary Female Writing in the Caribbean." In

West Indian Literature and Its Political Context, edited by Lowell Fiet, 79–91. Río Piedras: University of Puerto Rico, 1988.

Ismond, Patricia. "Jamaica Kincaid: 'First They Must Be Children.'" *Sargasso* 4 (1987): 37–46.

Lanser, Susan Sniader. "Compared to What? Global Feminism, Comparatism, and the Master's Tools." In *Borderwork: Feminist Engagements with Comparative Literature*, edited by Margaret R. Higonnet, 280–300. Ithaca: Cornell University Press, 1994.

Ledent, Benedicte. "Voyages into Otherness: *Cambridge* and *Lucy*." *Kunapipi* 14, no. 2 (1993): 53–63.

Lenk, Cynthia Ruth. "Race, Gender, and Personal Power in Selected Contemporary Caribbean Works of Fiction." Ph.D. diss., University of Arkansas, 1990.

Louis, James. "Reflections on the Bottom of the River: The Transformation of Caribbean Experience in the Fiction of Jamaica Kincaid," *Wasafiri* 8–9 (Winter 1988–1989): 15–17.

Mangum, Bryant. "Jamaica Kincaid." In *Fifty Caribbean Writers*, edited by Daryl Cumber Dance, 255–263. Westport, CT: Greenwood Press, 1986.

Martin, Janette May. "The Dynamics of Expatriatism in the Writing of Jean Rhys and Jamaica Kincaid." Ph.D. diss., Bowling Green State University, 1994.

McDonald-Smythe, Antonia. "Making Herself at Home in the West Indies: The Gendered Construction of Identity in the Writings of Michele Cliff and Jamaica Kincaid." Ph.D. diss., Ohio State University, 1996.

Morgan, Paula Eleanor. "A Cross-Cultural Study of the Black Female-Authored Novel of Development." Ph.D. diss., University of the West Indies, 1994.

Morris, Ann R. and Margaret M. Dunn. "'The Bloodstream of Our Inheritance': Female Identity and the Caribbean Mothers'-Land." In *Motherlands: Black Women's Writing from Africa, the Caribbean and South Asia*, edited by Susheila Nasta, 219–237. London: The Women's Press, 1991.

Murdoch, H. Adlai. "The Novels of Jamaica Kincaid: Figures of Exile, Narratives of Dreams." *Clockwatch Review* 9, no. 1–2 (1994–1995): 141–154.

———. "Severing the (M)other Connection: The Representation of Cultural Identity in Jamaica Kincaid's *Annie John*." *Callaloo* 13, no. 2 (Spring 1988): 325–340.

Natov, Roni. "Mothers and Daughters: Jamaica Kincaid's Pre-Oedipal Narrative." *Children's Literature* 18 (1990): 1–16.

Niesen de Abruña, Laura. "Family Connections: Mother and Mother Country in the Fiction of Jean Rhys and Jamaica Kincaid." In *Motherlands: Black Women's Writing from Africa, the Caribbean and South Asia*, edited by Susheila Nasta, 257–289. London: The Women's Press, 1991.

Oczkowicz, Edyta Katarzyna. "Jamaica Kincaid's *Lucy*: Cultural 'Translation' as a Case of Creative Exploration of the Past." *MELUS* 21, no. 3 (1996): 153–158.

———. "The Metaphor of 'Translation' in Multicultural Writing by Contemporary American Women Writers." Ph.D. diss., Lehigh University, 1994.

Payette, Patricia Ruth. "*Jane Eyre* and the Postcolonial Bildungsroman." M.A. thesis, University of Louisville, 1995.

Perlman, Karen Beth. "Memory Speaks: The Revision of History and the Subject in Contemporary Women's Fiction." Ph.D. diss., University of Michigan, 1994.

Perry, Donna. "Initiation in Jamaica Kincaid's *Annie John*." In *Caribbean Women Writers: Essays from the First International Conference*, edited by Selwyn R. Cudjoe, 245–253. Wellesley: Calaloux, 1990.

Rafi, Iris Fawzia. "You of Age to See about Yourself Now! So Pull Up Your Socks!: Themes of Bildung in Select Novels by West Indian Women." Ph.D. diss., Emory University, 1994.

Ramchand, Kenneth. "West Indian Literary History: Literariness, Orality and Periodization." *Callaloo* 11, no. 1 (Winter 1988): 95–110.

Renk, Kathleen J. "The Shadow Catchers: Creole/Womanist Writers in the Anglophone Caribbean." Ph.D. diss., University of Iowa, 1995.

Schlosser, Donna. "Recurring Vocabularies: Narrating Voices in *Annie John*, *Jasmine*, and *Middle Passage*." Ph.D. diss., Florida Atlantic University, 1997.

Simmons, Diane Ellis. *Jamaica Kincaid*. New York: Twayne, 1994.

———. "Jamaica Kincaid: A Critical Study." Ph.D. diss., City University of New York, 1994.

———. "The Mother Mirror in Jamaica Kincaid's *Annie John* and Gertrude Stein's *The Good Anna*." In *The Anna Book: Searching for Anna in Literary History*, edited by Michey Pearlmn, 99–104. Westport, CT: Greenwood, 1992.

———. "The Rhythm of Reality in the Work of Jamaica Kincaid." *World Literature Today* 68, no. 3 (1994): 466–472.

Smyth, Heather. "Psychoanalytic Feminism and Caribbean Women's Relationships in the Works of Jamaica Kincaid and Paule Marshall." M.A. thesis, University of Guelph (Canada), 1994.

Stewart, Karen. " 'A' Is for Annie: A Post-It Note on Autobiographies and Postcoloniality in Jamaica Kincaid's *Annie John*." Ph.D. diss., University of Vermont, 1996.

Tapping, Craig. "Children and History in the Caribbean Novel: George Lamming's *In the Castle of My Skin* and Jamaica Kincaid's *Annie John*." *Kunapipi* 11, no. 2 (1989): 51–59.

Tiffin, Helen. "Cold Hearts and (Foreign) Tongues: Recitation and Reclamation of the Female Body in the Works of Erna Brodber and Jamaica Kincaid." *Callaloo* 16, no. 4 (1993): 909–921.

———. "Decolonization and Audience: Erna Brodber's *Myal* and Jamaica Kincaid's *A Small Place*." *SPAN: Journal of the South Pacific Association for Commonwealth Literature and Language Studies* 30 (April 1990): 27–38.

Timothy, Helen Pyne. "Adolescent Rebellion and Gender Relations in *At the Bottom of the River and Annie John*." In *Caribbean Women Writers: Essays From the First International Conference*, edited by Selwyn R. Cudjoe, 233–242. Wellesley: Calaloux, 1990.

Trotman, Althea Veronica. "African-American Perspectives of Worldview: C. L. R. James Explores the Authentic Voice." Ph.D. diss., York University, 1993.

Ty, Eleanor. "Struggling with the Powerful (M)Other: Identity and Sexuality in Kogawa's *Obasan* and Kincaid's *Lucy*." *International Fiction Review* 20, no. 2 (1993): 120–126.

Reviews

Annie, Gwen, Lilly, Pam and Tulip

Hoffert, Barbara. "Image, Imagery, Imagination." *Library Journal*, 15 September 1989: 37.

Keleher, Jean. *Library Journal* 114, no. 20 (December 1989): 118.

Annie John

Allen, Zita. "Close, But No Cigar." *Freedomways* 25, no. 2 (1985): 116–119.

Bonnell, Paula. "Annie Travels to Second Childhood." *Boston Herald*, 31 March 1985: 126.

Braunschweiger, Jennifer. "The Last Word." *Seventeen* 55, no. 6 (June 1996): 85.

Bruner, Charlotte H. *World Literature Today* 59, no. 4 (1985): 644.

Cole, Diane. *Ms.* 12, no. 7 (January 1984): 14.

Harris, Helaine. *Belles Lettres*, May 1985: 10.

Kenney, Susan. *New York Times Book Review*, 7 April 1985: 6.

Onwordi, Ike. *Times Literary Supplement*, 29 November 1985: 1374.

Trelles, Carmen Dolores. "Dos novelas del Caribe inglés: *Annie John* y *My Love, My Love or the Peasant Girl*." *El Nuevo Día*, 8 March 1988: 12.

VanWyngarden, Bruce. *Saturday Review* 11, no. 3 (May–June 1985): 68.

White, Evelyn C. *Women's Review of Books* 3, no. 2 (November 1985): 11.

Annie John (Audiobook)

Baskin, Barbara. "Audiobooks: *Annie John*, Written and Read by Jamaica Kincaid." *Booklist* 92, 1 January 1996: 868.

Hilyard, Nann Blaine. "Audio Reviews: *Annie John* by Jamaica Kincaid." *Library Journal*, 15 February 1995: 196.

Annie John (French translation)

Liberation, 15–16 November 1986: 31.

At the Bottom of the River

Bardsley, Barney. *New Statesman*, 7 September 1984: 33.

Freeman, Suzanne. *MS* 12, no. 7 (January 1984): 15–16.

Grierson, Letitia. *Wall Street Journal*, 20 January 1984: 26.

Homar, Susan. *Sargasso* 4 (1987): 76–80.

Leavitt, David. *Village Voice*, 17 January 1984: 41.

Maguire, Gregory. *Horn Book* 60 (1984): 91.

Milton, Edith. *New York Times Book Review*, 15 January 1984: 22.

Salkey, Andrew. *World Literature Today* 58, no. 2 (1984): 316.

Tyler, Anne. "Mothers and Mysteries." *New Republic*, 31 December 1983: 32–33.

Wieche, Janet. *Library Journal*, 1 December 1984: 2262.

Lucy

Als, Hilton. "Don't Worry, Be Happy." *The Nation*, 18 February 1991: 207.

American Visions 6, no. 2 (April 1991): 36.

Antioch Review 49, no. 1 (Winter 1991): 156.

Davis, Thulani. "Girl-Child in a Foreign Land." *New York Times Book Review*, 28 October 1990: 11.

Hawthorne, Evelyn J. "Antigua: *Lucy* by Jamaica Kincaid." *World Literature Today* 66, no. 1 (Winter 1992): 185.

Jaggi, Maya. "A Struggle for Independence." *Times Literary Supplement*, 26 April 1991: 20.

Jones, Malcolm Jr. "Read All About It: *Lucy*." *Newsweek*, 1 October 1990: 68.

Kakutani, Michiko. *New York Times*, 12 October 1990: 31C.

Listfield, Emily. *Harper's Bazaar*, October 1990: 82.

Mendelsohn, Jane. "Leaving Home: Jamaica's Voyage Around Her Mother." *Village Voice Literary Supplement* (October 1990): 21.

Nelson, Sara. "Picks and Pans." *People Weekly*, 5 November 1990: 40–41.

New Yorker, 17 December 1990: 122.

Passaro, Vince. *Self*, October 1990: 98.

Steinberg, Sybil. *Publishers Weekly*, 17 August 1990: 50.

Thompson, Bibi S. *Library Journal*, 1 November 1990: 125.

Virginia Quarterly Review 67, no. 2 (Spring 1991): S58–S59.

Warner, Mary. *The Christian Science Monitor*, 26 November 1990: 13.

Warrior, Robert Allen. "Good Reading." *Christianity and Crisis* 50, no. 14–15 (October 22, 1990): 313.

A Small Place

Brodsky, Mollie. *Library Journal*, July 1988: 88.

Covi, Giovanna. "Jamaica Kincaid's Political Place: A Review Essay." *Caribana* 1 (1990): 93–103.

Ellsberg, Peggy. "Rage Laced with Lyricism." *Commonweal* 115, no. 19 (4 November 1988): 602.

Giddins, Paula. "Book Marks." *Essence*, August 1988: 24.

Harvey, Miles. "The World's Great Places: *A Small Place* by Jamaica Kincaid." *Outside* 21, no. 5 (May 1996): 38.

Hill, Alison Fresinger. *New York Times Book Review*, 10 July 1988: 19.

Maja-Pearce, Adewale. "Corruption in the Caribbean." *New Statesman and Society* 1, no. 18 (7 October 1988): 40.

Peterson, V. R. "Pages." *People Weekly*, 26 September 1988: 37.

The Autobiography of My Mother

Boland, Eavan. "Desolation Angel." *Village Voice*, 6 February 1996: SS11.

Brice-Finch, Jacqueline. *World Literature Today* 71, no. 1 (1997): 202.

Ermelino, Louisa. "Picks and Pans." *People Weekly*, 19 February 1996: 27–30.

Essence, March 1996: 96–98.

Giels, Jeff. "A Cold, Bleak Caribbean." *Newsweek*, 22 January 1996: 62.

Groszmann, Lore. *The Nation*, 5 February 1996: 23–25.

Ingraham, Janet. *Library Journal* 121, January 1996: 142–143.

Kakutani, Michiko. *New York Times*, 16 January 1996: C17.

Keller, Johanna. *Antioch Review* 54, no. 3 (1996): 368.

Marcus, James. "Alone with the World." *Harper's Bazaar*, January 1996: 66–67.

Mead, Rebecca. "Innocence Isn't Bliss." *New York*, 22 January 1996: 52–53.

Pinckney, Darryl. "In the Back Room of the World." *New York Review of Books*, 21 March 1996: 28–32.

Publishers Weekly, 1 April 1996: 38.

Rochman, Hazel. *Booklist*, 1 December 1995: 587.

Schine, Cathleen. "A World as Cruel as Job's." *New York Times Book Review*, 4 February 1996: 7.

Segal, Lore. "The Broken Plate of Heaven." *Nation*, 5 February 1996: 23–25.

Skow, John. "Sharper Than a Serpent's Pen." *Time*, 5 February 1996: 71.

Steinberg, Sybil S. *Publishers Weekly*, 9 October 1995: 75.

Stewart, Andrea. *New Stateman*, 11 October 1996: 45.

Stone, Laurie. *Ms*. 90, January 1996: 62.

Turbide, Diane. "Motherless Child." *Maclean's*, 8 April 1996: 72.

Us, March 1996: 41.

Valentine, Victoria. "A Story of Life Through Death." *Emerge* 7, no. 5 (March 1996): 60–61.

The Autobiography of My Mother (Audiobook)

Ives, Nancy R. *Library Journal*, 15 June 1996: 105.

Publishers Weekly, 1 April 1996: 38.

My Brother

McNatt, Glenn. "Kincaid's My Brother: Elusive Closure." *Baltimore Sun*, 5 October 1997: 5M.

———. "When a Brother Dies of AIDS." *Chicago Sun-Times*, 19 October 1997: 20.

Quindlen, Anna. "The Past Is Another Country." *New York Times Book Review*, 19 October 1997: 7.

Interviews

Bonetti, Kay. *Conversations with American Novelists*. Columbia: University of Missouri Press, 1997.

———. "An Interview with Jamaica Kincaid." *The Missouri Review* 20, no. 1–2 (1991): 7–26.

Cudjoe, Selwyn. "Jamaica Kincaid and the Modernist Project: An Interview." *Callaloo* 12, no. 2 (Spring 1989): 396–411.

Ferguson, Moira. "A Lot of Memory: An Interview with Jamaica Kincaid." *The Kenyon Review* 16, no. 1 (1994): 163–188.

"Interview." *New Yorker*, 17 August 1981: 25.

Jacobs, Sally. "Don't Mess with Jamaica Kincaid." *Boston Globe*, 20 June 1996: 57.

Kreilkamp, Ivan. "Jamaica Kincaid: Daring to Discomfort." *Publishers Weekly* 243, 1 January 1996: 54–55.

Mantle, Larry. "Airtalk" (A discussion of Kincaid's *The Autobiography of My Mother*). KPCC Pasadena. 17 February 1996.

———. "Airtalk" (A discussion of Kincaid's *My Brother*). KPCC Pasadena. 24 February 1997.

Muirhead, Pamela Buchman. "An Interview with Jamaica Kincaid." *Clockwatch Review* 9, no. 1–2 (1994–1995): 39–48.

O'Conner, Patricia T. "My Mother Wrote My Life." *New York Times Book Review*, 7 April 1985: 6.

Perry, Donna. "An Interview with Jamaica Kincaid." In *Reading Black/Reading Feminist*, edited by Henry Louis Gates, 492–509. New York: Penguin, 1990.

———. "Jamaica Kincaid." In *Backtalk: Women Writers Speak Out*, 127–141. New Brunswick, N.J.: Rutgers University Press, 1993.

Snell, Marilyn. "Jamaica Kincaid Hates Happy Endings." *Mother Jones*, September–October 1997: 28–32.

Vorda, Allan. *Caribbean Writing*. Hattiesburg, Miss.: Center for Writers, University of Southern Mississippi, 1996.

———. "I Come from a Place That's Very Unreal: An Interview with Jamaica Kincaid." In *Face to Face: Interviews with Contemporary Novelists*, edited by Allan Vorda and Daniel Stern, 77–106. Houston: Rice University Press, 1993.

———. "An Interview with Jamaica Kincaid." *Mississippi Review* 20 (1991): 7–26.

Miscellaneous

Brady, James. "Ross, Kincaid Cross Sabers." *Advertising Age*, 12 February 1996: 19.

Cook, Mariana. "Eight Portraits." *Yale Review* 83, no. 3 (July 1995): 28–36.

Edwards, Audrey. "Jamaica Kincaid: Writes of Passage." *Essence*, May 1991: 86–90.

Funny, Nikki. "Jamaica Kincaid: *Annie John* 10, no. 6 (June 1995): 414–415.

Garis, Leslie. "Through West Indian Eyes." *New York Times Sunday Magazine*, 7 October 1990: 42.

Gilkin, Ronda. *Black American Women in Literature: A Bibliography, 1976–1987*. Jefferson, N.C.: McFarland, 1989.

"Jamaica Kincaid." In *Black Writers: A Selection of Sketches from Contemporary Authors*, edited by Linda Metzger, 326–328. Detroit: Gale Research, 1989.

"Jamaica Kincaid." *Contemporary Literary Criticism* 43 (1987): 247–251.

"Jamaica Kincaid." *Current Biography* 52, no. 3 (March 1991): 19.

"Jamaica Kincaid." *Current Biography Yearbook* (CBY). New York: H. W. Wilson, 1991: 330–333.

Kaufman, Joanne. "Jamaica Kincaid." *People Magazine*, 15 December 1997: 109–114.

Lee, Felicia. "Dark Words, Light Being." *New York Times*, 25 January 1996.

Listfield, Emily. "Straight from the Heart." *Harper's Bazaar*, October 1990: 82.

Rubin, Muriel Lynn. "Adolescence and Autobiographical Fiction: Teaching *Annie John* by Jamaica Kincaid." *Wasafiri* 8 (Spring 1988): 11–14.

Related Works

Allfrey, Phyllis Shand. *The Orchid House*. New Brunswick, N.J.: Rutgers University Press, 1996.

Brontë, Charlotte. *Jane Eyre*. London: Penguin, 1993.

Chodorow, Nancy. *The Reproduction of Mothering: Psychoanalysis and the Sociology of Gender*. Berkeley: University of California Press, 1978.

Fanon, Frantz. *Peau noire, masques blancs*. (Translated as *Black Skins, White Masks*.) Paris: Editions du Seuil, 1952.

Fox-Genovese, Elizabeth. *Within the Plantation Household: Black and White Women of the Old South*. Chapel Hill: University of North Carolina Press, 1988.

Frye, Karla. Y. E. " 'An Article of Faith': Obeah and Hybrid Identities in Elizabeth Nunez-Harrell's *When Rocks Dance*." In *Sacred Possessions: Vodou, Santería, Obeah, and the Caribbean*. Edited by Margarite Fernández Olmos and Lizabeth Paravisini-Gebert, 195–215. New Brunswick: Rutgers University Press, 1996.

Paravisini-Gebert, Lizabeth. "Introduction" to Phyllis Shand Allfrey's *The Orchid House*. New Brunswick, N.J.: Rutgers University Press, 1996

———. *Phyllis Shand Allfrey: A Caribbean Life*. New Brunswick, N.J.: Rutgers University Press, 1996.

Pattullo, Polly. *Last Resorts: The Cost of Tourism in the Caribbean*. London: Cassell, 1996.

Rhys, Jean. *Wide Sargasso Sea*. New York: Norton, 1982.

Spelman, Elizabeth V. *Inessential Woman: Problems of Exclusion in Feminist Thought*. Boston: Beacon Press, 1988.

Index

About the Author

LIZABETH PARAVISINI-GEBERT is Professor of Hispanic and African Studies at Vassar College. She is the author of *Phyllis Shand Allfrey: A Caribbean Life* (1996) and co-author of *Caribbean Women Novelists* (Greenwood, 1993).